FRAY SERVANDO TERESA DE MIER

Writings on Ancient Christianity and Spain's Evangelism of Mexico

Translated from Spanish and Notes by

Gary Bowen

FRAY SERVANDO TERESA DE MIER: Writings on Ancient
Christianity and Spain's Evangelism of Mexico

© 2020, A. Gary Bowen

In association with:

Elite Online Publishing
63 East 11400 South Suite #230
Sandy, UT 84070
www.EliteOnlinePublishing.com

Printed in the United States of America

ISBN: 978-1513655772

TABLE OF CONTENTS

Introduction

The President of Mexico (1824-1829), Don Guadalupe Victoria, assigned Fray Servando Teresa de Mier a very decent abode in the National Palace, where he went to live the remaining years of his life. Three years of a peaceful and tranquil life loved and respected, in contact with the best society of Mexico and in relations with the most notable men of the nation. He had three years of rest after thirty years of outrageous persecutions, jails, labors, and sufferings. He was very highly respected by President Victoria and his Vice President Don Nicolas Bravo who consulted with him on their gravest concerns. From all the States, inquiries were directed to him, and he came in this time to be the most popular man in Mexico. Two centuries later Fray Mier is unknown even in his native Mexico.

Gary Bowen married Herlinda Briones-Vega de Bowen resident of Los Mochis, Mexico, in 1964. Three years later visiting family in Los Mochis and shopping in a bookstore, Herlinda slapped a book in Gary's hand, declaring: "We have to buy this. I studied it in school." Thus, began Bowen's study of: "*Servando Teresa de Mier, Escritos y Memorias*," Ediciones de la Universidad Nacional Autonoma, Mexico, 1945.

Twenty years later Bowen came to know a Deputy in the lower house of Mexico's Congress, the Chamber of Deputies. Bowen spoke of Mier in his conversations with the Congressional Deputy, only to learn that an educated Mexican politician had never heard of this "most popular man in Mexico." Today, no knowledge of Fray Mier is common, even in Mexico. Two years after their first meeting, the Deputy phoned Bowen to tell him of a political conference he had attended in Monterrey, Mexico, Fray Mier's hometown. The Deputy's Monterrey colleagues recommended a book, of which the Deputy bought two copies, one for himself and one he mailed to Bowen. Thus,

1

Bowen came in possession of: "Biografia del benemérito mexicano D. Servando Teresa de Mier Noriega y Guerra," by José Eleuterio González, 1876, Commemorative Edition 1977, published by the State of Nuevo Leon and the Autonomous University of Nuevo Leon, Mexico.

Early 1990's, Bowen attended a class at a Catholic Jesuit University in Mexico. His introduction to the University faculty of Jesuit Priests included this: "Gary studies the writings of some silly guy Fray Mier. Have any of you ever hear of Fray Mier?" There was a silent nodding of their heads, by the Jesuit Faculty. The teacher asked, "Really, how do you know him?" The Jesuits unanimously responded: "We studied Fray Mier and his writings when we were preparing to become Jesuit Priests." The Fray Mier topic was immediately dropped by the class instructor.

The source of Bowen's translated writings by Fray Mier are published by respected public Universities of Mexico and honored by Mexican Jesuit Priests. Bowen study of Fray Mier has led him to conclude that Fray Mier's life and writings are knowingly and willfully hidden from common view. Fray Mier's life and writings are true, authentic history that deserve to be studied.

Preface

Fray Servando Teresa de Mier (1763-1827) was a 31-year old ordained priest of the Dominican Order of the Roman Catholic Church with a Doctor of Theology when he was invited by Mexico City's Council to deliver a sermon December 12, 1794 at the Collegiate Church of Guadalupe, honoring the tradition of the Virgin of Guadalupe, Mexico's Patron Saint. His Virgin of Guadalupe Sermon caused a notorious scandal. Fray Mier was accused of denying the tradition of the appearance of the Virgin of Guadalupe triggering removal of his Doctorate of Theology, an ecclesiastical suspension of his license to preach, imprisonment, exile, and his Catholic Church Inquisition for the next 27 years of his life.

Fray Mier's *Apologia* defends his innocence of the accusations and judicial proceedings incited by his December 12, 1794 Guadalupe Sermon and strongly declares the Gospel of Jesus Christ was preached in America before Spain's conquest. He abridges the few surviving records of the ancient people of Anáhuac (Mexico), and the many records of the Catholic missionaries of New Spain as evidence of the truth of his Sermon. Dr. Mier's, *Apologia,* written in Spanish with a stilted Latin grammar, reads like a doctoral thesis written for a PhD, or a legal deposition to be filed with a court of justice for legal judgement. Neither the Spanish nor the translated English text is a quick read. Dr. Mier's details of how he came to know the propositions he preached in his 1794 Guadalupe Sermon provide due diligence to the truth of his Sermon.

Fray Servando Teresa de Mier: Writings on Ancient Christianity and Spain's Evangelism of Mexico." is a translation from Spanish of Fray Mier's writings with biography and comments by Mexico's State of Nuevo Leon Governor José Eleuterio González (1813-1888). Governor González published *Biografía del benemérito mexicano D. Servando Teresa de Mier Noriega y Guerra* ("*Biography of the Distinguished Mexican Don Servando Teresa de Mier Noriega y Guerra*"), 1876 in Monterrey, Nuevo Leon, Mexico. A Commemorative Edition, Facsimile of the Original, was republished by the State of Nuevo Leon, Mexico and the Autonomous University of Nuevo Leon upon the Sesquicentennial of the Death of Father Mier, 1977. The Biography's primary focus is Fray Mier's *Apologia*, with additional writings, and speeches to Mexico's Constituent Congress. Fray Mier's writings are an academic historical labyrinth in defense of his December 12, 1794 Guadalupe Sermon.

This is well documented Mexican history, which is sadly hidden and occasionally classified as Christian myth. *Fray Servando Teresa de Mier, Writings on Ancient Christianity and Spain's Evangelism of Mexico.*" is the first publication in English of Fray Mier's original Spanish writings. Quoting Fray Servando Teresa de Mier from his *Apologia*: "If these things appear deliriums, they do not appear so much to those who have studied our antiquities."

—Gary Bowen—

SECTION I

DR. MIER'S APOLOGIA
(1794-1821)

WRITTEN IN DEFENSE OF HIS GUADALUPE SERMON,

RECITED IN THE SANCTUARY OF TEPEYACAC,

THE 12th DAY OF DECEMBER 1794.

PROPOSITION ONE

"And other sheep I have, which are not of this fold:
them also I must bring, and they shall hear my voice;
and there shall be one fold, and one shepherd."
The Bible, St. John 10:16

PROPOSITION TWO

"And there appeared a great wonder in heaven;
a woman clothed with the sun, and the moon under her feet,
and upon her head a crown of twelve stars: And she being with child
cried, travailing in birth, and pained to be delivered."

The Bible, Revelations 12:1-2

Chapter 1

Apologia
by Dr. Mier Introduction[1]

Powerful and sinners are synonymous in the language of the scriptures, because power fills them with pride and envy, it facilitates their means of oppression, and ensures their impunity. Thus, the Archbishop of Mexico, Don Alonso Nuñez de Haro achieved it in the persecution by which he ruined me for the Guadalupe Sermon that then being a monk of the Order of Preachers,[2] I recited in the Sanctuary of Tepeyacac the 12th day of December 1794.

But: *I saw the unrighteous man exalted on high and lifted like the cedars of Lebanon. And I passed by, and behold he was not.*[3] It is time to instruct the posterity upon the truth of everything that happened in this affair, in order that you might judge with your accustomed impartiality that you might take advantage and do justice to my memory, since this *Apologia*, cannot now serve me in this life that naturally is near its end at my age of fifty-six years. I owe it to my very noble family in Spain and in America, to my Mexican University, to the Order to which I belong, to my character, to my Religion and to the native land, whose glory was the object that I had proposed in the sermon.

I will follow in the *Apologia* the same order of the events. I will first tell for your intelligence what preceded the sermon and followed it up to the opening of the process. I will then prove that I did not deny the tradition of Guadalupe in the sermon; I will explain it with some proofs, and it will be seen that far from contradicting it, its theme was all calculated to sustain it against the arguments, if it were possible; and if not for that it takes away from the native land a glory more solid and greater without comparison. From there the passions appeared in a conspiracy prosecuting the innocent, slandering it under the disguise of censors, defaming it with a libel called Pastoral Edict, incriminating it with a public prosecutor's indictment that the same is no more than a horrific crime, and condemning it with a sentence worthy of such a tribunal; but with the cruel derision of naming the most absurd and atrocious penalty, piety and clemency. And I left for exile, but always under the tremendous escort of the false testimonies disguised with the title of confidential reports. Always the oppression accompanied me, always the intrigue, and I found nothing in all my resources but venality, corruption and injustice. Even with twenty-four years of persecution I have acquired the talent of painting monsters; the discussion will show that I do no more here than copy the originals. I have nothing now against who bloodied me; all my enemies disappeared from this world. They have already given their account to the Eternal; I desire that He has pardoned them.[4]

Chapter 1, Notes

1. *Memorias del Dr. Servando Teresa de Mier*. Published for the first time by Manuel Payno en: *Vida, aventuras, escritos y viajes del Dr. Servando Teresa de Mier*. Mexico City, Imprenta Abadiano 1856. Reprinted in a Father Mier Biography written by José Eleuterio Gonzáles, Monterrey, Mexico. 1876. Published again, in part, by Nicolás Rangel in *the Antología del Centenario*, Vol. II. Mexico City. 1910. A Fourth Edition, with Prologue by Alfonso Reyes, published in Madrid, Ediciones América, Colección Ayacucho. 3 Vol. Finally, parts of these Memories were published in *El pensamiento del Padre Mier* by Alessio Robles, Biblioteca Enciclopédica Popular. No. 16. Mexico City. 1944. The bibliographical provenance of this footnote is from Edmundo O'Gorman, op. cit. page XLIII. Chapter 1, Dr. Mier's *Apologia*, is translated from the José Eleuterio Gonzáles Biography cited above by O'Gorman, republished 1977 as a Commemorative Edition, Facsimile of the Original, by the Government

of the State of Nuevo Leon, and the Autonomous University of Nuevo Leon, on the Sesquicentennial of the Death of Father Mier, 1827-1977, pp. 9-142.

2. The Order of Preachers is more commonly known as the Dominican Order, or Dominicans, of which Fray Mier was a member.

3. The First Epistle of Saint Clement of Rome to the Corinthians, Chapter 14: 5 written circa 80-140 A.D. was translated by Charles H. Hoole, 1885.

4. The preceding is Dr. Mier's Introduction to his *Apologia*. - Chapters 1, 2, 3, 4, 5, 6, and 7 are Dr. Mier's complete *Apologia*.

Chapter 2

Antecedents and Consequences of the Sermon up to the Opening of the Process

Some seventeen days before that of Guadalupe, the Councilman Rodriguez assigned me the Sermon for the fiesta of the Sanctuary; and as a practiced orator, and that I had already preached three times on the same image with applause, quickly I made up my theme, and it was checked, when the Father Mateos Domínico told me that a Lawyer had told him some curious things about Our Lady of Guadalupe, that had delayed him the entire afternoon. I began listening to him in curiosity, and he himself led me to the home of Licentiate Borunda, who told me: "I think that the image of Our Lady of Guadalupe is from the time of the preaching in this kingdom of Saint Thomas who the Indians called *Quetzalcóhuatl.*" I was not surprised by this preaching that since a child I learned from the mouth of my wise father. Everything I have later studied, has confirmed it to me. I believe that there is no instructed American who is ignorant of it or that doubts it. But against being of that time, the image of Our Lady opposes the tradition. "It does not contradict my opinion," he responded, "because according to the image was already painted when the Virgin sent it to [Bishop] Zumárraga." "It would not be," I retorted, "on the cape of Juan Diego that then did not exist." "It is not an Indian's cape," he told me; "I rather believe that it is on the cape of the same Saint Thomas who would give it to the Indians as a symbol of the faith, written in his way, since it is a Mexican hieroglyphic from those that they call composed, that encrypts it and contains it. Then the painting would not be supernatural." "Earlier in my system it can only be tested. Doctor Bartolache has ruined all the basic essentials that the painters had in one thousand six hundred sixty-six; but the hieroglyphics that I see in the image are linked to the most refined little phrases of the *Nahuatl* language, with such skill and delicacy, that it appears impossible that the neophyte Indians at the time of Saint Thomas, as after the conquest, could encrypt the articles of faith in such a sublime manner. Even the conservation of the image can only be miraculous in the passage of so many centuries. And if it is that it is damaged, as it already was in one thousand six hundred sixty-six, it could come from the assault of the apostates, during the persecution of Huemac, King of Tula, against Saint Thomas and his disciples. And this can perhaps allude to the allegory of the flaying of *Tetehuinan,* so celebrated in Mexican histories. The Christians would hide it and the Virgin was sent to the Bishop with Juan Diego etc. according to the current tradition."

This is the result that Borunda told me, and it is also the analysis of my sermon. He proceeded like this: "I more than being a *Nahuatl* language native, I have most of thirty years studying its composed and figurative sense, from reading manuscripts, confronting traditions, examining monuments, with travels to that end, training myself in deciphering hieroglyphics, that I believe to have encountered the key; and what I have said about the image of Guadalupe, is the result of my studies. All is disclosed in the volume of a folio, titled *Clave general de jeroglícos* americanos [1] that I have written in honor of the Royal order, with that request from the Royal Historical Academy I was invited to write upon our antiquities, and with the occasion of three manuscripts excavated in the Plaza Mayor.

"They have been explained there, alluding to the ancient superstitions attributed in all to the Indians; but there is not such a thing: what they contain are the dates of the principal events of the Christian writing and religion." Then, I interrupted; "They are precious monuments to your credit, because the incredulous could not say that we have feigned the Christians. This should be printed." Borunda continued, "I protested at the time in the literary *Gazeta*; but I have lacked the funds for the printing. If you wished to give notice to the public in your sermon to excite the curiosity, perhaps that would attain what is necessary for the printing." I responded; "I would gladly do it, but it is necessary that I have certainty of the essentials, and you already see that I do not have time to examine your work." I believe that only nine or ten days were lacking until the sermon. He told me; "Oh! the proofs are incontestable, only that they do need extension to present their strength. This can be remedied, exhibiting only some light, adaptable proofs to a sermon, remitting them to a public discussion, in which they are all exhibited, and there is no fear. I have reviewed my work with the Minister President Luengo de San Agustin, and I also took it to the Canon Uribe, who told me that his occupations did not give him time to examine it, but he did not condemn it."

These recommendations were good: neither could I imagine that a lawyer, acting for the Royal Court, had damaged brains as the Canons censors pretended. I am also simple; I have liked this pension from the great geniuses, even if I do not have it. I saw a system favorable to the religion, I saw the native land was assured of an Apostle, a glory that all nations crave, and especially Spain, that being a tiny county, it is not content with less than three Apostles of the first order, even though all dispute it: I finally saw, that without harm to the fundamentals of the tradition, the image and the Sanctuary were exalted, and above all that it opened a way for responding to the arguments against the history of Guadalupe, otherwise irresolvable in my opinion. The religion, the glory of the native land, of the image, of the Sanctuary, fills me with enthusiasm, and this upset me, if it is that I could be upset. *Huic uni forsan potui succumbere culpæ* (*"Perchance, I might have succumbed to this one weakness"*). [2]

I retired to my convent cell after having heard Borunda. I

meditated two or three days on all that he had told me. I reduced it to four propositions, I traced some proofs, and once the outline became apparent, I returned to filling it out and gathering all that was necessary. It is true that some propositions given to me were of little weight; but I already believed according to the antecedent that substantial evidence remained in the depth of the work. I asked especially for notes on the explanation of the Mexican hieroglyphics that Borunda believed to see in the image, because my knowledge on this genre is very superficial; and he dictated them to me, either by speaking or reading from his work.

With this material I returned to work, and as I had to prove four propositions, to link the proofs, give all the oratorical tone, and since I did not possess the material, I scribbled (Most of it was thrown out to scribble as all speakers do, before putting together a perfect piece). It turns out that my scribbles, with Borunda's notes, amounted to eighteen pages in the judicial decree, even though the sermon only has five.

When there were then no more than two or three days before the sermon, having achieved a draft such that is legible for me, I went to read it to Borunda, who approved it. I likewise read it to various doctor friends: no one found it theologically reprehensible; no one believed that it denied the Guadalupe tradition, all judged it ingenious, and some participated in my enthusiasm, even offering me their pens to appear in my favor in the literary fray that it provoked.

I confess nevertheless, that my enthusiasm had diminished with time, and that to have had two days more to do another sermon, I would not have preached the same. But the urgency of the time, the vote of my friends, the incontestable proofs that Borunda said he had, and some not exactly worthless that I found in the depth of my research, and upon which I will establish later in my defense, they made me dive into the water.

The sermon preached, I had as always what they call praises, and there was no lack among the Canons of the

Collegiate Church who asked me to archive it, as an erudite piece that did honor to America. However, among the individuals of the Municipality of the City there were those who counseled me not to give it, because it would be printed. I even had to preach in the Capuchin of Mexico to the nuns, and I had no sermon (because at the end I had not finished composing, except the first part). I preferred to walk by the more public places and to visit various respectable homes to observe the impression that my sermon had made. I found nothing scandalous, save among some the notice that I had preached a new kind of sermon.

But *miserabile dictum* (*"Miserable to relate"*)! the Señor Archbishop sent an order to the Churches that Sunday, the sixth festival day, must formally be preached against me for having denied the Guadalupe tradition, affirming that the image was painted on the cape of Saint Thomas and not on that of the Indian Juan Diego. And, as for this day, almost all the Guadalupe Fiestas in Mexico are reserved for the people being occupied this primary day of pilgrimage to the Sanctuary, and by consequence the speakers are many, and their declamation simultaneous and heated, immediately and necessarily produced a terrible scandal. The purpose to stir the populace against me and to begin an inquiry, was so infallible, that before it was proven (since at eight-thirty in the morning of the same Sunday even though no sermon had been preached), already he asked me for mine through my Provincial, so that I had the simplicity to hand it over as I had it in a rough draft, and he intimated to me the suspension of preaching, at the same time that I was to do it in the Capuchin.

Consider a similar proclamation in a people so lively as the Mexicans that only the sight of an Aurora Borealis a few days before, had been taken as a sign of the day of judgement, and so excited by the image of Guadalupe, that nevertheless believing that the celestial fire came from the north, all night the people flocked upon Tepeyácac to die burned, they said, with our Lady. *Hic dies primus laeti, primusque malorum &c.* (*"Here is the first joyful day, and the beginning of evil, etc."*) [3] If I did not perish, victim of the popular indignation, perhaps I owe it to the prudence of keeping myself a prisoner in my convent. My community believed itself exposed, and the Provincial warned him, when they marched in the procession of images of the Virgin of Los Remedios to do so with utmost care, to avoid the insults of the mob. Especially outstanding, it was known among the educated people of Mexico that the Archbishop did not believe the Guadalupe tradition, and that he himself when I was preaching, was saying to his companions that it was hardly believable; and this uproar was no more than a maneuver to begin an investigation of me, to take from me the trust that the people had in me, and lose me by envy, or for his notorious hatred against everything American. But even had he believed the tradition, and had my sermon been scandalous, it was not he who ought to judge me, because his proclamation was even so. And in the end, unjust in every sense, because certainly I had not thought to deny so great a tradition as Guadalupe. The good Shepherd of the Gospel looked for the sheep that had strayed. He lifted it lovingly upon his shoulders to bring it back to the fold, and did not lash out at it, throw it to the dogs, nor did he disturb the flock. And, had I denied the tradition of Guadalupe? It had not even passed through my imagination.

It was easy that I deceived myself in my own cause, but the same Guadalupe Collegiate Church who ought to consider itself the most interested, having seen the scandal provoked the fourteenth day of December, the grey-haired met, the sixteenth, and after having agreed on that which I had preached was most glorious to the native land, to the image and to the Sanctuary, than that which they had, they said that their opinion had been turned over to four or five chapter members to convene with me; and if it turned out established as probable what I had preached, it would invite me with a sermon that could be preached as true; and if not, that I could recant it. But that His Illuminate had taken up the cause to himself. The Canon of Guadalupe Gamboa was the same day by night in my convent cell to advise me on it, and the Canon Leyva, Secretary of the Church Chapter, later confirmed it to me. Both marveled that I could have delivered the sermon, knowing the antipathy of the Archbishop against Creoles and their glories. This opinion, thus as proof that the Archbishop proceeded to give his proclamation without the petition of the party, thus it proves that the Canons had not believed that I had denied the tradition, nor was there in the sermon anything worthy of censure or a theological note, still they did not want that I preach it as true, if it were established.

It is evident from the judicial decrees and certainly *in verbo sacerdotis* ("*On the word of the priest*") [4] that from the beginning of the sermon I offered this protest: "I warn that I do not deny the appearance of Most Holy Mary to Juan Diego and Juan Bernardino; on the contrary to deny them appears reprehensible to me. Neither do I deny the miraculous painting of our image, on the contrary I have to prove it in a plausible way." I later warned that nothing denied how much I was thinking about the tradition being genuine and legitimate. Such ought to consider those rites of the Sacred Congregation, after the accustomed examination, whether it served to express itself in the prayer's lessons. To the end of the third of the second night, after having spoken of the woman of Apocalypse clothed with the sun and having the moon under her feet, [5] it goes on: "In this figure, they almost tell what appeared in Mexico the year 1531—an image marvelously painted of the Virgin Mary, who they say appointed a pious neophyte there near the city with a wonder, the place where she wanted a temple consecrated to her." I do not say more in the entire official letter. Have I denied some of this? On the contrary I have admitted more, as one sees by the protest; nor with it said could I substitute the complexity of my sermon. Later I did not deny in it the tradition of Guadalupe.

It is true that I added one or another detail, to exalt as I already said, the native land and the image, and suppressed some circumstances, likewise not admitted by the Congregation of Rites, not essential to the tradition, and necessary in my judgement of omitting to save the tradition from insuperable difficulties. Nevertheless, from the sermon's introduction, I anticipated this other protest, that also consists, and certainly *in verbo sacerdotis.* " I subject my proposition to the correction of the wise; and even though to some they appear strange, to me they appear probable. And at the least if I deceived myself, I have disturbed the reluctance of my countrymen that by my proving, they better clarify the truth of this history that the disaffected do not cease to criticize." And then, more enjoyable, I will gladly retract all my proofs, of which now I can only exhibit a few, consulting the brevity and the intelligence of the greater part of the audience." My clear intention was only to promote a literary discussion to better secure the tradition, and that meanwhile, I presented the means that to me appeared conducive.

If however, the Archbishop infers that my protests with what I added to it were damaging to the tradition, it was not for this lawful for him to have me accused before the people of denial as an express doctrine of mine, being only a consequence of his, that I had previously denied in the sermon. Our most Holy Father Innocent 9th in his celebrated dogmatic Brief, [6] directed to the Churches of France to give them peace about the disputes of Jansen and Quesnel, defined that even though one agrees to principals that follow heretical consequences, they ought not to attribute to him that he denies them, even though it has established the principles of which they infer. If this is a doctrinal and dogmatic point, he ought to impute much less to me against my objections to the consequence of having denied the tradition of Guadalupe, being a historical point composed of many circumstances, some of which can be denied, as happens to each step in many points of history, without for this saying you denied the same history.

Even though the thing is evident, I will put forth a couple of examples of approved traditions. The Spaniards have by tradition that the Most Holy Virgin appearing in mortal life to

Saint James, ordered that a temple be erected to her in Zaragoza to be from there the protectorate of the Spanish lands. But, when a prayer was said on this to the Congregation of Rites, Benedict XIV, as Promoter then of the faith, objected that it appeared indecent to the humanity of the Mother of God in mortal life to order that a temple be erected to her. And thus, this circumstance is omitted, only putting in the prayer that the Virgin ordered Saint James to raise a temple, and she left it to his devotion to have it consecrated to her. Thus, it was done: and it must be said, for this will the Congregation of Rites deny the tradition of Our Lady of the Pillar?

Another example: It is a tradition of the Spaniards recorded in their Compendiums that Saint Leocadia, raising herself from the tomb in front of the people of Toledo, said to Saint Ildefonso: "Alfonso, for thee my Lady lives who the summits of heaven have." But, when it was negotiated to insert this in Saint Ildefonso's lessons in the Roman Compendium, the same Benedict XIV put forward that these words were hyperbolic and exaggerated, far from the simple language of the blessed person in their apparitions, and truthfully not sincere. And so, that even though the Spaniards permit it in their Compendiums, they ought to omit them in the Roman, that ought to be composed with more weight and mature examination; and so much more, all that was before the Spanish could have put those words in the mouth of the people. That is how it was done: and one has to say is that why the Congregation of Rites denied the appearance of Saint Leocadia to San Ildefonso?

Much less ought this to affirm that I had denied the tradition of Guadalupe, upon which the same Guadalupe authors contradict themselves, alternatively denying many and very grave circumstances, as will be seen in the lecture series, without which anyone might say by this they have denied the same tradition.

I argue *ad hominem* against the same Archbishop. All the witnesses *nemine discrepant* (*"no disagreement"*) of the information on Guadalupe from 1666 that he so much praises in his edict, and all the Guadalupe authors that it calls very serious (except one recent, who doubts because of a Mexican inscription from the Sanctuary), they affirmed that the Bishop Zumárraga in obedience to the mandate of the Virgin to erect a temple to her in Tepeyácac, there a provisional chapel was constructed, to where he moved her within fifteen days from the appearance, it is to say, on December twenty-four of one thousand five hundred thirty-one, he going in the procession barefoot and crying from devotion, some add.

But the Señor Archbishop affirms in his edict that the image was not moved until the year one thousand five hundred thirty-three, Zumárraga spent that entire year in Spain, for which he departed some six months after the apparition, and he did not return until one thousand five hundred thirty-four. It is recorded by Torquemada in his life 3rd Volume, and the 1st of the same, from a Royal Letter that Tanco cites in his warning and from the Royal order that the Royal Chronicler Muñoz cites in his dissertation on Guadalupe, of which I will speak later. From which one infers that the Bishop neither moved the image, nor made such a chapel, even though before going to Spain he did the Amor de Dios Hospital and his Palace that was given to him, as it appears from his account book of receipts and expenditures that Don Cárlos de Sigüenza had in his control; nor did he make a case of her after he returned from Spain, even though he lived ten more years, the year one thousand five hundred forty-four he was still at the Santiago College, and that at that time it cost nothing to build but to order it, since the Indians (as Torquemada says) did all for free. It was Casas who in one thousand five hundred forty-two released the first laws that one must pay the Indians for their work.

Would it be possible, if the tradition were true, that a venerated Bishop would have disobeyed an order so decisive from the Mother of God, and would he have ever made the case of the image that the same had been placed to his care as a wage for the protection of his sheep? And nevertheless, had the Mr. Archbishop affirmed a proposition of such terrible consequences against the apparition, he would not want that we should say that he had denied it in the same edict in which he pretended to uphold it. Later, His Illuminate neither ought to say it of me against my protests however much that it appears to infer his denial of some circumstances.

And what would he have said if I had come forth to announce from the pulpits that His Illuminate had not only denied this and other much graver circumstances of the tradition, without undermining everything from their foundations? At the least with his approval, Dr. Bartolache's Manifesto was printed, from which I am persuaded, even to believe I can demonstrate that it is a complete and fundamental refutation of the tradition of Guadalupe, even though concealed with great skill to avoid public hatred. The Archbishop could have said without doubt that he had not believed it so that my private opinion was not sufficient reason for him to take off on the fury of popular resentment; and he would ask highly the justice against me, even when I could have been his superior, for having discredited him without having heard nor convinced him. This is the same that I should have said and asked on the matter of my sermon.

To penetrate his object and artifice it was necessary to have first taken charge of the state of the question. In 1648, it is to say, one hundred seventeen years after the apparition, there came to light in Mexico its first history by Sanchez, without founding it on any document, and there was born with it the difficulty and the opposition. The same Chaplain of the Sanctuary Licentiate Lazo later wrote to the author, congratulating him for the notice that entirely caught up with him anew, because until then neither he nor his predecessors, the Chaplains of the Guadalupe Hermitage, had known the Eve that they there possessed.

After some years the Priest Becerra Tanco printed his history and complains of the malcontents who had blocked his first account written a little after the first author. Father Florencia followed him to write in the same century of the miscreants complaining to him over the matter. They have grown so much since then, it has been years since the sermons of Guadalupe in Mexico have become apologetic dissertations, and no one lectures in this way where there are no opponents. Dr. Bartolache says that he titled his manifesto *Satisfactorio*, because it was to satisfy the many in Mexico who deny or doubt the tradition. The same has multiplied them, since with one hand it silently destroyed its foundations, and with the other not only firmly restored the ancient difficulties, but excited new ones, without giving solution to none, but apparent to most. There will be few Americans in Mexico who have not had debates on this with the Europeans that as they were not born into this belief, and show some rivalry, the difficulties that are jumping to view do not cease to oppose us, and even assured that the Archbishop was one of those who objected to them. Nevertheless, as no one without the vocation of martyrdom dares to publicly arrest a popular pious tradition, no matter how false it may appear to him, the contradiction had been forbidden and covered up until then. But then already it was not.

Doctor Don Juan Bautista Muñoz, well known for his works in the literary republic, Royal Chronicler of the Indies, which history he has already brought to light a volume, and Secretary of His Majesty in the Secretary of Grace and Justice of the same Department, found in the Royal Archive of Simancas the information that in one thousand five hundred seventy-five the Viceroy Don Martin Enriquez sent to the King, who had asked him about the origin of the devotion or history of Guadalupe, and expressly contradicts it. Neither, is the Venerable Father Sahagún favorable to it, the most erudite of the first missionaries, who in his universal history of New Spain, three volume folios that the Chronicler found in the library of San Francisco de Toloca in Guipuzcoa, proceeds to declare suspicious of idolatry the devotion of the Indians to the Virgin of Guadalupe.

With this and other case documents, the Chronicler formed a neatly written dissertation, in which he proposed to prove that the history of Guadalupe is a fable. He presented it in September of one thousand seven hundred ninety-four to the Royal Historical Academy that having finished examining it, approved it, ordered the printing among their records, and issued to the Chronicler the academic patent number. Since we already had gone against the tradition the dictum of a Royal Academy, so wise as that of history, which were the Campomanes, the Capmanys, the Riscos, the Tragias, the most distinguished in the nation; and we had the arguments of a Chronicler justly celebrated so much more terrible when it is evidenced to me by the sworn testimony of Don Carlos de Sigüenza, one of our major scholars, that the Mexican Manuscript that was considered very ancient that is the only document of the tradition that counts, and from which all the Guadalupe Authors are no more than paraphrases, traditions and copies; it is the work of the Indian Don Valeriano native of Azcapozalco, written from eighty to eighty-two years after the apparition.

To avoid, if it were possible these arguments against it, the sermon was calculated, far from having thought of denying the tradition. And, if it was not possible to sustain it so that a thing so much more glorious might stay with us, when it goes to not having deserved the major part of the world a glimpse of the compassion of Jesus Christ nor of his Mother until one thousand six hundred years after the death of the Redeemer, or to have it achieved at the same time as the other parts of the world no less sinful than America.

For this I proposed as probable two propositions, to which in substance one can reduce the entire sermon. The rest was nothing more than episodes of little importance to cover some holes which the critics have opened in the tradition. The first was, that the gospel has been preached in America centuries before the conquest by Saint Thomas, whom the Indians also called Saint Tomé in the Syrian language, as the Christians of Saint Tomé in the Orient, also Chilancambal, in the Chinese language, things much to be noted, also, Quetzalcohuatle (syncopated Quetzalcoatl) in the Mexican language. Because *quetzal* for the preciousness of the plumage of the Quetzalli, corresponds in the Aztec images to the halo of our Saints, as with shoots and rays surrounding the face was a distinction of the divinity, consequently it is as good as to say Saint. And, *coatl*, corruptly *coate*, means the same as Tomé, this is akin to the root *taam*, since in Hebrew one says, *Thama* or *Taama*, and with Greek inflections *Thomas*, to whom the same Greeks also called him *Didymus* in their language. *Thomas qui dicitur Didymus* (*"Thomas called Didymus"*). [7]

This preaching has been defended by many and very serious Spanish authors, foreign and American, even in works concerning not only manuscripts but printed in Spain, such as Diego Duran, Gregorio García, Alonso Ramas, Antonio Calancha, Nobrega, Mendieta, Remesal, Torquemada, Betancourt, Rivadeneira, Abraham, Justo Lipsio, the Spanish author of the Excellence of the Cross, Sigüenza in his *Fenix del Occidente, El Apóstol Santo Tomé* (*"Phoenix of the West, the Apostle Saint Tomé"*), [8] the Jesuit author of the *Historia del verdadero Quetzacohuatl el Apóstol Santo Tomé*(*"History of the True Quetzacohuatl, the Apostle Saint Tomé "*), [9] Becerra Tanco, Boturini, Veytia, and many others. In addition, holy and wise Archbishops and Bishops of America, for example Dávila Padilla, Casas and Zárate; nor Cardinals of the Holy Roman Church, such as Gotti.

This opinion is the most similar to the Sacred Scriptures and to the Holy Fathers, most worthy of the mercy of God with an immense portion of the human lineage, the most appropriate to confound the blasphemies of the incredulous against the divinity of the Christian religion, and at the same time that this is upheld by unimpeachable monuments, the most glorious not only to the Americans, but to the Spaniards.

This preaching was, undoubtedly, the real stone of the scandal, for the Archbishop and other persons of equal antipathy to the glories of America: and for thus I will insinuate the same in his support, of much that one could allege without further work than to copy from the voluminous printings and manuscripts that exist upon this matter, and which I have brought forth, also in another work.

I have said that this opinion is like the Sacred Scriptures, because Jesus Christ sending his Apostles to preach, told them, "Go to all the world, preach the Gospel to every creature that is beneath the heaven, and be my witnesses from Jerusalem and Judea unto the ends of the Earth." Would it be possible that an order so strong, general, and absolute would not have included half the globe? And, what excuse could the Apostles have had for not having complied, their Master having expressly conveyed the powers of his Omnipotence for standing up to the obstacles? The Gospel is not planted without the force of miracles; and if according to Saint Luke the Apostle Saint Philip was seized by the airs to go and announce the Gospel to only one city of the Philistines called Azotus, to which he could go by foot; would it have been a major difficulty or minor interest for Saint Tomé to bring it to almost half the world? Saint Mark concludes his Gospel affirming that the Apostles having left, preached everywhere; and the greater part of the world is America.

Saint Paul wrote to the Colossians that the Gospel was among them, as it is in the entire world; he said to them be fruitful and increase. And writing to the Romans twenty-nine years after the death of Christ, he says to them that in truth the prophecy ofDavid about the Apostles has already been fulfilled: "His words came to all the Earth."

Jesus Christ having said to his disciples that the Jerusalem temple, which they were admiring, would not remain stone upon stone, and their asking Him the time of its destruction, the most decisive, last and near sign of all those that He told them, was: "This Gospel shall be preached in all the world, and then will come the destruction." He spoke of Jerusalem and of its temple. This is the literal meaning that Calmet follows, and Jesus Christ himself appears to confirm, since He concludes like this in his discourse: "Of truth I tell thee that the present generation will not pass without all these things having been fulfilled." And that effectively, all the signs were fulfilled that He then gave before the destruction of

Jerusalem, which was forty or forty-two years after His death, the distinguished Bishop Tostado proves it with his erudition upon Saint Matthew.

This is the way a multitude of Popes also understood it, who defended the Gospel having been preached to the entire world from the time of the Apostles. One can read the collected writings of Maluenda in *De Ante-Christo*. Saint Crysóstomo to prove it even composed an entire homily that is the 21st. It is true that Saint Augustine appeared to doubt, but without happening that the learned Titelman on purpose put about to prove the arguments of the Saint but did not conclude his intent. Saint Thomas reconciles it with the other Popes explaining and saying that he only meant to say that the Gospel was not preached in all the world from the time of the Apostles in such a way to come to fruition until churches are founded in all the kingdoms and provinces (and in reality this is what proves the reasons of Saint Augustine); but what he did not deny is having given a general announcement of the New Law in all the world, conforming to the orders of Jesus Christ.

Well, I know that despite Saint Thomas's explanation, and Bossuet saying that in Jesus Christ's last speech which he quotes, the signs can very well be discerned that pertain to the end of the world of those who touch upon the destruction of Jerusalem; that the theologians still divide themselves and subdivide, each one quoting the Popes; nor do I intend to decide the question. I well imagine that in order to save the truth of the texts of the quoted scripture and others that could be quoted, it is not necessary that the Apostles preached in every place, neither province, nor kingdom, it being enough to announce it in the capitals of the kingdoms, or founding churches in the contiguous provinces, from where little by little it would be spreading with benefit to the rest by his disciples. But when it relates to a separate continent, so vast that appropriately one can call it a New World, and of a period, without news of the Gospel, for fifteen centuries, it seems to me that the sacred texts acquire an extraordinary power, and that no Father having had knowledge of America, would have denied the preaching in it from apostolic times. And much less Saint Augustine, who agreed to the interpretation of the scripture by Canon that it ought to always agree to the letter when it is not followed by something absurd; and such did not follow in this case, that rather it would be absurd that it had not been preached.

Yes, it seems absurd in mercy to the entire world, equally redeemed with His blood, to have left to perish in the darkness of infidelity during sixteen centuries, the major part of the world, of which the King was informed, the year 1542, as witnessed by sight the Venerable Bishop Casas, that God seemed to have put the biggest blow to the human lineage. No, no, much worthier seems Our Savior's mercy without limits to have it later extended to all mankind, to whom His law is meant to apply. I will not argue, only quote the peoples' Apostle. *Et quomodó credent ei, quem non audierunt? Quomodó autem audient sine predicante? Quomodó autem predicabunt nisi mittantur? Sed dicó: Nunquid non audierunt? Et quidem in omnem terram exivit souus eorum, et in fines orbis terræ verba eorum.* (*"And how shall they believe in him of whom they have not heard? And how shall they hear without a preacher? And how shall they preach except they be sent? But I say, have they not heard? Yes verily, their sound went into all the earth, and their words unto the ends of the world."*) [10] Those who pretend that God made a distinction among nations, transfer to Him our miserable passions; but God, says Saint Peter, is no respecter of persons; nor in Christ Jesus, says Saint Paul, is there distinction of Greek nor Jew, Barbarian nor Scythian, He wants that all mankind be saved and they might come to the knowledge of the truth: *omnes homines vult salvos fieri et ad agnitionem veritatis venire* (*"Who will have all men to be saved and to come unto knowledge of the truth."*). [11]

It is the general tradition of the Church, affirmed by the Popes, that the Apostles before parting from Judea distributed among themselves the parts of the world, to not crowd all together in one spot. And, we do not read that they did it to the exclusion of some part, and much less of the greater. To the contrary, having first preached the gospel in Judea according to the orders of Jesus Christ, they received an order to carry it to the Gentiles, by virtue of a vision received by Saint Peter, of a square linen full of unclean animals. These were the Gentiles from the four corners of the world, according to the interpretation of the Popes: *ut per universas quadrati orbis partes*, (*"As in all parts of the world."*) [12] says Saint Leon, *lux evangelii omnibus inferretur* (*"Light of the gospel introduced to all"*).

To say that America was then not known is nonsense, because the Apostles had inspired knowledge of how much the fulfillment of their mission meant. Besides which it is false that America was not known in the first centuries of Christianity. Masdeu (*Historia crítica*, Title 1, Illustration 1, page 324) proves with evidence that notwithstanding the submersion of Atlantis, which interrupted communication between the old and new continent, from Solon to Origen, it is to say, nine centuries clear knowledge of America was known in Europe, which only began to be obscured by the theological opposition of Saint Augustine, the struggles of Lactantius, to which were later added Pope Zacharias's anathemas against the Priest Virgil, always conserving the memory among the Arabs or ancient Orientals, who called America *Jesu-Dunico*, or New World. Saint Clement disciple of Saint Peter and his successor to the twenty years of his martyrdom, in his celebrated letter to the Corinthians, which was read in the churches of the East more than thirty years as a scripture, tells them like thus: "in the immense ocean there are other worlds governed by the Creator with the same laws with which ours is governed." Origen, Saint Jerome, and other Fathers spoke in the same way.

And, who does not know of the blasphemies of the incredulous against the Christian religion, who's Divinity, they say, was testing them for sixteen centuries, up to crushing their bones, with its expansion into all the world by only twelve men, and with the universality of the Church; and in the end a New World was discovered where nothing was known of it? It is false. Throughout America, monuments and vestige evidences of Christianity were found, according to the unanimous testimony of the missionaries.

There was no more difference among them except that some fearful of the opinions of the time, in which the preaching of the Gospel served as the title for the Conquest of America, they feigned attributing them to the devil's mimicry, who had (they say) in America the strange witticism of meddling in the catechist of Christian doctrine, whose mysteries all our Indians knew, in some parts pure, and in others more or less turned upside down with fables, and of meddling without fear to fabricate crosses which the Indians worshiped, so that since the Spanish surged onto the coasts of Yucatán, seeing so many crosses painted and of many materials within and outside of the temples and even upon the breast of the anciently buried dead, they began to call our America, *New Spain*. This is the origin of this name that the King later confirmed to a petition from Cortés. And the missionaries not yet understanding the devil's mantle to explain the most ancient prophesies, individuals, and circumstances that the Indians held upon the arrival, religion, and domain of the Spaniards, because the catechist that the fabricator of crosses did not understand to foresee so much, they opened a new cradle of numerous prophets and truths among idolatrous Gentiles. Such were according to them in New Spain, Quetzalcohuatl, Chilancambal, Cozas, Toltoxin and some others, in Brazil, Eguiara, in New Granada, various others, in Peru, Viracocha, and everywhere Tomé. Subterfuges so miserable and ridiculous, resources so desperate, only served to demonstrate that the facts in favor of the ancient preaching, which they pretended to satisfy, were incontestable.

For the same political motives Señor Solórzano had opposed *de jure in indiarum* ("*By Indies Law*") the preaching of Saint Thomas. But having come to light *La predicación del Evangelio en el Nuevo mundo viviendo los Apóstoles* ("*The Living*

Apostles Preaching the Gospel in the New World") by the Dominican Fray Gregorio García, and *La predicación de Santo Tomas en América* (*"The Preaching of Saint Thomas in America"*) by the Augustinian Fray Antonio Calanche, he retracted his opposition in the *Política indiana* (*"Indies Politics"*), saying that one does not dare to deny it even though one still cannot entirely dismiss belief in the demons, the reading of said works is recommended for the mighty diligence; they testify what the authors have put forth, and assures that this in no way is prejudicial to the rights of His Majesty; which the same Emperor Carlos V wrote disjunctively to the Indians, telling them, "the gospel which thou may have never heard, or which you may have forgotten, etc." The vassals well ought not wish to be more sensitive than their Sovereigns.

I say this because some accused me that I had intended to take from the Spaniards the glory of having brought the Gospel. How could I have thought of taking from them a glory that is very much ours, since it was from our fathers the conquistadores, or the first missionaries, whose apostolic succession is in midst of us? *Gloria filiorum patres eorum (*"The glory of children are their fathers.")* [13] Neither does the glory of the Apostles damage that of their successors; and so glorious it is to have introduced the Gospel at the beginning, as to reestablish it after it had been forgotten or changed.

I even believe that the ancient preaching of Saint Tomé is a more glorious thing for the Spaniards than had he not gone before, because evidencing from their own histories that they owed the possession of America less to their sword than to the ancient prophecies of their coming and dominion, generally believed in all America as from Saint Tomé, it is more glorious without doubt to have owed this favor to an Apostle of Jesus Christ rather than to the devil, or to his thing such as idolatrous prophets.

The Spaniards barely landing the prow on New Spain, they found in Cozumel the Indians forming a procession to ask for rain surrounding a grand Cross they called "the true tree of the world" lifted by Chilancambal that in the Chinese language, as I have said, signifies Saint Tomé. He had preached to them in Campeche that people would come from where the sun rises, armed with that sign, to rule these lands: and once they saw that the Spaniards revered it so much, they believed that they were the same ones designated in the prophecies and they submitted themselves to them.

Our Aztecs had even marked in their paintings the year *ce acatl*, in which they would come, it corresponds precisely to the year 1519 on which Juan de Grijalva arrived in Chalchihuican, today Veracruz, and he left his name on the Castle of San Juan de Ulúa. As soon as the notice of this arrival reached Mexico, the wise King Nezahualpilizintli ofTescuco came to Mexico to give to Mocteuhzoma his condolence of the end of his Empire, he was unfaithful to his kingdom and disappeared until today, without having left a designee among his sons, according to the law of the Acolhuans, the inheritors of the kingdom, because it was not necessary anymore. From the belief of said prophesy, the magnificent gifts emanated that Mocteuhzoma sent to Cortés after he disembarked; and if we give credit to Torquemada, Cortés still being on the ship, the envoys believing that he was the same Saint Tomé, put on him the episcopal garments which had been conserved in Cholula. With said prophesy and the fulfillment of so much that must precede it, Captain General Maxiscátzin of Tlaxcala convinced his Senate to submit themselves to Cortés.

Mocteuhzoma left to receive him in person, believing that he was the Ambassador of Quetzalcohuatl or Saint Tomé, because as such would he come, as he himself wrote it to Carlos V. "My duty," he says, "was to have him believe that Your Majesty was the same which the people were awaiting." "If it is so, Noble Captain," Mocteuhzoma, told him, "that this grand Lord who sent thee is our Lord Quetzalcohuatl, this Empire is yours, and I will do whatever you command." Because the Emperors or Huetlatoanis of Mexico were only titled Lieutenants of Quetzalcohuatl, who were therefore called Teteolt, or Our Lord. Mocteuhzoma, gathered in courts the Kings of the Empire, the Princes and Lords of vassals, and haranguing them with the prophecy that they had in their monuments, he paid homage to the Empire of Carlos V; and following his example all the Princes and Lords were presenting their tributes.

"Regarding the religion," he continued saying, "What thou have proposed to me, we agree: I see that it is the same that Quetzacohuatl taught us. With time, we have forgotten or changed it: thou who comes now from his court, will have it more current. Thou goest saying that which we ought to do, and we shall go about practicing it." For which, Acosta says, the best way to sow the Gospel was opened without opposition, nor the shedding of any blood. The same is easy to have seen happen in the Antilles, in New Granada, in Brazil, and in Peru. If later there were wars, it was because our people were not content with anything, and their customs so unworthy of the disciples of Saint Tomé later they had doubts of their being those designated in the prophesy.

Thus, the ancient preaching of the Gospel in America is as true as glorious to Americans and Spaniards; but who was the preacher is not equally indisputable because of the burning that Bishop Zumárraga did of all the archives and libraries of our Indians, and that other Bishops have continued, has left us in this uncertainty.

Of the remains Boturini managed to gather, it appears, says Veytia, that there were two preachers in New Spain. One around the sixth century, and other more ancient, twelve years after a great eclipse, that the same Veytia and Boturini calculates to be that at the death of Christ.

If it is so, the most ancient could not be other than the Apostle Saint Thomas, as they think, and this is the general opinion of the authors. Not only because in all the Americas the name Tomé was preserved, which they did not learn from the Spaniards, who would have taught them to say Tomás. Not only because they mean the same as other names they used in their respective languages, such as Quetzalcohuatll, Cozas, Chilancambal, etc., which means twin or pal; only because it is the only one of whom the Popes speak that goes back to barbarian and unknown nations. And it appears from Syrian Church monuments it is established, that from the further India where they called and call him Tomé, he passed over to preach in China.

Now, from this not only was it easy to come to America, passing the narrow strait that separates it from Asia, or passing from island to island, of which there are on the coasts between both a range of mountains, but also in the ships of China which were in communication with both Americas in the first centuries of Christianity. It appears from Monsignor Wache, who studied in Peking the same geographic maps of the Chinese; and in his memoir on an unknown island, presented to the National Institute of France, and printed among his Memoirs, he refers to the names the Chinese gave to both Americas, describes the course by which they came, and even mentions the year 450 of our Lord Jesus Christ, that monks came to our America, where they extended the Judeo-Christian religion that is so similar to Christianity that it could be mistaken for it.

As for the second preacher that was in Anáhuac, if it was in the seventh century, I would say that it could have been Saint Bartomé, Apostle of that century in China, and whose name we encounter here in the famous Copil of Tula, who the King Huemac martyred, and ordered his head be thrown into the lagoon, where it is called *Copilco*, which is meant to say, "where the Son of Tomé is;" and this means Bartomé. His sepulcher was conserved with much veneration in the main temple of Mexico until the conquest according to Acosta and Torquemada.

If this preacher was in the sixth century; in which colonies of Irish monks, whose abbots were all Bishops, dispersed themselves by different paths to preach the Gospel, it could be the abbot Saint Brendano, commonly Saint Borondon, who according to their Records came in the sixth century from Ireland to a very large, remote, and unknown island with seven companions; and with them, ordained Bishops, he founded seven churches and returned to Europe. The truth is that his acts in this part are considered apocryphal by the circumstances of his journey, which smell of fables; but always in the ancient and rare much marvels are exaggerated, but at its core it remains the truth. Already since the beginning of the discovery of the Americas, the same happened to Oviedo, first general historian of the Indies, to explain the traces of Christianity they found everywhere. What I warn you is that this admirably fits with the history of the celebrated Quetzacohuatl, as Torquemada recounts it. According to him about this time he disembarked in Pancuo with seven disciples who were later much venerated under the name Chicome-cohuatl, or the seven Tomés. He was Pope or high priest in Tula, where he gave penance to the people, and from where he sent his disciples to Oaxaca and other parts to preach a holy law and he fasted forty days; he raised the crosses which the conquistadors found in Tlaxcala, Tehuantepec and Cuatulco, to whom he gave his famous cross the name, since it means "where the stick is adored"; he destroyed the idols, prohibited the wars and human sacrifices, not admitting other than that of bread, flowers, and perfumes; he always lived in chastity, and he performed many miracles.

Huemac King of Tula, having raised a cruel persecution against the religion from which some apostatized and others suffered martyrdom, came to settle in Cholula. And Huemac going even there with an army to persecute him [Quetzacohuatl], after having been here exactly twenty years, he embarked to where the sun rises in Cuatzacoalco, since then it was called thus, that is, where Tomé hid himself. He sent from there four disciples to govern Cholula, which they divided into wards or parishes, a division that lasted until the conquest; and he foretold the year in which people of his same religion would come from the east to dominate these countries. Of the future fulfillment of this remote prophesy, he gave them, in the style of the prophets, a sign of a nearer event, and it was that the immense pyramid of Cholula would break into pieces; that having it verified, as also the persecution of Christianity in Tula followed by four years of famine and epidemic so horrific they almost ended the Tolteca nation, they had him from then as a Saint, and they believed the prophecy. For this as in significance of him who they were awaiting, they had his image laid down in his Cholula Temple, where for having been this father or apostle's cathedral in the community of the Aztecas, it was his Rome, and it had as many temples as days of the year.

He [Quetzacohuatl] was tall, white, blond, blue eyes, long hair and beard, and the face striped with blue, also his seven companions, as at that time the Irish did. He wore a crown in his hair, had a miter and staff, and upon his black tunic a white cape strewn with red crosses, which is faithfully the ancient cloak of the Bishops. The country to which he returned and from where he had come was called Huehuetlapal-lan, that means Great Red Land, and this can mean Ireland, *Land* at least I know that it is Earth. Torquemada also conjectures that he came from Ireland with the same facial characteristics they attributed to Saint Tomé in the other America. Regarding, being the same San Brendano, there is only difficulty with the Tomé name; this or that Saint also had this name, or perhaps it will mean the same in the Hibernian language.

On the other hand, I find in the names, in the vesture and miter, in the long hair of the Bishops (whom in all languages of our America they were called Popes), in the marriage of the Priests (which the Mexicans in their language were called Elders), in the ceremonies of their mass that they had according to Acosta and Torquemada, in that the bread that the Teopixquis or ministers of God consecrated they believed it converted into the true flesh and blood of the Lord of the Crown of Thorns and they took it while fasting with much repentance and tears, in the fast after Septuagesima, in the period of flood that they marked in accordance with the seventy interpreters, in the invocation of the Trinity or form of baptism in Hebrew, in the anointing of all the body that precedes it, and in the ceremonies of the other six sacraments that they practiced according to Betancourt, in the confession even of the neophytes that they demanded of them according to Remesal, in the images of Jesus Christ tied and not nailed on the Cross, as we will later see etc. etc. I find this, I say, in all these Eastern rites and customs. It is true that the monks of Ireland founded by the Greeks could retain much, as they were it, but can it be that one of the two apostles of Anáhuac may have been Eastern and the other Western, and later they may have mixed and confused the rites? Here the decision depends on our astronomers finding out the date of the great eclipse that came twelve years before the first preacher.

For the preaching in later times ought not to have been difficult, because since the tenth century there were already in America colonies of Normans or Danes, of Irish and Scots. The clear proofs can be seen in the Geography of Maltebrum. Certainly, our authors, even disregarding Saint Tomé, agree that at the least four ages before the conquest, what others call four generations, and others very mistakenly four years, already America had clear and distinct knowledge of the Christian religion and of the coming of the Spaniards. Each one, do your calculations on this. That which I dare to preserve is that if the aforementioned preachers did not have the same name, the most celebrated was called Tomé, and his preaching and his name are the key of the ancient Aztec history, of its theology, of the foundation of Mexico, of its Empire and of the conquest of the Spaniards. It would be very easy for me to give the proofs, which I omit, because they need much extension, and because many Mexican authors have already advanced the major part in manuscript works that can be consulted. I will return to speak of this subject when I speak of the judgement of the two Canons, censors of my sermon, which agree with me in being true to the preaching of the Gospel in America before the conquest of the Spaniards, and it is likely by the Apostle Saint Thomas.

The Second Proposition of my sermon was that Tonantzin, the Mother of the true God, given to be known to the Indians by Saint Tomé, had from those times a temple and worship on the hill Tepeyac in the image of Guadalupe. At the least she was identical, and the Indians called Tonantzin, Guadalupe, for forty years, according to Father Sahagún, until the years 1560 when the Spaniards began to baptize her with the name of Guadalupe, as I will look at later with official testimony of Viceroy Enriquez. In consequence I said, the Most Holy Virgin appearing to Juan Diego would give him her ancient image so that he could carry it to the Bishop etcetera, according to the tradition.

This Proposition is not new, nor should it appear strange. Not the first, because it is found in manuscripts of respectable authors, which they kept and read with esteem in Mexico where they have many supporters. Not the second, because the first missionaries found in the hands of the Indians the Bible in images and figures, and the wise Father Gregorio García says that fearing it would not be believed in Spain, he asked the missionaries in Veracruz for their written testimony, and they gave it to him. Torquemada tells of a book that the Otomies had with the doctrine and image of Jesus Christ, and they buried it to hide it upon the arrival of the Spaniards. Equally accountable that the Dominican missionaries also found described in the paintings of the Indians various articles of our faith such as the Annunciation to our Lady or the Incarnation, and the Resurrection of Our Lord; and that these had images painted of the Most Holy Mary with a tiny cross in the hair, and of Christ crucified with the circumstance of being on the Cross not nailed, but tied, and thus they believed that it was. This circumstance is much to be noted because thus the Christians of Saint Tomé in the East painted him; the reason for all this, he gives himself not to the torture of the Cross with nails, but with cords, as one can see in the histories of the martyrs of Japan.

This supposition is still necessary to not confound the most ancient religion of Anáhuac with the additional fables introduced with the lapse of time that confuses and turns everything upside down, and by the nature of their own hieroglyphics since it causes the code with antiquity to be forgotten. The same missionaries so concerned in the beginning against the Indians, whose images so disgusted them for being filled with extravagant hieroglyphics for their intelligence that they knew to distinguish among the primitive gods of the time of the Toltecans, introduced by Quetzalcohuatl, who they called *Tlaloques* or of the Paradise, or of the mountains, and of the waters (known as Teotlipalmenohuan or Tenteotl, Teohuitzahuac or Teotlaloc, and the Tonantzin or Tzenteotinanzin), and in the theogony later forged, upon which the same missionaries also invented not a little from their prejudices, from the ignorance of the language; and of the Azteca theology, and from the ineptitude of the *Nahuatlatos* or interpreters of the paintings.

Under these assumptions, the sermon's second proposition seems to me that it can be proven, by way of the ancient Mexican history, as with the same Guadalupana history. According to that, who was the *Tzenteotinanzin*, or *Tonanzin* given to be known by *Quetzalcohuatl* who from those times was venerated on the hill *Tepeyac*, to whom he conveyed the name *Tonantzin*? To read Torquemada and Cabrera is enough to know it. She was a Virgin consecrated to God in the service of the temple, that through the work of the heaven she conceived and gave birth to the Lord of the Crown of Thorns or *Teohuitzahuac*, without lesion to her virginity, He appeared in human and divine nature, he was born made a perfect male, *fæmina circundabit virum* ("*A woman shall compass a man*"), [14] and he was destroyed in being born a serpent that tormented his Mother, *tu insidiaberis calcaneo mulieris et ipsæ* (according to the Hebrew and Greek text) *conteret caput tuum* ("*The heel of the woman shall bruise your head. And the women will lie in wait for you*") [sic]. [15]

This Lord of the Crown of Thorns who they also painted naked and with a cross in the hand, formed with five spheres of feathers, was called by another name *Méxî* that pronounced in Mexican as in Hebrew with the same Hebrew letter *shin*, means the same as anointed, and they even said that they had the name of Mexicans since their God ordered in both languages, that is Anointed or Christ. For this they celebrated his fiesta all of them anointing their faces with a certain ointment. It is to say that "Mexicans" means the same as "Christians," consequently Mexico means *where Christ is worshiped*. Even though one encounters this whole word, as the Indians pronounced it, in the 2nd verse of Psalms 2nd the Hebrew says *Mescicho* where the Vulgate reads *Christum eius* ("*His Anointed*"). And the Christians could give him this name, fugitives of Tula from the persecutions of Huemas, and saved themselves in this lagoon upon an island of sand, or *Xaltelolco*, that later they named *Tlatelolco*, and from there they established *Tenochtitlan* named *México* to the assembly of the two wards. See *de Ante-Cristo* by Maluenda.

Nor is this the only Hebrew word that our Indians used, since the Christians of Saint Tomé in East India also used Hebrew in their liturgy. In the West the *Cocómes* or *Tomés* Priests baptized with the name of the Trinity in Hebrew (see Maluenda *ubi supra*) according to the testimony of the Venerable Bishop Casas, who adds that in Yucatan the Indians had full and clear knowledge of the Christian religion taught by Cozas or Tomé, who arrived there with twenty disciples and they named the Most Holy Virgin with Hebrew words that mean: Mother of the Son of the Great Father.

In Mexico they also called her *Tonantzin Tonacayohua*, or Lady of Him that has embodied in us, as to the Crosses that they worshiped, they called *Tonacayoüitl* the tree of Him that was embodied among us. Anyway, they called her *Tzenteotinantzin*, this is, Mother of the true God, what that means is *Tzenteotl*, by another name *Teotl-ipalmenohuani* or the Lord by whom we live; pure spirit, Omnipotent, Omniscient, eternal, immense, incomprehensible, just, merciful; to whom alone they paid adoration that she would reveal by deed and by word, since they only knelt before his images, and to him only did they say this prayer: "Oh Omnipotent God, who we call thee *Titlacahua* (whose slaves we are) open the hands of thy piety and have mercy on us."

The Virgin Mother of this true God was the beloved mother of all the peoples of Anáhuac, and for this they called her *Tonantzin*, or Our Lady and Mother. They much enjoyed raising temples to her, for her ancient and grand beneficence, and they were such devotees of her image on the hill Tepeyac, that no one passed without going up to pour upon her altar the flowers that were found there, an offering which was pleasing to her because she detested and prohibited human victims, the same as Saint Tomé, and for this they called her *Cihuacohuatl* or Tomé woman.

But they also called her *Coatlautona*, because they said that she was the mother especially of *Quetzacohuatl*, and of the Priests *Coatlan* or Tomés, who made a vow of poverty, obedience, and chastity, living from charity that they went two-by-two to ask for with their white belted tunics, their eyes lowered and the arms crossed. They bathed in the fountain *coapan* or of Tomé that was discovered when they opened the foundations of the (Spanish) cathedral, and even thought of good water, as it was superstitiously covered; they rose up to pray at midnight, they did great penance, they carried the figurative crown of thorns with the hair of each one, *senchonhuitznahuac*, and they served in the temple of the Lord of the Crown of Thorns, *huitznahuac-teocalli*. This last word is entirely Greek.

The figure in which they venerated this Virgin was that of an Aztec child or little girl, dressed in a white resplendent and belted tunic, and with a sea-green blue mantle studded with stars. This is the same figure of Our Lady of Guadalupe. And they said that in such a figure she appeared many times, even though always to one alone and revealing to him secret things, principally a little before the conquest. And a little after this one saw her walking in the same clothes lamenting by the hill the ruin of her temple, fallen during the siege of Mexico, that it might be restored to her.

Various fiestas celebrated her, the principal one being the 2nd day of February or the Purification of Our Lady and the presentation of the Child Jesus in the temple, with the circumstance by which children were presented to her, and they had to be precisely purchased with money *omne primogenitum pretio redimes* ("*Redeem all the firstborn*"); and they made sure that part of them were white and blond, in memory of it having been *Quetzalcohuatl* who instituted the fiesta. The other celebration to her was the day of the winter solstice that in our America is the 22nd of December. According to the Priest Becerra Tanco on that day was the apparition of Our Lady of Guadalupe, which, the author adds, lacks no mystery, for having been another day of the Apostle Saint Thomas, who it was that brought the Gospel to this kingdom, of which I have seen painting and tradition that cannot be applied to another of the Apostolate for having conserved the name *Dydimus*. It means that he was *Quetzalcohuatl*.

If we appeal to the Guadalupe history, the same Most Holy Virgin came to be known as the ancient *Tzenteotinantzin* since the first message that she sent with Juan Diego was. "Tell the Bishop that the Mother of the true God sent thee, with an order that he shall build me a temple in this place, to show from here the ancient Mother's heart that I conserve towards the peoples of thy lineage." And how would the Virgin say to Juan Diego, or this to the Bishop in good Mexican, that the *Mother of the true God* sent him without saying *Tzenteotinantzin*? Because, *Diosinantzin* is an amalgam of Spanish and Nahuatl, subsequently introduced by the Franciscan missionaries out of spite to the Dominicans? Nor how could the Virgin, if she were not the ancient *Tonantzin*, who asked for a temple there to show in that place, the ancient Mother's heart that conserved the Indian's lineage, when in one thousand six hundred years she had not thrown them a compassionate glance, nor had notice of her been tolled except after three or four years between slavery, desolation, and death?

Juan Diego, at the very least, could not understand everything in this message, except that the Indian's most beneficent Mother and Lady sent him, in whose identical dress they then used to tell that she was seen walking on the hill lamenting the ruin of her temple, that it be rebuilt to her. The same apparition within a rainbow, while the entire hillock represented a flower garden, even with lucid and harmonious little birds never seen in these regions, as the Aztecs imagined paradise, it was manifesting that it was the ancient *Tlaloque* or of the paradise, that they venerated in ancient Tepeyácac. To judge it so was so natural that the same Juan Diego, according to the Guadalupe history, exclaimed amazed: "Am I in the paradise of my elders, who were called the origin of all flesh?" Such is the Christian paradise, and the Indian clearly supposed Christianity to have been the religion of his elders, and by consequence the *true Mother of the true God*, was she who they venerated in Tepeyácac. No one has ever been able to remove from the Indians' head that their ancient religion was ours, and in this meaning and belief here one makes Juan Diego speak and work.

I said in the sermon that perhaps I would make the case of the proposition that I am proving, the famous number 8 that the image of Guadalupe has at her feet. It can be a coincidence, but it can also be some number, or the remainder of some Syro-Chaldaic sign, because without doubt it is not a number 8 as they call it, but a character of said language that one sees in the trimming of the famous Cross of Saint Tomé in East India Meliapur, whose inscription was expounded by the order of Cardinal Don Enrique, Prince of Portugal. The very same is found in the famous stone excavated in China, relative to the preaching of Saint Bartomé in the seventh century, explained in Rome by Father Kirker. From this same language, appears to have been or to be the inscriptions engraved on stones that were found in both Americas with the tradition of being related to the preaching of Saint Tomé. And, for this Saint Toribio Archbishop of Lima, ordered chapels built to cover those inscriptions that remained in Peru. Thinking a similar tradition very worthy of respect, Father Calanche brought one of the said engraved inscriptions. The Venerable Bishop Casas saw other large signs on the large buildings of Mictlan in Yucatan and was also induced to believe that Saint Tomé had preached in Onahualco, as our Indians called the city of Campeche. These things should have deserved, and they do deserve more attention than that of stirring up the ignorant masses.

In a word, I will have seen that the history of Guadalupe includes and contains the history of the ancient *Tonantzin*, with her hair and with its soft curls; what I have not warned you of is that her history is dispersed in the writers of Mexican antiquities. And so one of two; or what I preached is true, or the Guadalupe history is a comedy of the Indian Valeriano, built upon the Aztec mythology regarding *Tonantzin*, for that they carry it out in Santiago, where he was professor, the young collegiate Indians that in their time were accustomed to represent in their language this way in verse as in prose the farces that we call sacramental dramas, much in vogue in 16th century Spain and in America. And for this Valeriano made Santiago the place for the stage object of the travels of Juan Diego, even though a native and parishioner of Cuautitlan, and even though perhaps neither did the Church of Santiago then exist. It is necessary to opt between the horns of this dilemma because there is no solution.

I will say more: if that which I preached is not true, the image of Guadalupe would be one of those prohibited in the decree of the Second Mexican Council, for having mixed in her painting mythological traces of the Aztecs. Such is the color of the moon that is under her feet, and that they painted black or ash-gray, because they believed the moon transformed itself into a being full of sores, having thrown her into a bonfire when already she was almost into charcoals and ash, envious of having seen her leave the penitent Ycápan converted into the sun. Is it credible that the Mother of God appearing when the Indians were almost all Gentiles and idolaters seems to thus confirm them in their mythological genesis of the sun and the moon, contrary to the sacred Scriptures? It was to avoid these and many other arguments against the tradition that I believe necessary to end a little of the customary course. I will exhibit later to them that I may have proved that nothing of the above mentioned until here contradicts the genuine and legitimate tradition of Guadalupe.

This teaches that the image was already painted when the Virgin sent it to Bishop Zumárraga. This is what the Mexican Manifesto says, the original source of the history in question. The Priest Becerra Tanco, a distinguished master of the Nahuatl language, proves it with his own words. And this author who was one of the witnesses of the information of one thousand six hundred sixty-six, and according to Florencia he alone is worth many, whose vote is of such weight that his account was inserted in the records sent to Rome, and that in the end according to Bartolache, he is the most classic, erudite and judicious of the Guadalupano authors. He spoke expressly thus: "It is warned, that the tradition does not say that the image was painted at the unfurling of the mantle by the Indian in the presence of the Bishop; but that he saw it then, and not before; and the image for being already painted, the Virgin ordered Juan Diego not to show to any person that which he carried, other than to the Lord Bishop. To say that it was painted before this with flowers is an imagination by which some have wanted to make the miracle greater."

Also, the Licentiate Lazo, Chaplain of the Sanctuary, in the Mexican account that came to light in the year one thousand six hundred forty-eight clearly says, according to Bartolache, that the image was already painted when it was taken to the Bishop. When then, how, or where was it painted? "No one knows," replied Father Anaya, whose octaves on Guadalupe are much esteemed. Later, I have been able to set back the epoch of the painting, without prejudice to the genuine and legitimate tradition, to save this from the arguments, and to make that more glorious to the native land.

Only one objection is jumping to view by natural consequence, and it is that the painting put back to the time of the preaching of Saint Tomé cannot be painted on the cape of Juan Diego that then did not exist. But one thing is that the

Indian takes the image to the Bishop around his neck, as they were accustomed to wear his cape. That is the only thing that could build on an established tradition, and another thing is that the image's cloth must be Juan Diego's same usual cape.

I said that the second one denied it, only in the intelligence that such was not the genuine tradition, because such cannot be what would contradict the Mexican Manifesto in its source, what cannot be sustained as true, and what the sacred Congregation of Rites did not want to admit or to express in the prayer, despite the effort with which they reported it in favor of the circumstance.

I say that it would contradict the Mexican Manifesto, because according to it what the Priest Tanco has given to us literally translated, Juan Diego coming from Tepeyac with the flowers on his cape, he came opening it from time to time to regale himself with them. Also, the Bishop's domestics forced it opened, they reached a hand to the flowers that suddenly became painted or woven on the cape, but they did not see the painting. Neither had Juan Diego seen it, since the flowers burst out before the Bishop who was left stunned to see the image. So, it is that this could not be if the image was already painted on his cape. Nor even if he could have stretched it out to the people of the street, according to the Virgin's mandate, bringing it around the neck as the Indians wear the cape. Then it is not on the cape of Juan Diego, or the Mexican Manifesto contradicts itself.

In vain, I will say that this proves that the image was not painted in front of the Bishop, because the Mexican Manifest affirms, the original source of the Guadalupe history, that it was already painted, or it must be said that it was not on the cape of Juan Diego in order to raise the contradiction, or the Royal Historical Academy will answer back with Cardinal Baronio, that God never permits impostors who might weave so well their cloth, that some thread does not escape them whereby in the end his scheme unraveled. It is necessary to take charge that we do not now throw on the tradition folk songs to our whim: we have the war declared by enemies as clever and respectable.

I also say that it cannot support itself as true that the cloth of the Guadalupe image could be the usual cape of Juan Diego for three reasons. First, because the cape of a Mexican Indian consists precisely of three parts, as everyone knows and Tanco affirms; and the cloth of Our Lady has no more than two.

To respond that he would cut the third is a guess. The loose threads that it has from one side toward the foot, or they ought to be even to the top to prove something, or they only prove what Tanco himself says, that they have kept the tiny pieces that they have been cutting for relics. And it is even clear that being as the parts are united with a thread thicker than that of the cloth, according to the painter Cabrera y Bartolache, one should have cut the thread and not a cloth so precious.

To respond that from Tanco one infers a part has been cut, as Bartolache responds, is manifestly untruthful. Tanco thinks that the image was painted at the foot of Mount Tepeyácac, when the Indian was showing the Virgin the flowers in his cape that he would have diagonally on the shoulder, as they were accustomed when they take something in it. For this image that the Virgin gave him then the sun arose by the back, toward his right shoulder, and in this position some Angel with the colors prepared by some painter, would paint her image following the optical inflection of her shadow on the cloth and middle of the cape that Juan Diego kept in front, toward his right shoulder. If this poetry is valid for inferring something, what it could infer is that one-and-a-half part has been taken from the image's cloth. This inference is false, because there are those that have two equal parts, with only the difference of two finger breadths, according to the dimensions given by Bartolache himself.

The second reason for not being true that the image's cloth is Juan Diego's cape, arises from the Indian's quality, that was *macehual* or lower class; and by consequence his cape or *tilmatli* ought to be of *ixtle* or the thread of maguey, especially as before the recent conquest. This was etiquette so rigorous among the Aztecs that the son of the Emperor of Mexico could not wear the cape of another class before having won a battle. For this, all the witnesses of the information on Guadalupe from one thousand six hundred sixty-six, assuming with Sanchez the first Gudalupano historian who printed that the image's cloth is Juan Diego's cape, agreed with him that it is of ichtle, and they pondered much about its coarseness. The Mexican common people, also supposing the same even today, still call the cloth of our image *ayate,* that is, woven from maguey. Thus it is that it is verified that it is not such, from the time of the Priest Tanco, and Bartolache has juridically demonstrated with the faith of writers and painters that it is from the *iczotl* palm, soft as cotton, so fine and well woven that Bartolache having brought, without excusing cost nor fatigue, the best Indian weavers and spinners of the materials of the country, and he himself presiding one whole year, his work could not equal the fineness of Our Lady's cloth. Therefore, it is not Juan Diego's cape or blanket.

The third reason for proving the same is that the cloth of Our Lady conforms to the declaration of the first physicians that inspected it in one thousand six hundred sixty-six, and it also conforms to Bartolache's inspections, it is softer on the front side than on the backside. This is the same way that all the paintings are done on the cloth of *iczotl* palm that the Indians allocated for fine paintings, because Boturini says that they first burnished the part that they were painting. Therefore, the cloth of Our Lady is a cloth prepared to the style of the Indians for painting on it, and it is not the cape of the Indian Juan Diego.

The image of Our Lady from the village of *Tecaxique* is identical in paint and cloth to Our Lady of Guadalupe, and no one says for this that it is on the cape of an Indian, although there also an apparition is counted, as innumerable others in the recent kingdom conquest, because then, Torquemada says, the Indians were given to painting many images that they took and left in the churches, where each day they appeared without knowing who had brought them.

Last, I will say that it cannot be the genuine tradition that the image is on Juan Diego's cape, because the Sacred Congregation of Rites did not want to admit or express in the prayer this circumstance, despite the determination with which they reported in its favor.

Effectively, such is not expressed anywhere in the prayer, nor is it indicated if you wish by some illusion, like the flowers. And not only was it reported that it was on the cape of the Indian in the honors of the postulant López, which includes the Concession Brief, *In Eodem Linteolo* (*"On the Linen Cloth"*); but that in the Acts sent to Rome it was made to consist of the principal of the miracle on the cape of the Indian, for being of iztle, and by consequence rough, thin, and full of holes, incapable naturally in the end of having painted on it the image without priming. This information evidences from Nicoselli, who translated to Italian the Latin account sent from Mexico with the Acts which are summarized and beseeched by them before the Congregation of Rites for the concession of the prayer that they had lost.

Nevertheless, the Congregation suppressed in it the circumstance so relevant. Therefore, it did not believe it true, or at least it did not believe it essential to the tradition. In any case of the two, I could deny it without prejudice to the genuine tradition, and so much more that the Doctor Bartolache assures by his experiences and very solemn inspections that there is not half a word of truth in all the half page that contains the information sent to Rome on this. Since neither is the cloth of the image of ixtle, but of iczotl, soft as cotton, as fine as well woven, and that not only can one paint on it naturally without another priming than the same compound of the colors, but that on a cloth of iczotl that Zamorátegui managed to make, more fine than theirs, he painted fiber to fiber and without any priming, as is the image of Guadalupe, his copy to put in the Church of the Pozito (Mexico City).

The result of everything with evidence is that I did not

deny the Guadalupe tradition in the sermon. Yes, the circumstance that I earlier conditionally denied cannot be sustained as true, and denied it saves the tradition's significance against thearguments, resulting in greater glory for the image and the native land, one ought to absolutely sacrifice without dispute and to adopt my method.

Not being able to, nor owing to the truth, to say that the image is on Juan Diego's cape, I adopted through a consolatory result, and precisely to guard against the sentiment or scandal of the ignorant, the Borundiana species that were on Saint Thomas's cape; but modifying it under these terms: "One could say, even with the very lowest probability. . ." This was not to be affirmed, as it was proclaimed by the preachers of the Sunday following the fiesta, and it was asserted in the famous Episcopal Edict, without having ventured a conjecture, warning that it was extremely weak. All this was suppressed, my protests in favor of the tradition were kept quiet, the intention of my most glorious sermon to the native land, to the image, and to the Sanctuary was hidden, and a lot was written only about the adventurous fragment of Saint Thomas's cape, totally impertinent to the substance of my sermon, for mentioning it to the people in contradiction with Juan Diego's cape, one might be persuaded that I had emphatically denied the tradition, the scandal was incited and resulted that it was cause for a pretext to prosecute me and ruin me, as the Archbishop had already intended it with the Archdeacon Serruto, whose sermon of the condemned Saint Peter was approved and printed in Spain by His Illuminate with so much fanfare. *Hoc opus hic labor erat* ("*It was this work, this labor*").

Without so sinister an intention, what motive was there to have excited such an exorbitant scandal? Is the image of the Mother of God on the cape of an Indian more worthy, than the cape of an Apostle of Jesus Christ? If they left in America, according to the same Spanish authors printed in Spain, the Sacred Scriptures in images, images of Christ and of the

Virgin and of the selfsame Saint Tomé, vestiges of his feet and his hands, and inscriptions engraved on stones; if in Peru they think to have one of his shoes, if here in Cholula his cape or episcopal pallium is conserved and all his clothes, that the Indians looked over Cortés believing that he was the self-same Saint Tomé, why did it have to be a scandal that we have his cape in the linen of Our Lady of Guadalupe? The cape of the Apostles was a Jewish cape like that of the Indians. What Saint Tomé wore in America, according to Father Calancha, was of two cloths like that of Our Lady of Guadalupe; and to this, if it is the image of the *Mother of the true God* that the Indians worshiped in Tepeyácac, also called *Coatliene*, that means to say, "her garment is from the Tomé." I have here enough for a very weak conjecture, as warned that it was what I preached. If these things appear deliriums, they do not appear so much to those who have studied our antiquities.

It was already time that the Lord Bishops should have learned a lesson from their hasty judgement of them. The first Bishop of Mexico felt that all the symbolic manuscripts of the Indians were magical figures, witchcraft, and demons; and he made it a religious duty to exterminate them by himself and by means of the missionaries, throwing to the flames all the Aztecs' libraries, of those of which Tezenco on its own was their Athens, raised as tall as a mountain when by order of Zumárraga they took it out to burn. And, as the Indians redid their manuscripts or hid them to conserve the history of their nation, the missionaries made use of the Christian children, in whom they invested their mistaken zeal, so that they were robbed from their parents, and from this came the death of the seven Tlaxcalteca children reputed martyrs. Thus, this Bishop caused a loss, as irreparable as immense, to the Nation and to the Literary Republic.

Mr. Palafox finished destroying all the Aztec statues there were in the streets and corners of Mexico and deprived us of much light of their ancient history. At the end of the XVIII century the Bishop of Nicaragua destroyed in a bonfire another portion remaining of the symbolic-historical manuscripts of the Indians, with an inevitable edict, as that of Mr. Haro, in which he declared they contained errors, impieties, demons, and deliriums: and there were no others, according to Boturini, other than those that the Bishop's Pastoral contained.

The Canon censors after agreeing that the preaching of the Gospel in America before the conquest is certain, and it is probable that it was done by the Apostle Saint Thomas, they say that the rest of the sermon is also found in many manuscripts that they keep and read in Mexico with esteem, and especially in the work of one author, for another respectable part, as identical in the ideas to Borunda, that they believe he has copied it. And, since many persons of sound judgement in Mexico, for this carry on the same opinions, they asked His Illuminate to gather said manuscripts, dispossessing their owners. And what is the reason for such violence? It is peremptory. The dictum of Uribe and Omaña, which no Mexican knows, is worth more than that of the respectable authors and the just people of Mexico.

When will they cease these truthfully scandalous operations for destroying our monuments, depriving us of the sweat of our wise men, and impeding us from the knowledge of our antiquities, using religion as a pretext? The King, on the contrary, had a little before issued at the request of the Historical Academy a Royal order not only that all the monuments of the American antiquities be conserved, but also inviting us to study them and write about them. The Royal order was communicated to us by the hand of Mexico's Royal Court.

If we can write, we can preach, especially having in our support respectable authors and people of true judgement, and not giving our opinions as beyond any doubt. It is not prohibited to preach probable things. Almost all that we preach, outside of dogma, is no more. And, it pleases God what many times was the material of the funeral prayers, upon which adulation he never says a word to us. Above all when the speaker warns the people, as I do, that he does not announce like a Master in Israel the eternal truths of the law, but a probable discussion that he submits to the correction of the wise, there is no inconvenience, because there cannot be seduction, there is not under this protest some Papal prohibition, and the scandal that results is purely passive, welcomed, and not concluded, or pharisaical. When a scandal is born of truth, Saint Gregorio Magno says about the ninth chapter of Ezekiel, it is more useful to leave the scandal to be born, than to abandon the truth.

But there was not even this scandal, before the Archbishop excited it on purpose. Nor ought there to be any, because not only did I not deny the tradition of Guadalupe as I leave already proven, but that the sermon was all outlined to support it against the arguments, if it were possible, and if not that the native land keeps a greater glory. Forced by the necessity of defending my honor, I am going to exhibit these arguments, not all, nor in all the extension of force that they allow, because this alone would necessitate a volume, they are so many, but as many as are needed to make known the difficulty that I intended to overcome, and I do not believe to have been defeated.

To commence, permit me to go back to the year one thousand five hundred and sixteen, a wretched period to the heresy of our encomienda system, more true than plausible. Harassed by the missionaries to not teach the Christian doctrine, nor to give time to the Indians for teaching it to them, when for this they had been principally entrusted, they finally turned to saying that they were unfit for the Gospel, and therefore neither mankind, nor competent knowledge, etc. And the worst was that by force, to repeat it, they came to firmly believe the principle and the consequences.

This heresy was born says the precise Remesal, on the island of Santo Domingo; and this then being like the metropolis and the way of the Spaniards to the New World, spread throughout it with the rapidity of an infection, causing most solemn slaughters of human flesh.

I will not stain my discourse with them; but I cannot omit

that with the departure of Hernan Cortés for Honduras in one thousand five hundred and twenty-four, Mexico was made into a daily camp of civil war, and such was the disorder that the Bishop Zumárraga left for Tlaxcala with his clergy singing the Psalm *in exitu Israël de Egipto* ("*When Israel went out of Egypt.*"). [16] The Bishop of this, the only consecrated that there was, came to Mexico but nothing could contain and calm the scandal. Both Bishops in one thousand five hundred twenty-nine wrote to the Emperor, that in those five years four hundred thousand Indians died, and if a remedy was not soon put in place, they were finished.

Since the government was stirred up, a sailor took the letter inside a buoy well covered with pitch and put it in the water, and for this the Second Court came to disembark in Pánuco. This Court sent to the Bishop Zumárraga some six months after the time of the apparition, to justify himself before the King of the crime of defending the Indians. Their celebrated Royal Protector Fray Bartolomé de las Casas came to Mexico at the same time and having seen the devastation that the brutal heresy of the conquistadores did everywhere, Mexico's San Domingo Prior Fray Bernardino de Minaya was made to leave in all diligence for Rome to get a dogmatic decision. Paul III effectively issued two Briefs on the fifth of April of one thousand five hundred thirty-six. In the first he defined the Indians as true men, who are fit for the faith and for the Gospel, and true owners of their goods, of which one ought not to dispossess them, nor to destroy them with slavery. In the second Brief directed to the Archbishop of Seville, then the metropolitan of the Indies, to have executed the first, it strikes down excommunication reserved to the Supreme Pontiff against the impious sectarians of the mentioned opinions.

And what documents did the San Domingo Prior take to Rome for such a crucial decision? The most classic, and of what we know, was a beautiful Latin letter from the already cited Bishop of Tlaxcala, the Venerable Garcés. In it, he asked permission to test the capacity of the Indians in order to the faith, with the wonders that the heaven had worked to their favor, or with them; because even until now, it says, no miracle in the Indies has been authenticated, religious and prudent men ought not to be denied the credit on this, it being very normal that God repeats in the new church what he has done in the ancient one.

One sees of course by this authentic testimony, written three or four years after the pretended apparition, that they had not produced the information of it, as the Apostolic Chair asserted for the attainment of the prayer, *extitisse compertum est* (*"It occurred when it was discovered."*); since the Bishop could not ignore them, that was then, the only one consecrated, the center of the religious communications and intimate friend of Zumárraga. Today one is already convinced that there was no such information.

But, how was it possible, if the apparition is true, that a Venerable Bishop could have omitted, a decision as important to the spiritual and temporal life of his sheep and of millions of men from all over America, an act so recent, public, and marvelous when he does not express an opinion on other similar obscure events, like Our Lady of the Rosario to have appeared with two women Saints to an Indian woman, and gives her a crown of roses?

The same Guadalupano authors increase the difficulty, because they discuss that the Virgin appeared on purpose for confounding the heresy already said of the conquistadors. And certainly, a more urgent argument could not be invented, than for the Mother of God herself to come down to ask for a temple where her maternal affections are shown to the Indians. She chose one of the most insignificant, judging by his condition, as her Ambassador, and she authorized him with the corresponding credentials. His poor cloak served as her altar, in the painting she takes the figure and attitude of a *cihualpiltzin* or Indian woman chief, and even though the Indian could not pronounce Guadalupe, because their language lacks *g*, *y*, and *d*, she orders that he call her by this Arabic and dreadful sounding name, since it means, "river of wolves," for it being her most celebrated image in Extremadura, where the greater part or the most important of the conquistadors were from, like showing them that she does not differentiate them from her affection for the Indians. Who then would imagine that a Venerable Bishop,writing to the head of the Church in order that he might decide that the same Virgin had come down to test; to frustrate him with her silence, her Divine and conclusive logic?

And Zumárraga, could he have stopped a piece of news to confuse the heresy of the time, so deadly, to defend his sheep with the testimony from heaven, and to defend with them his cause, that was the same, before Mexico's Court and Spain's King; to convert the Indians, almost all then Gentiles, since the courage to ask for baptism did not begin until the year one thousand five hundred thirty-four, according to Torquemada; to confirm the neophytes in the faith; to repair with this miracle the scandal of the bad example of the Spanish Christians, and to replace it with it the language of the missionaries who scarcely began to babble a few Mexican words? Bartolache says that they did not make up the news because they could not make it up, since all had passed only between the Virgin and the Indian and he was untrustworthy for rude, novice, and self-interest. But this is nonsense. If the Virgin authorized her envoy to petition the Bishop with the correspondent credentials of a miracle, in accordance to the tradition, he ought to be believed on his word as with any legitimate Ambassador.

At the least, if the Bishop believed it, he could not refuse to obey the Virgin in raising the temple that she asked for, being from the Mother and protector of her sheep and more when it cost him nothing but to order it. He did nothing: nor did he come to agree to such an image in the sixteen years that remained of his Bishopric. And what is most incredible, the Indians rebuilt for free the cities, and only because the Friars told them they were for their people, they came for the models of the churches and convents, and when the Friars went, they found them already done. They did not take the image of

Guadalupe from an adobe hermitage to the reasonable church until forty years later, and this for another incident that I will tell later.

Yet even more incredible it seems to me that the beloved Father of the Indians, Fray Bartolomé de las Casas, who spent his long life in their defense, kept a difficult silence on such a wonder to the favor of his clients, when in those years he wrote his four hundred sheet defense of the Indians without margins, in which he poured out the rest of his knowledge, without omitting anything in order to exalt them in any genre, and he filled the world with histories, memorials, representations, treatises, accounts, and shouts.

Many monks of all the orders wrote by order of the King and of his generals, histories and chronicles, always defending the Indians and speaking of the spreading of the Gospel and of so many miracles accompanying it, descending to the smallest details, and all kept quiet about the greatest of all the miracles that happened.

The conquistadors, even though bad, were so highly devoted to the Virgin that they brought painted on their flags with enough resemblance to that of Guadalupe; and to that of Extremadura of whose name they had so much devotion, that there were in all the cities of America commissioners for gathering the bequests that they did in their last wills. None were done for that of Mexico, nor memories of her apparition in so many reports that they wrote and so many apparitions of the Virgin that they told. Gomara, Cortés's Chaplain, was the echo of all things, since he wrote for their reports, filling it all with miracles and apparitions in the battles, in such a manner that Bernal Diaz del Castillo, who wrote of the years one thousand five hundred sixty, erupts in anger, because it seems to him that nothing was left to be done to the sword of the conquistadors. And, he said nothing of Guadalupe. The same Bernal Diaz is sure to also tell of the apparitions of the Virgins, like in Nautla because he says that thus they told them. And pledged to doing the defense of the conquest by the good spirits that resulted, he puts forth the miracles that

Our Lady of Guadalupe did in Tepeyaquilla; but of her apparition that was the greatest, and that by the name that the Virgin had wanted to take, he did more to his purpose and favor, not one word.

Neither did the Royal Chroniclers, who the Kings named for writing the history of the Indies, speak of it even though they do not omit miracles; the Master Gil Gonzalez Dávila heaped up stubble and fluff in his ecclesiastical history as soon as a wonder came to his notice. At least he would not have kept quiet the history of Guadalupe, writing the life of Zumárraga. And what will we say of the Indians' silence, those most interested in the matter, even when they wrote in our and their language many volumes of history, of which not a few exist?

These arguments are not all negative, since when the authors were found on occasion and even an obligation to speak and they did not speak, the argument is mixed; although the silence also proves in the history, and yes shows it is universal. The words of Father Papebroquio, celebrated writer of the Acts of the Saints, are: *Silentínm in historia probat, et quandoque demonstrat; ut quando historici omnes silent* (*"Silence proves in history, and sometimes pointed out when all the historians are silent."*).

Neither do they lack constructive case documents against the tradition. The Royal Chronicler Muñoz alleges two. The first is from the Venerable Father Sahagún who came to Mexico with the first Franciscan missionaries in one thousand five hundred twenty-eight and wrote the *Historia universal de la Nueva España* (*"Universal History of New Spain"*) first in a trilingual Dictionary, and later with said title. The paragraph that Muñoz produced, says that Sahagún wrote it in one thousand five hundred sixty-four, when the devotion of Guadalupe was at its greatest fervor. Speaking of the gods of the mountains and hills he continues. "There was another near Mexico, called Tonantzin, to who a great concourse of people came, and from very far lands. And now that Our Lady of Guadalupe is there, they also call her Tonantzin, an opportunity taken from the preachers who thus called the Mother of Our Lord, and her name is not *Tonantzin*, but *Diosinantzin*. And they come to this Tonantzin as before and as far as before. Which devotion also is suspicious, because there are other images near their villages, and they do not go to them, and they come to this Tonantzin as before and as far as before."

Would a monk as instructed as Sahagún have the devotion of the Indians towards theimage of Guadalupe and the pilgrimage to her Sanctuary for suspicion of idolatry, if it had been half the apparition that one supposes?

But the second document Muñoz alleges is much more decisive, in that it is constructive and official. From one thousand five hundred fifty-six until one thousand five hundred seventy-five, the devotion of Guadalupe was the great fervor in the sixteenth century. It was taken from a hermitage to a sensible church, that today we call the old church, or of the Indians; the Congregation was founded, dowries that still exist were set up for orphans, they put priests there, and asked the King for a license to start a parish and a monastery. The kings at that time desired to know everything that happened in America, and they ordered that it be referred to them in the greatest details, and thus the King by motive of that devotional movement ordered Viceroy Don Martin Enriquez that he inform himself and then inform him on the origin and the rest concerning Guadalupe as one infers from the same report. This could not be mistaken at a time so near, almost all the missionaries living who had placed the image on Guadalupe, according to their own history, and the immediate successor of Zumárraga, [Fray] Montufar.

I received it, says the Viceroy, from Your Majesty dated in the Royal San Lorenzo, the fourteenth of September of the past year (one thousand five hundred seventy-five). He proceeds informing him of many things appertaining to the Government; because the letter is very long; and then at paragraph fifteen he continues thus: "And on order to the hermitage of Our Lady of Guadalupe, and have the

Archbishop visit her, visit her and take the accounts as has always been done by the prelates. And the origin that this had, as one commonly understands, was that a poor shepherd, who walked by there about the year one thousand five hundred fifty-six; raised his voice that an image of Our Lady that was there in a hermitage, had healed him: which voice ran through the Region and the people began to meet, and they gathered alms which the Church now has. And they called her of Guadalupe, to say that she looks like the Guadalupe in Spain. From then was founded a brotherhood that had about four hundred brothers; and for which alms were gathered, and from what this yields I then send to Your Majesty the sum; and if more is gathered, I will also send it. I have said to the Archbishop that it would be good to be applied to the Indians' Hospital, that as it bears the name of Your Majesty, but nobody gives it anything, yet it is the most needed of all. The Archbishop wants to apply them to orphans' dowries. It is not the place for the parish, even less for the monastery; and there are so many around that would be useless. I have spoken with the Archbishop who would agree to put a Priest there who could say mass and could hear the confessions of the people who go to the novenas. The Archbishop has already placed two clergy; and if the income grows more, he will also want to place more; in such a way that everyone will come to be reduced to what two or three clergies eat." This is an official and authentic document, to which one cannot put fault because it has been copied in the Royal Archive of Simancas from among the correspondence of the Viceroys, by a Secretary of His Majesty's Royal Chronicler, and has been examined by the Royal Academy of History in an approved, prizewinning dissertation and ordered printed among their Acts.

The distinguished historian Torquemada finished writing his General Chronicle of New Spain the year one thousand six hundred twelve; but he says that he worked on it more than twenty years before. Bartolache has pretended to raise some clouds against its criticism and veracity; but I have them well examined, there are objected quibbles of bad faith, or doing him a favor, hallucinations of a man who had read very little and in leaps and bounds. Torquemada is the depository most copious and authentic of the events appertaining to the Kingdom. He swore in his prologue, to have said nothing but the pure truth, investigated with all the diligence possible and he carried it out. He was raised since a child in Mexico; he was Provincial Priest of the Indians, in whose favor he principally wrote, he had all the manuscripts of the former missionaries; he also wrote their lives, and with the same notable prolixity and fondness that of Zumárraga. He was guardian of Santiago, the target of Juan Diego's travels, he lived there with Don Valeriano, Professor of that College, and original author, as I will now prove, of the history of Guadalupe: he witnessed his death, receiving in legacy some manuscripts, and in conclusion was architect of the Avenue of Our Lady of Guadalupe of which he speaks many times. This historian by way of explaining to us about the point in question, proposes in effect to tell the origin of the most celebrated Sanctuaries of New Spain, and of the fiestas that are celebrated in them, and see here the essence of what he says.

There was in New Spain three celebrated places for the devotion and gathering of people from very far lands to adore the idols that they venerated in them. The monks of Our Father Saint Francis, who were the first who came to prune this vineyard for the Lord, determined to substitute analogous images to their name or history in order that they were more suitable with the fiestas and their motifs, though not idolatrous in abuse or intention. And thus, in *Tianguizmanalco* where the God *Telpuchtle* was adored, which is to say *young man*, they put the image of Saint John the Baptist; in *Chiautempan*, near Tlaxcala, where the *Toci* or grandmother was, the image of Saint Anne; and in *Tonantzin* next to Mexico, the Most Holy Virgin who is *Our Lady and Mother*; which is to say *Tonantzin*. And repeating a few pages, the same paragraph in essence, better specifies the place, saying where Our Lady of Guadalupe is now. And proceeds *ubi supra* ("*the above*") saying that these are the fiestas, and this is their origin, even though not all know it: that in his time for the most part the devotion and audience had already ceased (although less in *Tianguizmanalco*), for having brought down the Indians, or for having other images near their villages.

All efforts have been useless, done to dodge a testimony so clear from the Prince of our historians, that is put forth on purpose to account for the origin of the suspicious images and of the fiestas that they celebrated. The same festival of the Guadalupe Sanctuary, that the Indians today still celebrate on September eight is proof that the purpose was not the apparition, just as the Spaniards celebrate it the twelfth day of December, proof that this one was born after the accredited apparition . The same Torquemada says in another part that many images were venerated up to his time on the altarpieces of New Spain painted on the back of Saint Francis in the paint shop set up for the Indians by the Flemish Envoy Fray Pedro de Gante, one of the first monks who came.

The year one thousand six hundred twenty, Father Betancourt, a Franciscan monk no less instructed and distinguished than Torquemada his contemporary, wrote the history of Our Lady of Los Remedios; he speaks of Our Lady of Guadalupe and compares her with Los Remedios, and he never leaks the word "appeared." But when it seems entirely impossible to me that no one speaks of the apparition of Our Lady of Guadalupe, is during the five years that she was in the Cathedral of Mexico by reason of the flood of one thousand six hundred twenty-nine, the biggest that Mexico has suffered, till a Royal Decree was sent out to move the City to the heights of Santa Fe; which was not executed for costing more than the six hundred million pesos already spent. How was the fanatic devotion possible with such a calamity that the tradition would not have implored assistance in pulpits and writings, if it had already existed? With everything no one spoke one word, and Father Florencia says that it cost him much work to investigate why the freedom of Mexico is attributed to Our Lady of Guadalupe, since she was here five years without decreasing the waters; and in the end there was an earthquake and they dissipated. And then she comes forth with what they told him that the Virgin appeared to a Jesus Mary nun, and she told her that she had saved Mexico. It is certain that for those times the history of the flood was printed with legal exhibits, and according only to them that in five years it did not rain in Mexico, and the waters dried up, without talking about Our Lady of Guadalupe.

The history of the apparition came to public light for the first time in one thousand six hundred forty-eight surrounded among many discussions preached by Father Miguel Sanchez, Chaplain of Our Lady of the Remedios. But immediately the Licentiate Lazo, Chaplain of Our Lady of Guadalupe, wrote congratulating him as I already said, for being the most fortunate Creole, for having discovered the Eve (says he) that we possess in this Guadalupano Paradise, without me nor all my antecedent Chaplains of the hermitage knowing anything. And was there a tradition before the work of Father Sanchez and it was unknown in the Sanctuary itself, when in the entire world the incidents most pertinent to the miracles are always conserved for the temporal and spiritual interest that concern them? It was necessary that Guadalupe had no festival relative to the apparition, paper, inscription, nor memory. And faith was not for lack of devotion or zeal. As soon as Lazo heard the first news to Sanchez, even though this does not claim any document supporting a miracle of this scope, and he only says that he took the account from the papers of an Indian, the Licentiate Lazo printed it in six months in Mexican to spread the devotion among the Indians; and he heated up the devotion in such a manner that to him is owed originally the munificence of the current sanctuary and all relevant to it. Also, a Jesuit cleansed Sanchez's account from the preached discourses and printed it to make it more manageable and more current among the Spaniards.

The three accounts in Spanish and Mexican now considered current in Mexico, where so few are printed, and the printed page is considered an oracle, even more so in that time of so little critique. However, the matter would take root, news so glorious for the native land! However, the authorized orators would sensible manage it with the dolts of that century and with the approbation of the Ordinary! At twenty years information built with hearsay witnesses was tried, and I do not know what the Canon Siles went to look for as far as Cuautitlan, because they never lacked for a pious thing, and less could they lack after twenty years of continuous proclamation.

But the Canon Siles, himself, author and promoter of this information in one thousand six hundred sixty-six, was the approving agent of Father Florencia's Guadalupe history which brings about abridgements of said information; and says in his report that he will not dare to assure that the tradition was previously known. Then what case would be made of his witnesses, or better said, can he call that which was not a known, tradition?

Florencia's second approving agent was Licentiate Maldonaldo, Judge of this Royal Court, who says that the tradition of Guadalupe has happened, the same as Flavio Dextro, a stranger of antiquity, and today resurrected with annotations. It is thus that for this same ignorance of antiquity that today all agree Falvio Dextro came out of the fraud office of Roman de la Higuera: Later the Guadalupe tradition was likewise a stranger of antiquity before the authors' printed matter came from the office where they were printed.

The witnesses themselves of the information of one thousand six hundred sixty-six were mistaken the same way the first printed author was mistaken. For example, they were mistaken with him in assuring that Bishop Zumárraga moved the image in fifteen days from the apparition to a provisional adobe hermitage, and they were equally mistaken in saying with him that the cloth of the images is of rough and sparse fabric; proof that they had drank from that fountain. And what value can some hearsay witnesses have against the universal silence that I have proved and against positive and authentic case documents? Bartolache says that there could not have been recent miracle information, because all had passed only between the Virgin and Juan Diego, and this for rude, neophyte, and self-interest was unworthy of faith. Well, how could there have been at one hundred fifty-nine years later? Or, what are hearsay witnesses owed, when all the fame could come only from those unworthy of faith? Then the tradition is already defective in its origin. I will try to show with the passage of more than a century-and-a-half that it has been wrong.

Now I will only make note that one insist principally on the testimony of the Indians, for being the most ancient, on the reports; and the Priest Tanco, the most respectable of all the witnesses, at that time precisely wrote that one ought not to make a case of what the Indians said, already unworthy for having lacked the men of importance that were among them, and to not know, so little of their antiquities, confusion, without order, and scrambled with many fables and errors. And, so it is necessary on the tradition to rely only on the ancient Mexican Manuscript. It is right, because it is a rule of the most judicious critic, that no one ought to accept any tradition without a reliable ancient document that upholds and can sustain itself against the arguments, because otherwise it would be necessary to accept all genre of fables and errors that throughout time have claimed a passport under the name of tradition.

But this clamored manuscript, who is it from? What is its antiquity? It is necessary to investigate this, because it is the original fountain of the Guadalupe history, as one tells it, and yet of all the tradition we have found no earlier news. I already said that Sanchez, the first Guadalupano historian, says only that he took his account from the papers of an Indian, enough of the truth, and he left proof in the inkpot. The Mexican Lazo published six months later his account, without citing anybody, and as he testified six months before that he knew nothing. Boturini conjectures that he would print some ancient manuscript of some Indian from Azcatpozalco, by how much he knew of the Kingdom of the

Tepanecas, whose capital was that town. Bartolache says that the reasons that he noted do not prove his intent, and he least proves the antiquity that nevertheless he attributes with two or three short pure Mexican expressions, as if today we could not also use some in Latin from Augustus's century, especially Mexican being a living language. Tanco only cites the manuscript with the epithet of antiquity; but always anonymously, because its period and author ought to be ignored. Father Florencia says that he had an account in Castilian from the Indian Don Fernando de Alva Ixtlixochtl who lived during the years one thousand six hundred forty-eight, and a Mexican manuscript that according to its faded and rumpled condition ought to be very ancient, and that speaking of it with Father Betancourt, he told him this that it would be from the Venerable Father Mendieta one of the early missionaries.

But Don Cárlos de Sigüenza who was the third approver of Florencia's history, and who had loaned the two accounts that he cites, Castilian and Mexican, bitterly complains in his manuscript that I possess and Don Agustin Pomposo Fernandez gave me, that Father Florencia had added this and other species in his work after his approbation. And he says about the Mexican manuscript: "Not only is it not from the said Father Mendieta; nor can it be, because it contains events and miracles years after the death of that monk. I say, and I swear that I found it among the papers of Don Fernando de Alva that I have all; and it is in the handwriting of Don Valeriano, which I know, and he is its true author. And in the end some miracles were added from Don Fernando's letter. That which Don Fernando wrote was a paraphrastic translation of said account; and it is in his handwriting."

Comparing some things that Florencia brings up as taken from Alva's manuscripts and observing the difference that there is between the account printed by Sanchez and the translation from the Mexican manuscript that Tanco printed, one knows that what Sanchez printed in one thousand six hundred forty-eight was a paraphrasing of Alva. I am also of the opinion that what Lazo printed is Don Valeriano's manuscript, because in effect it was from Azcatpozalco, as Boturini conjectured him to be the original author of this account; and he agrees according to Bartolache, the already painted image was clearly put on when it was sent to Zumárraga, as Tanco says the ancient manuscript teaches. And for this I believe Florencia stopped the printing of it, even though he had promised it.

Now, let's look at the time of the manuscript. Sigüenza says that it brings forth miracles and events years after the death of Father Mendieta. Thus, it is that this monk died in one thousand six hundred fifty according to Torquemada: then it is still later in years. These cannot happen in the year one thousand six hundred twelve, because in this year the Father Torquemada finished writing an account of Father Mendieta's death and burial which he attended. Then the manuscript will be from near the years one thousand six hundred ten or twelve; later by eighty or eighty-two years for the same reason to the period of the apparition: and it does not appear that its author even came to a life of seventy. What credit then does he merit? I have here a critical Canon dictated for the sanest reason. Every author who tells of an event sixty or seventy years prior to the time that he writes, that is the normal life of a man, especially since he could form a precise idea of the things, to transmit his news with discernment to the posterity, or has told us to whom he owes it to add weight to his testimony, or has excused us from giving him credit, for he could not be a witness. And, what act, nevertheless, is it that he proposes for us to believe upon his word? At least one that includes twenty-one traditional miracles. To know; five apparitions of the Most Holy Virgin, others put forth seven; the apparition of little birds; the apparition of all the hill converted in a flower garden; the disappearance of Juan Diego in the view of the Bishop's domestics who followed him; Juan Bernardino's health; the apparition of the flowers on the hillock, the disappearance of the painting of the image in the eyes of Juan Diego every time that he would take his cape on the road; the same disappearance in the eyes of the assistants; an equal disappearance in the eyes of the domestics who recorded what the Indian brought on his cape; the transformation to their view of the painted or woven flowers; the apparition or painting of the image before the Bishop; and according to some the painting with flowers and the painting with priming on canvas naturally unfit; and in short the apparition of a thermal water well. There are still other allusions. And all this we must believe by the said anonymity of an Indian at the end of eighty-two years of universal silence? From an Indian, the most lying people, who therefore, according to Acosta, do not allow the inquiry of witnesses, and who even swore against their Priests, the Mexican Council III orders to exclude for their notorious propensity to perjury? *Quoniam manifestum est, dice, quam propensi sintad perjuria indi* ("*Since it is obvious, to say, that the Indian is prone to perjury*"). Oh well, favoritism from their gentilism to relate apparitions, especially from the Tonantzin of Tepeyácac.

This is not even the worst, but that the manuscript is full of anachronisms, falsehoods, contradictions, foolishness, and mythological errors. In a word, it is a mystery play, a farce, or comedy done by Don Valeriano, to the style of his time performed in Santiago, where effectively it was used to perform in Mexican prose and even in verse, Boturini says that Our Lady of Guadalupe had two comedies. In that of Don Valeriano, it is easy to designate from where he took the plot, the nexus, and storyline for each episode of the drama, having for object to persuade the same thing that I preached. This will certainly not be the first romance that has attained the honors of an ecclesiastical office1

Don Valeriano took for the first thread of his plot the same passage from the little shepherd, who Our Lady of Guadalupe healed in the year one thousand five hundred fifty-six, as His Majesty the Viceroy Enriquez reported. Certainly, the Little Shepherd ought to tell that Our Lady appearing to him had healed him. This is the voice that according to the Viceroy ran throughout the region, and the mentions of the apparition allude to her that are found in some anonymous little notes from the Indians and in some testimonies from the natives of Cuautitlan, all later not only to the year one thousand five hundred fifty-six, but to that of five hundred seventy, when the devotion was in all its fervor for the miracle with the little shepherd. These mentions prove the Guadalupe tradition for those who read them already preoccupied with her; but they only prove what I have said. If I were to say that the Virgin of the Rosario appeared to some guy, no one would think that the image of the Rosario was a ghost, but that the Virgin appeared to some guy in her figure; and not to say the notes and testimonies except that Our Lady of Guadalupe appeared to Juan Diego, it is proof of not having had more than the Indian having said that the Virgin appeared in the figure of the Guadalupe image and she healed him. This is the fame to which the Indian witnesses of one thousand six hundred and sixty-six referred, happened to them what always happens to fame, that acquires body and force with the passage of time and the circumstances added to it: and if the poets intervene with their songs to which the Indians were much given, or they put the thing in a comedy thrashing, one raises without dispute every tall story in a popular tradition, that if it is pious one cannot attack without risk, especially if it has been canonized by some imbecile devotee with print and the licenses necessary for it.

They even conserve vestiges of the Little Shepard's age and illness in the words with which the Virgin greets him. "My son Juan Diego whom I love as tiny and delicate, how are you?" Words more exaggerated and far from the simple language of the Blessed in their apparitions, than those that Benedict XIV reproved in the mouth of Santa Leocadia to San Ildefonso, the Virgin speaking according to the history with an adult, married, and healthy Indian; but they are speaking very tolerably with an innocent and ill little shepherd.

He [Juan Diego] was from Cuautitlan, then the most elderly Indian of the witnesses of one thousand six hundred sixty-six, who achieved seeing built the first Church that the Viceroy reports was built to the Virgin with the motive of the health of the little shepherd. He says that the Indians of Cuautitlan came by neighborhoods to work on it, and there could not be another cause for this devotion in a distant people but the little shepherd being their compatriot. This is Juan Diego, and from this time his uncle Juan Bernardino, since in one thousand five hundred thirty-one not only was there no Indian with two names; but even Christian Indians were very rare, because the monks not knowing the language could not catechize them. The little Creole children raised among the Indians went by the houses with the surplice doing the catechism. The fortitude of asking for baptism did not begin until one thousand five hundred thirty-four. And then they baptized them at the banks of the springs or rivers, giving each day to all the men a name, and another to the women on a little paper. And only after they warned them of the inconveniences of them having put forth at the beginning only a Saint's name, they began to add another that served them as a surname.

The account says that Juan Diego went to mass at Santiago, and that for having arrived late to the instruction, occupied with the message from the Virgin, they whipped him: all this in one thousand five hundred thirty-one is an anachronism. Zumárraga founded the Santiago College in one thousand five hundred thirty-four. In vain it will be said that a Church or Convent already existed to which it was added. It is impossible that in the primitive shortage of ministers the convents in Mexico would multiply, where there were already Dominicans in one thousand five hundred thirty, Mexico being all devastated, and the Kingdom full of great cities. Torquemada says that their monks at the beginning were in only four convents, administering as much territory as Spain and France, and they were those of Mexico, Tezcuco, Xochimilco and Tlaxcala. I even believe the fifth was Cuautitlan, a city then very populous. At the least in one thousand five hundred thirty-six their neighbors were already stirred up by disturbances because of the total shortage of ministers they wanted to take away their Friars. Certainly, they had them since they were Christians, and Cuautitlan was never a mission or parish of Santiago. But it could very well be that of the little shepherd who walked by Tepeyac. It is conceived equally as well that in one thousand five hundred fifty-six he came from there to hear mass on a Saturday, but Cuautitlan is very far for this devotion. Nor can it be that they whip him for having missed the instruction on a holiday, already being Christian. It is true that the custom of teaching with the whip and the catechumens was introduced with great outrage from Casas, who brought the law against this strange catechism; but it was later. In one thousand five hundred thirty-one even though almost all the Indian were Gentiles, very powerful, and they did not cease from getting excited despite the yoke. The missionaries had not dared to do such.

It is another anachronism to say, therefore, that he went to Santiago for the sacraments for his uncle. What sacraments did they have to take to him in one thousand five hundred thirty-one, when one could hardly be given baptism? Alva says that it would be the Eucharist and the extreme unction. But enough said of this, Torquemada says that in many years it was not given to the Indians for lack of ministers. When there were finally enough, it was given to them to understand what it was and administering to them began. He mentions the first Indians received it after one thousand five hundred forty, according to Father Mendieta. He also then refers to the first Indian who took communion. This Sacrament was then not delivered to the Indians even by the year one thousand five hundred sixty since a Lima Council ordered it was not to be given to them. And in so much shortage of ministers and when horses were a jewel, would one go four leagues to carry the Eucharist to an Indian peasant? When Alva says he found out by investigations that Juan Diego was given a permit to take communion everyday of one thousand five hundred thirty-one, therefore he commits another anachronism even more intolerable.

By the same investigations, he says he learned that Juan Diego was already married five years when the Virgin appeared to him, but that he had kept virginity in his marriage. This is entirely incredible if the apparition had been in one thousand five hundred thirty-one, because he would then marry as a Gentile, and there is no example of married virgins without the religion. And much less among the Mexican Indians, among whom the lack of virginity in the bride dissolved the marriage. And so, another day after the marriage the priests went, and they brought to keep in the temple the sheet where there was found the seal of the virginity. This was like the authentic writing of the contract. And, therefore, the missionaries warned in their writings, have great caution with the married Indians, because now that they cannot dissolve the marriage after Christianity for the corruption of the bride; the relatives of the husband go another day, and abuse all the furnishings of the house of the bride.

All these circumstances, a case for being truths, were only verifiable in one thousand five hundred fifty-six; and so there can be no doubt in that the Juan Diego of the apparition is the Viceroy's little shepherd, and the apparition that this one told, the first thread of the plot upon which Don Valeriano creates his comedy.

Nothing is believable not even that which refers to a Bishop such as Zumárraga. The Emperor knew him in the convent of Abrojo near Valladolid, says the Royal Chronicler Gil Gonzalez Dávila, and he sent him as Bishop to Mexico for having had a good hand in throwing out the witches from Vizcaya. He continued to see them here everywhere; he did autos-da-fe with all the Indians' manuscripts, as witchcrafts and magical figures; and he had, says Torquemada, in the San Francisco jail various Indian prisoners as sorcerers.

Of course, the first difficulty that presents itself in the accounts by Juan Diego, is that he receives his messages and dispatches without interpreters; and he never knew the

Mexican language, neither was he of the age for this, yet then even the interpreters were bad and very rare. However, we give in that he understood the messages were from *Tzenteotenantzin*, to show the Indians by her name the ancient Mother's entrails that preserved them. He ought also to find out about the apparition; and on comprehending birds, a flower garden, and a rainbow, proper things from the Goddess of Paradise who had been venerated there, inevitably he had to understand that she was the *Tonantzin* who walked by there, crying so that they might rebuild her temple. The clothes were identical: and on this coming two domestics to assure such Bishop that the Indian was a sorcerer who had gone missing from them, he would have gone to receive the warrant of his commission to the San Francisco jail, even if he had brought a thousand bundles of flowers. When these were not found at any time in Mexico, and for the Indians it had not been an indispensable etiquette to carry bundles of flowers when they went to his palace, the Bishop would believe that he had produced them by sorcery, and even more so the principal cult of the *Tonantizin* consisted of flowers.

With equal implausibility the domestics give to the Bishop what followed from his order to Juan Diego, and who entered and left the palace halls while the Indian suffered delays and difficulties to see His Illuminate. Garcés, the Bishop of Tlaxcala, who was consecrated, never had a domestic other than an old Negro woman: who else would he have from Mexico, a poor and persecuted elect? A Spaniard was then a personage, and in almost all the century they could not even get craftsmen, even those they brought by way of Spain; soon thereafter they were Lords; and even the Negroes were slave owners. Bishop Zumárraga who even though consecrated visited his Diocese on a donkey, went each day when chosen to say mass at San Francisco with his Breviary under arm, and he passed the days in the plaza behind a thick wall of his Cathedral that he was building, in the middle of the Indians, teaching them the Lord's Prayer and the Creed in

Latin, which was what he could do; in such a way that some Spaniards reprimanded him that he mixed so much with them. Look at the plot to suffer delays and difficulties in speaking to such a Bishop. All these things are episodes added later, for forming the comedy upon the apparition of the little shepherd, the first thread of the plot.

The second thread is taken, as I see it, from another apparition that Torquemada tells happened at the banks of the Lagoon on a Friday of the year one thousand five hundred seventy-five to an Indian from Azcatpozalco, who is mentioned with the two names of use among the Indians, to whom the Virgin appeared in the form of an Indian, with a blue robe, it is to say, in the figure of the *Tonantzin* the perpetual ghost to the Indians before and after the conquest, even though always only to one, and revealing to him secret things. She gave him an order to go to the Xochimilco Guardian, which infers it was Father Mendieta, and to tell him of her part, he must warn the people they should confess and do penance, because God was very angry. And indeed, at the time of Enriquez, then Viceroy, two million Indians died, according to the census that the Viceroy ordered taken; Dávila Padilla, eyewitness. The Guardian did not pay attention to the Indian; but this one repeated his journeys with the same demand, until seriously engaging the Guardian with his perseverance, he said in the church what the Virgin ordered, that by fortune (Torquemada concludes) was of some benefit.

Even though unsuccessful, this admiration of the perseverance of the Indian is very similar with what happened to Juan Diego, in taking the Virgin's messages; and there is no doubt that those served as a type for this one, because the Mexican manuscript also places the apparition to Juan Diego on Friday. Don Fernando de Alva in his paraphrase says that to have put Friday for Saturday with the Gregorian correction there could have been some change in the dominical letters. But as I have already demonstrated, the Mexican manuscript is very subsequent to the correction of the calendar, that was in one thousand five hundred eighty-two, it is most probable that Don Valeriano wanted to allude to the apparition of the Indian from his land, putting Juan Diego in his place, he palmed off Santiago, where he was professor, in place of Xochimilco, the place of the scene, and that was closer to Tepeyácac: in place of the Franciscan Guardian the Bishop also Franciscan, who founded the Santiago College, and gave more glamor to the piece; the illness and health transferred from Juan Diego to his uncle Juan Bernardino; and perhaps he switched the apparition to this one, so as to give a reason for the name Guadalupe, which the Spaniards gave to the image who before one thousand five hundred seventy was called *Tonantzin*, according to Sahagun and Enriquez, so that this apparition could be equivalent to that of the Indian of Azcatpozalco his land [the land of Juan Diego]. Oh well, he set all this in the past to the year one thousand five hundred thirty-one, because then was when according to Cabrera (*Escudo de armas de México*) ("*Mexico's Coat of Arms*")[17] the Tonantzin traveled around appearing on the Hill Tepeyac and asking that her temple be rebuilt.

Behold the entire plot we are going to see the nexus or crux of the comedy. This is composed of the history of the *Tzenteonantzin*, with all the Aztec's mythological errors on paradise, and of the apparition of God to Moses in the bush on mount Horeb. To understand the plan of the Indian Valeriano, who was a Latinist and of much ingenuity, it is necessary to agree that after the conquest the ten plagues of Egypt fell upon the Indians, as the Father Mendieta proved in a work of this title.[18] Especially, the free rebuilding of all the cities and towns that the conquistadors had destroyed and devastated, especially, took root, and even the construction of other new settlements to reunite all those who lived dispersed in the fields to support the agriculture conforming to the good political economy. The rebuilding of Mexico City alone cost the life of twenty-five or thirty thousand, because of Cortés having ceded the Governments of Santiago and San Juan to the Indians, so many were burdened and with so much determination to the rebuilding, that they neglected the sown lands, and they perished from hunger. With an equal work in all the country, their transfer to other countries going to conquer in favor of the Spaniards, and the yoke of slavery, such a plague overcame them around the years one thousand five hundred forty, that of the four parts of the Indians, says Torquemada, the three perished. Casas was he who in one thousand five hundred forty-two brought forth the laws that their work must be paid to them: and by the most solemn dispute in which Sepúlveda, lawyer of the war and of the slavery, won the year one thousand five hundred fifty, and he gave them in Mexico their freedom the year of one thousand five hundred fifty-four, a little before the apparition of Our Lady of Guadalupe to the little shepherd of Tepeyácac.

The Indian Don Valeriano proposed therefore to give to understand that just as the God of his parents appeared to the Shepherd Moses on the Mount Horeb, sorry for the affliction and slavery of his people, *quia ad amaritudinem perducebant vitam eorum operibus duris tuti et lateris, omnique famulatu quo in terrae operibus premebantur* ("*And they made their, lives bitter with hard bondage, in mortar, and in brick, and in all manner of service in the field: all their service, wherein they made them serve, was with rigour*"), [19] and he sent him to the afflicted promising them liberty, and to Pharaoh so that it was given to him in order that they went to him to sacrifice on that Mount, here also the Mother of the true God appeared to the little shepherd Juan Diego on the Mount Tepeyácac, the ancient Mother of the Indians sorry for their miseries promising them by Juan Diego the ancient tenderness of the Mother to the people of his linage *ad gentes generis sui* ("*Nations to their, own kind.*"), [20] (*) and she sent him to Mexico's Bishop with the order that he rebuild her temple on that mount, where her people would come to worship her, and she could continue to show them from there her maternal feelings that she preserved for the Indians.

To realize this plan, Valerian began by bring Juan Diego from Santiago by way of the western side of the little hill, that was the natural path, and he made the Virgin appear on the summit, where the ancient temple of la Tonantzin was, with ancient clothes or figure of this one, as afterwards was noted, and conforming to the mythology of the Aztecs touching upon the paradise where the Tonantzin lived, called for this *Tlaloque*.

One sees in Torquemada at the end of the 2nd Volume the history of the paradise that the Aztecs called Haloccan. They said that it was a flower garden full of flowers as beautiful, as fragrant, and glittering as if of emeralds and precious stones. The rainbow with its light and its colors adorned it all, and in the middle of it was the Tonantzin. To this place went the good ones who died of illness, just as the bad ones to hell, and to heaven only those who died in the war, because it appears that all their wars being of religion to extend the cult of the Lord of the Crown of Thorns, they considered them as martyrs. But the souls who went to the paradise usually do return to the world in the figure of little birds of beautiful song and colorful plumage.

We hear now the report sent to Rome with the Guadalupe proceedings, and printed by Nicoselli. The twelfth of December of one thousand five hundred thirty-one Juan Diego having just passed toward the Tónan hillside in Tepeyac, Mexico City, heard on the summit a harmonious music like the song of birds. He turned the face and stayed in suspense not only by the birds' chirping, like the birds' beautiful variety of colors never seen in these regions. Finally, like they had to be, if they were the souls of the Aztec paradise who came accompanying their Queen? Indeed, he continues the report saying that to Juan Diego all the mount looked like a garden of glittering flowers as if of emeralds and adorned with brilliant colors. He raised his sight and saw in the middle of a rainbow Our Lady of Guadalupe, it is to say, the *Tzentcotinantzin*, because such was her figure and robe. In such a way that the Indian exclaimed and could do no less than exclaim, I am in the paradise of my elders!

All the conversations that followed between the Virgin and Juan Diego are taken from the Scripture *mutatis mutandis* ("*with the necessary changes having been made*") as they say. The Virgin called to Juan Diego from the middle of the rainbow, as God to Moses from the middle of the bush, *Moses, Moses*: and Juan Diego rising, she does not appear, but she said *vadam et videbo visionem hane magnam* ("*and this will go over and see the great vision*"). If the first words: "My son, Juan Diego, to whom I love as tiny and delicate, how are you?" Valeriano did not preserve them perhaps for being the only ones the ill little shepherd would reference the Virgin to have said to him. They are copied to the letter from those of God in the Scripture *filius meus parvulus et delicatus ephrain*: [sic] ("*My son is young and tender, Ephraim*"). [21] All those [words] that followed were taken from those that God said to Moses, and He answered him [Moses} on the mount Horeb. "I am,"He told him, "the God of your fathers: I hear the affliction of my people in Egypt, and I have come down to liberate them. Go and say to Pharaoh that he set you free, so that you may come to sacrifice to me in the desert." The Virgin said to Juan Diego: "Go and say to the Bishop that the *Tzenteotinantzin* sends thee so that he can build me a temple here, where to show the entrails that I conserve as Mother of the peoples of your linage:" It is to say, to show that I am the ancient Tonantzin. Juan Diego returned to the Virgin: he recounts to her the little attention that has been made of the message, without doubt from the scorn of the Ambassador; and he begs her, send him to another of more worth. The words are identical to those that Moses says with which he excuses himself, and almost the same as those that God and the Virgin say to their envoys, to excite them to repeat the diligence, except that Valeriano adds the words that God said to Abraham, when he sent him to go to Canaan, *benedicam et magnificabo nomen tuum, et crescere te faciam in gentem magnam*; ("*I bless you and make your name great, I will make thee a great nation, and to increase.*") [22] appropriate promises from the ancient law, whose recompense was earthly, but very far from the new law. How was the Virgin going to excite in the mind of an unhappy Indian thoughts of ambition and fame? It is a rule of the mystics that any apparition that excites movements of pride in the mind is from the devil, and not from God.

The Bishop asked Juan Diego for a sign of being the Mother of the true God who sent him, and the Virgin who gave him the flowers, like there God to Moses the rod that also flowered. There, as I said, he gave him Aaron as a companion; here his uncle Juan Bernardino, there he says his name; and here she says that she wants to be called Saint Mary of Guadalupe. The copy is evident, and by consequence the fiction.

The rest are equally pretended incidents to complete the piece and to arrive at the outcome. The Bishop asked the Virgin for a sign of Juan Diego being her envoy, and he [Juan Diego] should ask for it. One does not accept an ambassador without credentials, and he who pretends to be one from heaven, ought to prove it with a miracle, says the 4th Lateran Council. This is the royal seal of the Omnipotent who no one can counterfeit nor can one prostitute to deception. So that it is not and avoids any diabolical illusion, it is even necessary that neither may it be any miracle but such that it is worth enough to prevent any mistake. Effectively the Virgin responded to Juan Diego she would give him such a sign that the Bishop could not doubt, ordering him come back the following day to receive her.

He disobeyed by occupying himself in looking for medicines for Juan Bernardino, who was found with a fever, because they say that even though rude, he knew that charity rather than obedience was first. In this case, it is false, and a Christian who knew the power of the Mother of God ought to return to present himself with complete confidence, and to ask her for the remedy or permission to attend to the sick. Seeing him in a grave state the third day he [Juan Diego] decided to come to take him the sacraments from Santiago; and against all likelihood the Indian pretended that in such a brief time he had completely forgotten his summons by the Bishop, and the strict orders from the Most Holy Virgin to present himself the following day, and he did not remember until arriving at the little hill. Then so that the Virgin would not hinder him with her messages about the destination that he was taking, he did not think of another road than the one taking him by the eastern side of the hill. Already one sees that if he had remembered that there was another route, according to Torquemada to go to Santiago, or had he taken any of the numerous small boats that then filled the Lagoon, that also was much more spread out than now. But the poet needed this incident to have the Virgin come down from the hill by the eastern side, to give this reason for having built the ancient hermitage there, to have the little thermal well spring up under the feet of the Virgin, to introduce the miraculous healing of Juan Bernardino in place of the little shepherd, to verify with notice from her to the nephew the circumstance connected to the apparition of the Tonantzin, revealing hidden things, to give to Juan Diego a companion like God gave Aaron to Moses, to tell him as like this one his name, and to embolden the image of Guadalupe, which the Europeans later gave to her image.

Without this poet's multiplex object, Juan Diego could not have worked except as an idiot. The first thing was because he thought to escape from the sight of the Mother of God. Second, because of his having always spoken up, he was seen so much going from one side to another, especially being then almost all surrounded by the Lagoon. Third, because he had also always appeared on the crest of the little mount that looks toward Mexico City, and from wherever he had to go to take his goat herd.

Neither is it credible that when the Virgin orders, she be given a name so irreligious and Saracen as *River of Wolves*, and so strange for the Indian that he could not pronounce it except for a miracle for his language lacked *g* and *d*. The conjectures of the authors on various assonant names in Mexican, that perhaps the Virgin would give, and they mixed it up with the time, all extravagant significances, are mere riddles contrary to the original manuscript, and they only serve to confirm the truth of that which the Viceroy Enriquez reported. Why had the Most Holy Mary given herself a reason to appeal her image, when they were prohibited by the Council of Auch and they provided the masses a continuous opportunity for idolatry, since in place of calling on the Mother of God, they call on statutes and paintings, as if they had some virtue. Was the Virgin in them, or was she heard better before her portrait, or before another? This would have us put our confidence in the images, or to worship, better in Jerusalem than on [Mount] Gerizim, [23] against what Jesus Christ taught in the new law. Anyway, I fear that all the impediments the poet introduces here, and the five days that had passed from the apparition of the Virgin to the manifestation of her image have not also been invented on purpose for verifying the five days that the Indians spent before the festival of the Tonantzin in making their small images that they called *tepictoton*. [24]

One supposes Tepeyácac, like a desert, in all the theatrical accounts of all the events when this is the name of a town that always existed and not very unfortunate at the time of the conquest. From there Juan Diego departed, carrying the flowers arranged in bunches, as the Indians always carried them as an indispensable etiquette for entering a palace, even though in the account he was not given time to do the bunches at least artistically, according to their custom. One ponders the admiration of the domestics on seeing flowers in December, even though Mexico City always is full of them, and there ought to be many more with the conquest so recent, since before, according to Torquemada, was all made a flower-garden for the affection that the Indians had for flowers, and the innumerable chinampas, or floating gardens, that filled the Lagoon. The Bishop notified of such a great news had the Indian enter; and although such Bishop, by the testimony of the domestics, ought to be persuaded that the Indian was a sorcerer, he remained very satisfied with the credentials of a few bunches of flowers, that every Indian according to their practice, would carry them every day. Were, not a few credentials very worthy of the Mother of the Omnipotent? Or is it not truly offensive to involve her power for such frivolities?

One responds that there were no flowers on the little hill. We grant that there were none then, even though the cult of the Tonantzin consists principally of flowers, even though they had an obligation to rise, throwing them on her altar when they passed near the mount, and even though the Indians were very diligent in the things necessary to her cult and that very celebrated Sanctuary. From where did the Bishop have evidence that the Indian had cut them from the hill? He needed the miracle of a piece of evidence, another cross-check. Does one not see that this is only to conform the Virgin of Guadalupe to all that which appertains to the Tonantzin?

Bartolache clearly knew that it was an absurdity to ascribe the flowers as Juan Diego's credentials, despite the fact that so says the unanimous tradition of the authors and witnesses. And making the pretense to not shock the masses, he put out that the Virgin sent her image to the Bishop as credentials. But they suffer the same defect as the flowers, since there were no Christian painters with whom to establish the miracle of the painting, nor is it a miracle according to Bartolache and his painters; and he says that the one thing to have assured the painters of one thousand six hundred sixty-six, came from the concurrence of persons of high character preventing purely optional operations. The fact is that among the Indians there were excellent painters, and at that time they painted all the altarpiece images for New Spain. Quickly I will return to speak of this very thing.

The Mexican manuscript concludes telling that Bishop Zumárraga put the image in her cathedral, in a basket while it was built where ultimately the Virgin appeared, a provisional adobe hermitage, to which it was moved at fifteen days. He went in the procession with the monks of his order; and with this motive there were grand festivals and mock sea-fights. But nothing then existed of the cathedral except the foundations, nor is the construction of the hermitage by Zumárraga true, nor his attendance at the movement, nor was this done until the year one thousand five hundred thirty-three all of which Zumárraga spent in Spain, as at the beginning all remained proven, neither before going there, nor after having returned did he made any case of the image even though his Bishopric lasted fourteen years, an absolutely impossible case if the apparition had been true. All this vignette of the comedy is taken from a procession that Zumárraga did to the Santiago College, built under his direction in one thousand five hundred thirty-four, to settle there, sixty Indian schoolboys. He paid for the entire function, he ate that day with the friars, and there were mock sea-fights and all these fiestas, so good that at the beginning they even made a cross to put up, in order in this way to call the attention of the Indians to everything that appertains to religion.

Reporting those things that in the whole discourse I have been pointing out are the arguments that I had intended to overcome in my sermon. Borunda from his study on the indigenous antiquities, had seen in the history of Guadalupe that of the ancient Tonantzin. Any other would have inferred that it was a comedy or novel copied about this. But Borunda was incapable of adopting a similar consequence, because he was such a devotee of the Guadalupe Virgin, that on sight of any print of her he used to begin crying from tenderness. Therefore, he contrived means to save the tradition, to set back the period of the painting until the time of Saint Tomé, without another sacrifice of the vulgar tradition, the cape of Juan Diego, which he thought to substitute with advantage for the cape of the same Saint. I imagined the same as Borunda; and believing as he believed the tradition, I could do no less than to adopt his scheme. I consulted so many friends; they also coincided on the same, because there is no other way to half-way save the tradition. I would have desired to know what other way they found; the Archbishop did not say that he did not understand these things, nor did he believe the tradition, except the theologist censors, and principally the famous Uribe who was the chief of the debate.

Because if the arguments have no solution, they are demonstrations; and as to the truth, the contrary cannot be demonstrated, thus the Guadalupano tradition would necessarily turn out to be a fable.

In conclusion, having to see that even the minor episodes of the sermon were directed to satisfy objections, or to repair some open breaches in the tradition, I will yet put forth some of the arguments that go up against the miracle of the painting.

There is no doubt in that Dr. Bartolache destroyed all the foundations on which the ancient painters had confirmed it. And even though he finally asked his own, if they considered it as miraculous, it was well guarded, even though so precisive, from their specifying if they held it as such by the painting of which only they could be judges, and it was what mattered. He wanted that they responded affirmatively to him to protect himself and them before the common people, and thus they did it by tradition.

The fact is that among the Indians there were very first-rate painters, says Torquemada; and principally after they had seen our images from Flanders and from Spain, they have very much beautified them, and nothing that they could not perfectly imitate and counterfeit. This supposes that they brought many images: and principally conquistadors, in large part as Extremadurans, brought from the Sanctuary of Guadalupe the image of Guadalupe placed on the choir, thirty-two years before the period of the apparition by order of the Hieronymite Chapter, of which one could say that it was *sicut mulier amicta sole, et luna sub pedibus eius*, ("*as the woman clothed with the sun, and the moon under her feet*"). [25] formal words from the chapter records, says Father Medaña, historian of the Sanctuary; and he adds that the one of Mexico is identical in form, color, adornments, and name.

The only difference that comes up is that it proves that ours is a copy of that done by the hand of the Indians. The cloth is of *iczotl* [26] that is what they used for fine paintings; it is burnished, which is the preparation that they gave to the part on which they painted; it is without priming, a genre of their painting; the substance of the colors is unknown, because they took them, says Torquemada, from the juice of herbs and flowers that they have hidden from our knowledge. The color of the moon is black, because thusthey painted it, alluding to the fable of Buboso, and it is a mixture of their mythology that they did in our images, and it motivated a decree from the Second Mexican Council prohibiting them. Anyway, the image has painting defects, to which the painter Cabrera pretended to respond, and he satisfied a few, says Bartolache, that in his courteous way of explaining himself means to say that he did not satisfy. And these defects prove as well that the painting is from Indians, just as they prove that it is not miraculous. They proved the first thing, says Clavijero, because he reached out to see the portraits done by the Indians of some of their kings, and they painted very well, according to the rules; only one will not dare to compare them with those of Europe in the light and shade. This is precisely one of the image's defects, such as the hands too small; if it is a defect, it is that of the poor Indians, etc. They equally proved that the painting is not miraculous, even though Bartolache insists in responding to the text: *Dei perfecta sunt opera* ("God's work is perfect."). [27] This is a text too general that embraces the works of nature, which often frustrates the general laws established by God for the perfection of his works. But when God works forthwith by himself; there is this theological axiom "the gifts of God conferred by a miracle are most excellent." And it is the touch stone for discerning the miraculous healings, etc. Then not having means to whom to attribute the defect, it would fall back on the principal agent; and this is impossible, being God.

What to respond to these arguments in the common system of the tradition? I do reach it, in the case of Borunda, on occasion. The basis of the miracle of the painting destroyed, he reasoned that the image was a Mexican hieroglyphic from those that are called compositions, that contain the symbol of the faith given to the Indians by Saint

Tomé in this writing in its own way; but in that the articles of faith are tied to the finest phraseology of the language with such sublimity and delicacy, it does not seem feasible the neophyte Indians thus encrypted them at the time of the Apostle, given the recently achieved conquest. I unveiled this idea in the sermon, deciphering the image piece by piece, and exhibiting the Mexican idioms and phraseology that Borunda had dictated to me. This will be an imagination; but the method is ingenious, and there is no other able to sustain the painting as miraculous on its own.

By this method many defects, converted into hieroglyphics, stop it being so, and it especially satisfies the gravest objections to the moon's mythological color that is said to then represent the eclipse at the death of Christ, which Boturini and Veytia effectively say the Indians had depicted in their paintings, as also had the Chinese, according to Benedict XIV. And Borunda believes that far from their having taken the color of the moon from the image of the fable of the Buboso, the Indians later figured out the color of that one, the same way the Egyptians took their absurd mythology from their ancient hieroglyphic writings, the other Gentiles forged a large part of their mythological history from the Sacred Scripture and even among the Christians some fables were introduced by the ancient paintings of the churches; for example, the gigantic stature of Saint Christopher. I find no other solution for this most grave argument, because to say as one of the Physicians of one thousand six hundred sixty-six said, that to some perhaps he felt like overlaying silver to the moon, and he made it black, and gold to the rays, and took their shine away, is to speak of pure imagination. The tarnished gold, the painter Cabrera says, is that of the tunic, perhaps it is from the touch of the prints, and it does not have that shine as that of the rays. Neither does gold turn black because they put silver on top of it. Nor the painters who easily would know the accident would continue painting the moon of Our Lady of Guadalupe always black. This is its natural color. Also putting the image so ancient, with the identity of that of Guadalupe from the Guadalupano Sanctuary choir in Extremadura, does not prove that it may be a copy, since all the most ancient images of the Virgin are painted, says Benedict XIV, with a blue cloak and a pink tunic, as one sees in those that they attribute to Saint Luke; and even a very ancient Eastern Council cites that it orders it should not be painted in any other manner than as in the Sacred Scripture, i.e. in chapter 12 of the Apocalypse. If it should seem that these were dressings of little benefit, it was surely not for lack of will or industry by the Physicians, since there is no greater ingenuity, except that the patient was already declared terminally ill. There was no study, no more was offered.

But at the least, if the tradition as it is told cannot humanely defend itself, the object of the comedy always remains with us, that even though it does not achieve a stand-in, as its author intended it, even foolish it is more glorious to the native land than the same apparition of Guadalupe. The two objects of my trial are set forth to persuade Don Valeriano. The first, that the Mother of the true God had a temple and cult in Tepeyácac [28] since the preaching of Saint Tomé in Anáhuac: [29] the other, that her image was the same as that we named after Guadalupe: and even though he does not dare to say it clearly, this is what he meant to say by implying it had already been painted when the Virgin sent it to the Bishop. This second argument is not as easy to recant, as one might think; because it is certain that the Indians had before the conquest images of the Virgin by testimony of the missionaries; and it is certain that they hid some because of the persecution of the Spaniards. It is common that when they saw them traveling around burning all the temples in Mexico, they hid their beloved *Tonantzin*. Torquemada says that the missionaries put Our Lady of Guadalupe in Tepeyac, but as they put nothing in the temple except the images that the Indians painted and gave them, they could give them their ancient *Tonantzin* to put her in Tepeyac. The fact is that it is identical to that of the ancient *Tonantzin* as I have proven; and it is certain that it is touched up, since all the authors confess that daring hands have been put on her, corrupting, says Bartolache, the divine original; and it is not evident that they had done this after it was put in the Sanctuary.

But even if though neither of this is true, what I have demonstrated is that the Mother of the true God, the Virgin Mother of Jesus Christ, conceived by the work of heaven, the Mother of the Lord of the Crown of Thorns, the Mother of He who became flesh for us and died on a Cross, announced by Saint Tomé, was since her time in Tepeyácac Our Mother and Lady, the Mother of the Christians and Patron Saint of Anáhuac. In a good hour, since the apparition of Guadalupe may be a fable or comedy: it is indubitable that since the law went forth from Zion, and the Gospel was ordered to be announced to every creature that might be under the heaven in the whole world, the kindness and humanity of Our Lord Jesus Christ appeared teaching us, and by his Most Holy Mother protecting us; and this is without a doubt much more advantageous and glorious for us; than the apparition of her image at the end of the centuries, which was not a favor, amongst the slavery, the desolation, and the blood, after having been watching us without compassion one thousand six hundred years to go down living into hell. *Popule meus, qui beatum te dicunt, ipsi te decipiunt ("O my people they who call thee blessed are themselves cause for thee to err").* [30]

Those from the Archbishopric to the Mexicans had on purpose erred on the glory that I secured to them with my sermon; but they were not wrong. And they said that it was a conspiracy of the Creoles [31] to take away from the Spaniards the glory of having brought us the Gospel, and to equalize the Indians with them, giving them their image of Our Lady of the Pillar. To the first calumny I have already responded: and to the second one I say that the will of the Mother of Jesus Christ exactly conforms to hers, she does not distinguish between Jews or Greeks, barbarians or Scythians. The Jews were those who imagined that the mercy of God was exclusive for them; but Saint Peter seeing the grace of the

Holy Ghost descend upon the Gentiles told them: *"Of a truth I perceive that God is no respecter of persons: But in every nation he that feareth Him, and worketh righteously, is accepted with Him."* [32] This is also the only way things are to his Mother. And he who, for having been born here or there, judges himself deserving of his predilection, nurtures an untruth and imprudent confidence in her who is only mother of the sinners who want to be converted (says Saint Bernard). Everyone else are abandoned, like her Son. *Odisti omnes qui operantur iniquitatem: perdes omnes qui loquntur mendacium* (*"Thou hatest all the workers of iniquity: Thou wilt destroy all that speak a lie"*). [33] It is not only Zaragoza that pretends the Apostles have built a temple to the Mother of God, still living in mortal flesh. The Cardinal Aguierre cites several others different regions and concludes with these words: "This certainly ought not to be denied anywhere where it may persuade them of some ancient tradition." *Sané id in particulari non est negandum ubi antiqua tradicio id suadeat.* [34]

Among us there is, despite whoever weighs in, I must not have my native land defrauded of this glory, nor the Mother of God that which results from her ancient mercy and beneficence. There is more: Canon censors made sure that the image of Guadalupe is not now conserved, so that all the colors are fallen off, and the cloth more than a little damaged. If I had said it, the Señor Archbishop would have made it proclaimed in the pulpits, so that the people would stone me. With that the question was *de sugeto non supponente* (*"You shall imbibe from not substituting"*), from an image that now did not exist. Then I had more right to stick to my proposition and to affirm to my native land a glory that was not exposed to the vicissitudes nor the rage of the times. The image may be ruined, and it has been this or that, it will always be certain that the Mother of the true God had a temple among us, and was from the beginning of Christianity, Our Mother and Lady, Our Tonantzin, that thus she was called even that of Guadalupe, until forty years after the Spaniards baptized her with a Saracen name, very strange from the sweet mouth of the Mother of God. My enemies persecuted me unjustly, and now I am going to make seen that there was no truth in their mouths, and the process that they did to me was a pure maneuver of their iniquity.

Chapter 2, Notes

1. José Ignacio Borunda (1740-1800), *Clave general de jeroglíficos americanos*, published by Joseph Florimond Loubat, Rome, Jean Pasqual Scotti, 1888; recent publications are available in French and Spanish. Pre-Hispanic pieces were found in the Plaza de Armas, El Zócalo, Mexico City in 1790, and more recently in 1978. Borunda first presented his writing in 1791 to the Historical Academy of Mexico.

2. *Perchance, I might have succumbed to this one weakness.* Virgil, Aeneid IV.

3. Virgil, Aeneid IV, edited by Mier: *Here is the first joyful day, and the beginning of evil, etc.*

4. *On the word of the priest*, a Catholic Priest swears an oath *in verbo sacerdotis* by Placing his right hand on his chest as a part of his consecrated duties.

5. King James Bible, Revelation 12:1. "And there appeared a great wonder in heaven; a Woman clothed with the sun, and the moon under her feet, and under her head a crown of twelve stars." This is a scriptural description of the image of the Mexico's Virgin of Guadalupe.

6. Mier probably references Pope Innocent X, and his Papal Bull *Cum Occasione*, issued May 31, 1653.

7. King James Bible, John 21:2. *Thomas called Didymus.*

8. *Phoenix of the West, the Apostle Saint Tomé*, publication is unknown.

9. *History of the True Quetzacohuatl, the Apostle Saint Tomé*, publication is unknown.

10. King James Bible, Romans 10:14. *And how shall they believe in him*

of whom they have not heard? And how shall they hear without a preacher?
Romans 10:15. *And how shall they preach except they be sent?* Romans 10:18.
But I say, have they not heard? Yes verily, their sound went into all the earth,
and their words unto the ends of the world.

11. King James Bible, I Timothy 2:4; *Who will have all men to be saved*
and to come unto knowledge of the truth.

12. Saint Bede the Venerable, (672/673-735), *As in all parts of the*
world.

13. King James Bible, Proverbs 17:6; *The glory of children are their*
fathers.

14. King James Bible, Jeremiah 31:22; *A woman shall compass a man.*

15. The quote is slightly different than Latin Vulgate Bible Genesis
3:15, but probably the source. *The heel of the woman shall bruise your head.*
And the women will lie in wait for you.

16. King James Bible, Psalms 114:1; *When Israel went out of Egypt.*

17. Cayetano Cabrera de Quintero (about 1700-1775) is a Mexican,
author of *Escudo de armas de México,* ("Mexico's Coat of Arms") currently
available in Spanish.

18. Fray Gerónimo de Mendieta (1525-1604), born in Spain, lived in
Mexico, where he wrote *Historias eclesiástica indiana.* Publication was
prohibited until 1870. The "work" which Fray Mier references was likely
an unpublished chapter of Mendieta's "Ecclesiastical History," which
does reference, "the ten plagues of Egypt."

19. King James Bible, Exodus 1:14; "*And they made their lives bitter*
with hard bondage, in mortar, and in brick, and in all manner of service in the
field: all their service, wherein they made them serve, was with rigour."

20. (*) This Note, (*), was written by Fray Mier. "Even though the
Indian Valeriano did not dare to express the full force of the comparison,
the Indians hope that the Mother of God must give them their complete
liberty, as God to the Israelites. This is one of their secret traditions. A
few years before my sermon, two lawyers were passing by the
neighborhood of La Candelaria, one of whom was Dr. Pomposo, who
told it to me; and going into an Indian's hut to flee from a heavy shower
of rain, they found one very gray-haired, so absorbed in studying an
Aztec painting on a mat that they had the chance of observing him
before astonished by their presence he could remove his eyeglasses and

gather the painting. The other lawyer, who had the face of an Indian, told him in Mexican do not be frightened, since he also was one, and asked him what he was doing. He responded to him, "Quetzalcohuatl," had already told them, "when the Spaniards were coming, but he also said that they had to go away. I was putting down the account, and now not much is missing." They returned another day to better inform themselves, and now they could not find either the Indian or the grass mat. Thus, I predict that in the case of revolution the Indians will imitate their conquistadors in carrying as a banner the image of the Virgin and it would be that of Guadalupe. Haro with his deliberations and uproars helped all species, the same way as he prepared the souls with so large an oppression of the Americans."

21. *My son is young and tender, Ephraim.* The source of the Don Valeriano Scripture quoted by Fray Mier is unknown. It appears to be a mix of I Chronicles 22:5 and Jeremiah 31:20. This is an example of *"mutatis mutandis"* (*"with the necessary changes having been made"*) that Fray Mier introduces at the beginning of this paragraph.

22. *I bless you and make your name great, I will make thee a great nation, and to increase.* King James Bible, Genesis 12:2 is the closest translation. "And I will make of thee a great nation, and I will bless thee, and make thy name great; and thou shalt be a blessing:"

23. Mount Gerizim is sacred to the Samaritans who regard it, not the Jerusalem Temple Mount as the location chosen by God for a holy temple.

24. Nahuatl Dictionary: mountain images or figures, "Small Molded Ones."

25. *As the woman clothed with the sun, and the moon under her feet.* King James Bible, Revelation 12:1, "And there appeared a great wonder in heaven; a woman clothed with the sun, and the moon under her feet, and upon her head a crown of twelve stars."

26. Nahuatl Dictionary: a type of yucca.

27. *God's work is perfect.* King James Bible, Deuteronomy 32:4; *He is the Rock, his work is perfect: for all his ways are judgement: A God of truth and without iniquity, just and right is he.*

28. Tepeyácac ancient name of Tepeyac (Hill of Tepeyac), located in Mexico City, was a pre-Hispanic worship site for the Native Mexican worship of Tonantzin, Mother of the true God.

29. Anahua was the Aztec name of a vast inland sea, now dried up and the site of Mexico City.

30. *O my people they who call thee blessed are themselves cause for thee to err.* King James Bible, Isaiah 3:12; "As for my people, children are their oppressors, and women rule over them. O my people, they which lead thee cause thee to err, and destroy the way of thy paths."

31. A Creole in the culture of New Spain was a person born in New Spain with pure Iberian Peninsula ancestry.

32. King James Bible Acts 10:34-35.

33. *"Thou hatest all the workers of iniquity: Thou wilt destroy all that speak a lie."* The quote is found in *William's Vision of Piers Plowman* written 1360-87 by the English author William Langland. The Latin quote from English suggests that Fray Mier may have studied English works.

34. The preceding quote is a translation of the Latin, a rare instance where Fray Mier translates the Latin to Spanish.

Chapter 3

The Passions Conspire Together for Prosecuting Innocence

After that Archbishop Haro, by means of the proclamation that he ordered given to the preachers on the Sunday of the eight-day festival of Guadalupe, incited the Mexican people against me. I had to disillusion him to contain such a scandal and to come back for my honor, to present an appeal to the Royal Court. But as the Holy Spirit counsels us: *"Do not enter into litigation with a powerful man, lest we fall into his hands,"* and the spirit of vengeance of that Prelate was as large as his arrogance, I swallowed my disrepute in silence, the hate and the imprecations of the people, and to give space to his ire and to avoid an attack, I put forth no further appeal than to keep myself a recluse in my convent until the Christmas Holiday. At this time in which even the prisoners are thrown out of the prisons, believing the people now calmed, by itself most sweet, I went out when the sun set in the evenings to breathe a little open air; and there were no more than four or five houses that I visited, all of distinguished people, where for my respect and the politeness of their upbringing, almost no word was spoken of the matter.

While, in the Archbishopric they had gone around inquiring if the friars would take a letter in my favor, and I had been asked by means of a relative of mine, a domestic of the Archbishop, named Savariego; to whom I responded with my accustomed simplicity that I did not know. When the Archbishop arrived to warn that I had nothing in Santo Domingo, except devouring rivals of envy, and that the Provincial Fray Domingo Gandarias not only was my enemy but sworn as well against everything American in the same manner as His Illuminate by public notoriety, began his campaign, Their understanding was that I should be made a prisoner.

The Day of the Innocents at the night's prayers, the Father Superior of the convent, Fray Domingo Barreda, presented himself in my cell to ask me for the key to my cell by order of the Provincial. I ought to have responded that he had no immediate authority over me, except in the case of a visit when someone was not found, since among the Dominicans all the immediate authority and economy of each convent belongs exclusively to the Prior, who for this takes the right side in any function, even when the Provincial is present; and it is by this proverb among them that *The Order of Preachers is The Order of Priors*. But he who was then Prior, besides being my envious enemy, had the honor of being the Provincial's very humble errand boy, as it almost always happens that he is European and the Creole Prior, even though this one was too ordinary, and the other one too proud.

Therefore, I responded that the Dominicans as well do not express another specific vow in the profession than that of obedience, thus neither do they promise it except under the specific *secundum regulam et constitutiones fratrum praedicatorum*, ("*According to the rules and regulations of the Friars Preachers*") that according to Saint Thomas the limit of one's sense is our obedience: That according to our Constitutions of *forma judicii* ("*Form of Judgement*") no monk can be arrested, without previous process in the Order, of which there may have resulted full or semi-proof: and so neither are they permitted to arrest him if he is a monk of distinction, and there is not risk of flight, by the note that always remains: That no process in the Order was done to me, and that neither was I a danger of flight, and I was a monk of distinction not only as a Lecturer, but as a Doctor, whose privileges they were obliged to preserve for me, not only because the University Prelates had sworn to it when I graduated, as well as for having received their degrees in our

Santiago Province of Mexico by our Constitution: *Ordinationes pro Provincia Sancti Jacobi de México* (*"Ordinations for the Province of Saint James in Mexico"*).

In addition to that I am a member of the nobility and a gentleman, not only by my Mexican Doctor's degree, conforming to the Law of the Indies, nor because of my well-known origin to the most elevated nobility of Spain, since the Dukes of Granada and Altamira are of my house, and that of Mioño with whom it is now linked, dispute the grandeur, but also because in America I am descendent of the first conquistadors of the Kingdom of Nuevo Leon, as reported in the judicial information presented and approved in the Order; and by consequence according to the terms of the Laws of the Indies I am a *Noble Gentleman, of a known house and ground with all the privileges and laws attached to this title in the Kingdoms of Spain.* Clearly, the habit of Saint Dominic that so many Saints, Bishops, Patriarchs, Popes, Princes, and Kings have worn has not taken away my bloodline, and I can claim as Saint Paul the privileges of my native nobility against the prisons and trampling.

The Provincial responded immediately even though verbally by the same Superior that my imprisonment was by order of the Very Reverend Archbishop. I handed over the key out of respect, and under the protest of representing my right against the force that was done to me. On the following morning I sent with the same Superior a message to the Provincial, in which I summarized eight Papal Bulls on our privileges, copied from the Order's collection of Papal Bulls, by which it is clear to them that not even for crimes committed outside of the cloister are we subject to the jurisdiction of the Commoners. Privileges that according to the Canons cannot be renounced neither by the Order's Generals, nor the entire Order without express license from the Apostolic See that it has conceded to them because it mediates their interest. I do not remember the place, but indeed the words directed to an Abbot General: *etiam si sponté volueris de iure tamen nequiveris sine consensu Sedis Apostolica* (*"Of the right of his own free will even if you choose however unable, without the consent of the Apostolic See"*). Beyond this there is a Bull inserted in the Dominican Constitutions by Bandele, according to which every Prelate of the Order who intends to renounce some of his privileges, remains *ipso facto* committed in the disposition of his employment.

The Provincial responded to the same Superior also immediately and verbally that he believed that yes, I was subject to the rude person. It was not enough that he believed it; it was necessary that he explain it to me, in response to my arguments. I answered with another message that Fray Agustin Oliva took to him, the lay executioner of the prisons, appointed custodian of mine, in that I asked his help to declare in writing if my imprisonment was by order of the Archbishop, as he had been sent to tell me, or if it were so by his own. He responded with the same layman that he did not want to: an answer, even though bad-mannered, very common in prelates of the cloisters, but even more illegal when by the Dominicans' Constitution they do not obligate them nor even the formal precepts of obedience, if they do not require them in writing. And to not receive any more of my messages, he forbade the friars to communicate with me, at all, and to prevent any type of communication, he became the designated sentry. Seeing my servant leave by the terrace roof, he also sent someone to take away from me the ladder I had. He ignored without doubt that my door, whose lock was of screws, opened within, and I could have left if I had wished to; but so much was my patience, that in place of opening the door, I opened a window that was blocked, and from there I threw a message for the Archbishop, in which referring him to what the Provincial said, I made him aware of the illegality of my imprisonment without my having been heard, and I asked to be heard, for I was prepared to present my counter charges; and in order to do so I asked to be allowed to name a procurator and attorney. Domingo Velasco carried and delivered this message to Flores, the Archbishop's secretary, who occupied himself in inquiring of him if I had carried on my behalf many short notes, which certainly I had not done, except a letter sent to the Canon Conejares, the Archbishop's Commensal, in order to placate the Archbishop on my behalf, who once he embraced the shield, like his countryman Don Quixote, was not capable of placating himself until the arrogant and evil creole who placed himself between his eyebrows was buried in complete ruin. I stood up too much in favor of my countrymen, to be worthy of mercy.

The response to my message was to call upon my Provincial the next day, who without doubt would complain of my having revealed that my imprisonment was by his order, which left his injustice in plain view, since the Provincial returned from the Archbishop furious, and he sent the Fathers Ponce and Leon, Senior, to take from me the books that I might have from the Convent's library, so that I could not study them in my defense, paper and ink, which Father Ponce forever retained, threatening me with severe punishment if I returned to writing another thing in my defense. Have you ever seen a similar despotism? In the Archbishopric my writing was completely shelved, later I saw in Spain that it had not been added to the case documents. Nevertheless, my message had been put in care, so at fifteen days of my imprisonment a Notary of the Archbishopric presented himself in my cell to read me an order from the Archbishop, directed to the Provincial, in which he said that relative to the Guadalupe Chapter Council having complained that on the days of the Christmas Holiday I had gone out to various houses to defend the same that I had preached, he had me at his disposition.

It was a lie, and the Order afterwards forged upon a probable judgement for mending the illegality of imprisonment and to cover the criminal connivance of my Provincial, since if it had existed before, he would not even have had difficulty in my confessing to it in writing, nor would it have been necessary in that so much time afterwards a Notary of the Archbishopric came to let me know about it. It is true that the date was delayed until the day of Saint

Sylvester because they could not delay it anymore; but this same thing proves the fiction, because my imprisonment had taken place the Day of the Innocents, and by consequence before the Order. How was it believable that the Canons had complained that I privately supported what they wanted preached as true if it was well-founded? Even on Easter it could not be known if it was, nor later, since I had not been heard. I believe that this complaint was hatched by the Chapter Council Procurator Don Francisco Cisnersos, a low-life Pancho dirty trickster, a go-between known by the Archbishop, who was already walking around causing me trouble. In the end none of this authorized His Illuminate to imprisonment me, since according to the Council of Trent, *Reformation Session 25* only in case of having preached heresy can a Bishop proceed by law against an exempt preacher; and so an accusation of heresy did not fit in this case, so that the heresy would be in accusing me of it, since this is a theological axiom of Ricardo de San Víctor: such a heresy is to deny that it is of the faith what it is, as to affirm that it is of the faith what it is not; and surely they are not points of peculiar history, upon which I had solely spun my sermon.

Even though it may have been certain that in private homes I had supported what I preached, and that this granted authority over me to the Archbishop, it did not follow that it was necessary to lock me up: it was enough to order that I must not leave the convent. But, my knowing that the Archbishop did not have jurisdiction over me, or the Provincial power to arrest me in any given case, except for danger of flight, to take from him all pretexts I presented a message, offering bail for the security of my person to his satisfaction, for monks, for seculars, or secular priests. He did not reply to me in compliance with monastic despotism.

The envious and lowly Prior, Doctor of seven obstinate arguments and also a consummate adulator, did not omit to give me vile molestations; and having taken me on Sunday as they usually do, to hear mass in the Infirmary Oratory, he ordered all the papers to be taken from my cell, even from my desks, in order to take from me the defense or case documents that I might have, to warn my correspondents and supporters upon whom I might rely or to find upon what to incriminate me. All by order of the Provincial, and the influence of the Archbishop: and the content of the least important of my papers was on every friar's lips communicated by the indecent Prior.

I, nevertheless, had firmness about my sermon; but my friend the Marquis of Colina arrived at my door, and counseled me to back down, because an Edict was threatened, and I already knew the furor with which these pieces were shot off by the Archbishopric. Later Father Ponce came to assure me that His Illuminate was not averse to putting an end to the matter if I submitted a retraction in the humble terminology written to Conejares; and since I knew about this private letter I thought he was privy to the secrets of the Archbishop. It was surely no more than a precursor, since the following day the Provincial summoned and welcomed me with the terrifying devise of an Inquisitor for taking my declaration; and even though it was not a matter regarding me he threatened me for his purpose. He then commenced to weigh me down with the toughness with which the matter went forth, and that I was destined to be exiled to the Caldas Convent near Santander in Spain. And even though the action had not been substantiated, nor had it been heard! He would have suggested the species that would not have occurred to the Archbishop. And thus, he carried on ending the matter in that he had no other means than that of a surrender, in which case he could promise me all the influence and protection of the Order. I fell into the snare and did two submissions that he did not like, and he ordered me that I must precisely put that I had erred and humbly ask for forgiveness. I obeyed but I had the foresight to put what I did for not being able to suffer more imprisonment that was now twenty days, without counting the fifteen days of my previous voluntary seclusion. This addition annulled the retraction; but he was not looking for more than a pretext to elude my hearing; and on the word he is wrong for having erred (that I did not understand except for an error of prudence, nor did I believe it possible to understand it beyond an error of private history, upon which I had spun the sermon) to tell me to my face all kinds of errors.

Will the Provincial now proceed with the intention of my disappearing? So far, I could not say it, because he immediately advised me to write many small notes to my acquaintances so that they can mediate with the Archbishop. Therefore, he wanted this to serve, more than it was for pardoning me, and that other hands, if they were able, may free me. I was so simple-minded, that I wrote to nobody, because it appeared to me that on a matter of so little importance, such as an error of history that I had only preached as probable, my offering since then to retract it if it was proved to me to be false, was more than enough with already having it retracted, and it was not necessary to inconvenience my friends. I ignored the power of jealousy and how large it was, because four excited rounds of applause had been given to my sermons.

I remained astonished when the following day my retraction, so clearly forced and void, a Notary from the Archbishopric appeared to ask for the ratification of having been done voluntarily and spontaneously. I responded that voluntarily I repeated what I had written the previous day, this is, that I did the submission for not being able to tolerate the prison. And to avoid explications I went from my study to my garden to speak with Fray Agustin, my custodian, and I only returned to sign when the Notary called me. He wanted to read to me, and I retorted to him that had he not put forth what I had said to him? He responded just the same; and without me reading it, I signed as the Apostle counseled the Corinthians in case of doubt if the meal had been offered to the idols; *nihil interrogantes propter conscientiam* ("*Asking no question for conscience sake*").[1]

I had sent to ask Borunda for his work, and he sent me only some sheets of the end, that came to me in this interlude. I read them very quickly and superficially, before they could take them from me in some new looting, as had been done already to my submission. I confess that far from having found the insurmountable proof that the man had assured me to have, I found a portion of true absurdities from a man that did not know theology, and full of antiquarian and etymologist rantings, that commences in riddles, followed by visions and concluding in deliriums. The man had read much, he conceived and could not give birth, and what he gave birth to he was unable to give it value for lack of other knowledge.

As a result, my spirit was low, because the Provincial having called on me five days after my first submission to tell me that it was indispensable to send another to the Guadalupe Chapter Council in order that their demand forced by the Archbishop be withdrawn for going against his dictum, I offered him in my submission every satisfaction, and even that of composing and printing at my cost a work contrary to my sermon. And I would have carried it out even though I had remained as bad as Bartolache, because there are not worst defenders of a hoax than men of talent: *malae causae peius patrocinium* ("*Bad cause worse than defense*"). The Chapter Council, which was in my favor sent their secretary Dr. Leyva to declare to me the Chapter Council remained pleased by my submission, and that it had passed it to their Prelate in order that he could there provide the desired effect. I was made to know of their resolution in my favor at the day's end December sixteen that on that same day the Canon Gamboa had already advised me that the Chapter Council was proceeding forced; and was amazed that I had not torn, burned, or denied the sermon, knowing the antipathy of the Archbishop with the Creoles and their glories. I protested to him that my retraction was only conditional, if they complied with what had been promised me to cut the matter off by its virtue. He responded to me that he would always counsel me the path of humility. And I contested that I agreed, if they complied with what had been promised me: if not, I was resolved to defend my honor until the last extreme. Since even though nothing useful was found in Borunda for my defense, the fundamentals that I had in the substance of my own instruction for adopting his system, and I have already expressed, were sufficient for maintaining me with glory on defense.

Seeing that days passed, and the thing proceeded, I wrote to the Canon Uribe, in whose power I knew were the judicial decrees for the censor, in the same manner that I spoke to Doctor Leyva; and he wrote to me that he begged me for the love that he had for me, to say nothing to anyone that my retraction had been forced. This plea as tender as perfidious, since at the same time he was asking for an Edict against me, and urging that the matter be passed to the Inquisition, that even though requested by the Archbishopric, he did not want to admit it for not pertaining to the faith, he held me up for some time. Moreover, he still held back from me the opinion of an Attorney, to whom I consulted whether the Archbishop effectively had jurisdiction over me. And he answered me that yes, as a successor of the Apostles. As I was without recourse to any books, I could not thoroughly instruct myself against such great a piece of nonsense. It is necessary to confess that the immense gossip of the people excited by the Archbishop, the immense noise that my rivals scored, the general abandonment of my timid friends, and the outrage of the friars had me indecisive, stunned, and bewildered, especially being very docile by my nature, and deferential to the dictums of others.

Melancholic therefore and sleepless at the window of my cell, I saw a friar who at an odd hour of the night escaped from the convent to go to see a vestal virgin who he had taken from the house of my barber. It then occurred to me that I also could leave to gain power with which to interpose a resource of force before the Royal Court, retracting the two retractions they had taken from me by violence and deceit. And calling a pious friend, I commissioned him to find out how that friar had managed to leave without any difficulty. But at the same time, I wrote Dr. Pomposo seeking advice, who responded to me that he did not agree that I should leave, even though my thought was to return on the same night to my cell. My friend the monk came at night to tell me that the rascal of the Third Order had escaped early from the convent; but that I could leave, because there was no difficulty in the exit. I responded to him that I had consulted an Attorney, and he did not agree.

However, he who had slept outside of the Convent was annoyed, because I in a tone of compassion had asked my barber to where that rogue had carried the unhappy girl who he had taken from his house. For this he came in the morning to tell the Provincial that I by means of another monk was making haste to go to San Francisco or San Agustin. Certainly, it would not have been a crime, being a prisoner illegally by incompetent authority, and oppressed even to the point of denying me of any access to the King's Tribunal, to take an asylum that the Canons concede to the monks. But to not go out of the convent even once, I needed to leave at night, or with the help of a monk. My door opens on the inside, and even though the Provincial, knowing that I opened it sometimes to receive something, he had ordered shortly before a tiny padlock put on my door, my servant could have removed it from outside, or I could lower myself from my window, I could have left between four and five in the morning, when the church was open, and the convent asleep.

Notwithstanding, the remark of a friar so discredited and disobedient was enough for our Sultan that even the Inquisition had to reprehend him, putting my friend without another preamble in a dungeon, and to transfer me from my cell to another that was already serving as a prison after many months of another monk imprisoned by Gandarias without another process than *for being our will,* and without another immediate authority than that of Father Libevo, whose powers he carried stamped on his face. All I was able to accomplish, after the first day in my new prison, was light and my Breviary; but I was not even given a tiny table for eating, nor did the Provincial wish to grant me some books from my library for my solace, because in all the books it seemed to him that I was able to study for my defense. The dear Indian who served me, lowering himself through some secret passages to the orchard, arrived at the bars of my prison the Monday of the week *in Passione* ("*The Passion*"),[2] and he advised me on behalf of my friend that the previous day, Sunday, someone had worked clandestinely on the printing press to print an edict against me. His Illuminate had excused this pious work, with the purpose that it not come to my attention, and he could intercept the publication as an appeal to the Royal Court. For this on another day getting breakfast, I quickly left for the Provincial's cell, and instructing him, I asked for a judgement and the resource for interposing an appeal of force. He responded to me outraged that he was not giving it to me, nor did he want to give it to me; that now there was not time (Why did it have to be?); that I was to keep quiet: and he reprimanded my jailer because he had not prevented my exit.

It was published the Day of the Incarnation *inter missarum solemnia* ("*In solemn mass*") in every one of Mexico's churches, including that of my convent, with the name of Edict, an inflammatory libel nominatively against my persona, likewise ordering it to be published on a festival day and in the same manner in all the Archbishopric's churches by a third party, and sent to all the Suffragan Bishops so that they would publish it, if it seems to them, as it seems they carried it out, except in the New Kingdom of Leon my homeland, where I am the synodal examiner, my family the first of the Kingdom, and the Bishop Valdez was my friend, a Creole, and he knew the Archbishop's weak points. The Edict was reprinted in small-scale so that it could be sold, finally it was inserted into the *Gazeta. Furor illis secundum similitudinem serpentiu* ("*Madness is in the likeness of snakes*"). [3] The dismayed Father Ponce was the first who came to my door to give me the news.

On another day, the Friday of Sorrows after eleven o'clock, on which the Royal Court had already gone on Holy Week vacations, a Notary came to announce to me the Archbishop's sentence at the request of his designated prosecutor and his known flatterer the one-eyed Larragoiti, Sacrarium Priest. He condemned me to ten years of exile to the Peninsula, confined all this time in the Convent of the Caldas near Santander; that is in a desert, and perpetual ineligibility for all public teaching in the Cathedral, the pulpit, and the confessional, abolishing by the sentence my title of Doctor that I have by Papal and Regal authority. All this, the Public Prosecutor said was by the mercy and clemency of His Illuminate. Present were Fray Juan Botello, the Provincial's most vile acolyte Father Ponce, Fray Agustin Oliva, and at the door the Prior Herrasquin, who finally remembered he was a Creole and exclaimed: "Jesus, he was not even a heretic!" It did not make any impression on me; I was already insensitive; as a man of honor and of birth I had received death's dagger with the Edict.

The sentence was void on all four sides; as illegal, as the process had been, as unjust, since I had not denied the tradition of Guadalupe, and I knew as a theologian that there was nothing in the sermon worthy of theological censor, even though the Archbishop said that according to the censors it was full of errors, blasphemies, and impieties. It was null, for being against the privileges of the regular priests; consequently, it was against the Laws of the Indies and the Royal Patronage that guaranteed them. I had to appeal, and I did to the Royal Court, to the Apostolic Judges, conservators of the privileges of my Order, and to the Bishop of Puebla as a delegate of the Apostolic See. But as such the sentence did not come announced to me until after the publication of the Edict, in order that the appeal that surely would had been put in place then could not prevent it; so, the sentence came announced to me when the Royal Court had already gone on vacation, to frustrate my appeal if I should try stopping it.

Branciforte, the Archbishop's buddy, a most corrupt crook would have given him help against me, and the Provincial would have helped the Archbishop to hide the appeal. We supposed that it was to come to the Judge Curators, the Canons Campos and Omaña; they were both an

Archiepiscopal. The Bishop of Puebla would not clash with the Archbishop because of a friar; they were wolves of one den. Would the Court admit it? And once admitted would justice be done to me, according to the immensity of my discredit, that was what most troubled me, principally having a new public prosecutor and judges, it is to say, indebted for their transport, and quick to sacrifice themselves to a Prelate, who did not care what means were used, and the money flowed like water to complete his vengeance? It was so notoriously inexorable that the entire world had abandoned me, and even those who seemed my relatives were ashamed of seeming so, even though in all America there was not another who could exceed me in nobility. With the friars nothing counts, when the opponent is the Prelate: they are slaves with bangs, like the military with epaulets. And if the persecuted stands out, he ought not to count on his community, but with enemies. The hell is unchained against him: now my life was not the life in the cloister: no means were exempted to tarnish, discredit, and ruining me even with anonymous letters to the Government. Nor had Gandarias left me any property other than the white habit that I had on the body. After all I feared a poison: this crime is not so rare; the same friar, who had accused me of wanting to take an asylum, had poisoned his novices' teacher, García the Malagueño. Principally since the Edict was published, I formed the resolution of living hidden far from my homeland, or having it withdrawn and prohibited; which I believed was only attainable in Spain, where I ignored the influence money had on the Archbishop.

Thus, reserving my protest before the King, I gave my hands to the executioner. Soldiers came to my prison after midnight, and after three o'clock in the morning I left Mexico, Palm Sunday, as disrespected as Jesus Christ on this day after so much applause. The troop was charged not to let me speak with anyone, and orders that they carried out ought to be so rigorous, that even though we arrived at night to Veracruz, and a north wind blew so strong and dangerous that it was still three days later without any City communiqué with the Castle of San Juan de Ulúa that is half a league inland from the sea, immediately they loaded me on a ship with all dispatch. While a jail cell was prepared for my lodging, the King's Lieutenant told me in a tone of admiration: "You are the first European who His Illuminate loses." "No," I responded to him, "I am a Creole: he has condemned me without hearing me; and so that I could not defend myself, they took from me my books, papers, ink, and communiqué." "Oh my God," he exclaimed, "the same prohibitions they order to be done here." The injustice and outrage were so manifest, that there on the sea in the depth of a jail cell the Archbishop, still feared the protest of an unhappy soul abandoned by the entire world for fear of drawing his ire.

The Provincial also had the indignity of writing to the Castle I was to be treated with stinginess, because the convent was poor. And it was clear to me that it was a bank of silver, then counting on a fund of sixty thousand pesos in haciendas and farms, except the Prelates who take some salaries more than regular priests, to the rest of the friars nothing more than lunch and dinner is given to them, and each one has breakfast, dresses and lives in his house or their own means. To bring friars from Spain, who come to socialize in the prelacies and honors leaving the Choir exclusively to the Creoles, the convent paid a thousand pesos per head brought to Mexico; and so many the Province has no need of them, that the major part of Creole youths are left without studies; in order that the Fathers from Spain have, when they come, donkeys to drive. So, they say, and often more. Only for a distinguished son of the Province was the convent so poor, that to fund the transport of his exile it was necessary to seize his library so that nothing was owed to the friars. This, nevertheless, was the same Gandarias that to defend an obscure Carmelite, had being Prior, made such a noisy resistance to the Carmelite's Provincial and to the orders of the Royal Court: and for a monk of his own Order, that he gave honor to his habit, sacrificed it against the privileges of his Order. The difference was clear; I am a Creole, and that one was a European. The Provincial came to the Archbishop as a ring on the finger.

I was in the Castle two months, a necessary delay for instructing his three powerful agents in Madrid, and to assemble the rope in the channels where I could solicit justice, and that the same iniquity and outrage could continue against me. The day of the Feast of Corpus Christi, I embarked, convalescent from fever, and under registry consignment on the mercantile frigate Nueva Empresa. While she sailed, I am going to give an account of the ruling that the two Canons Uribe and Omaña, chosen by the Archbishop for condemning me, gave upon my sermon

Chapter 3, Notes

1. *Asking no question for conscience sake.* King James Bible, Corinthians 10:25-26, "Whatsoever is sold in the shambles, that eat, asking no question for conscience sake: For the earth is the Lord's, and the fulness thereof."

2. *The Passion* is the Holy Week before Easter.

3. *Madness is in the likeness of snakes.* King James Bible, Psalm 58:4, "Their poison is like the poison of a serpent; they are like the deaf adder that stoppeth her ear;"

Chapter 4

The Passions under the Disguise of Censors Slander Innocence

The conquistadors said of the Indians that they were slaves *a natura* (*"by nature"*): Will their history be truth? Being put in battle by some powerful European against their fellow countrymen, there are no slaves more loyal, viler flatters, nor persecutors more malevolent and despicable. The Archbishop chose Uribe for Censor, because he already knew his opinion on what I had written on Guadalupe, and because everybody knew that he could not say as Saint Paul, *nunquam fuimus in sermone adulationis, sicut scitis* (*"Never used we flattering words, as ye know"*). [1] Omaña had as an image of his devotion a magnificent portrait of Flores, the Archbishop's Secretary; and in effect he assured me that he had done no more than to comply with Uribe's ruling like a *child*. Their censure will demonstrate what they were ordered to do.

Their censure scarcely went over my sermon in rough draft that I had delivered, when they represented to the Archbishop that it could not be the sermon that I had preached, because there was absolutely no motive for so much scandal; that surely, I had preached other things, according to what various persons said. Why doesn't their testimony check against the original? They would affirm or deny by the common people that everything is exaggerated and confused. When had I time to fabricate a rough draft that took up seven sheets in the case documents, when I failed to do the first part of the sermon that I was to preach the octave Sunday to the Capuchin nuns? I had not preached in a desert and with the reading of my sermon to three or four Guadalupe Canons the identity would be known. The Archbishop had already investigated it, since having known that before preaching I had read it to the Doctor and Lecturer Alcalá, he called him, and not only did he certify that it was the same, but that he let it be seen by the Canon Bruno the Archbishop's commensal and charged with the matter, by the signs of my fingers stamped on the paper, that right there I had studied it, but as an exercised orator I had left for the heat of the battle the last parakeets as they say. Effectively it was thus, and all my sermons without exception are in rough drafts, however complete like the present one. Since the true consequence that ought to be inferred from the representation of the censors, was that by their own confession my sermon contained nothing worthy of a scandal; that it was the Archbishop who excited it on purpose to motivate the process; and that if the censors afterwards found motive for censure, theyworked against their conscience to please their constituent.

Nevertheless, since they took away my rough draft, I have copied the sermon from my memory, that by consequence it was a clear copy; and as one sees in the court records, it does not distinguish from the rough draft except in some more refined expressions, and in one or another kind that like the copy was only for me, I added some of those that I had suppressed in the pulpit for its brevity. Well when upon the censors' petition I was asked for another sermon, I delivered it. And to have them see my sincerity contrary to what they unjustly suspected, I delivered them without their asking me for them, the fine points they I had from Borunda on the hieroglyphics that he believed to see in the image, all my jottings on slips of paper, and even the bit of the sermon that I had for the Capuchin nuns. So much was the candor with which I proceeded, unaware that on this Uribe had acted to lay down his censure. I had already been told that he was malicious, but I did not believe it to that extent.

All this delivered to the Notary, he took out a paper, and reading in it, all pensive and mysterious, he began to ask me on behalf of Uribe some questions so insidious, that the Notary was confused, and asked me some absurdities, such as if the proofs that I had of the sermon were from infallible, immutable, and invariable authors. All this jargon was reduced to knowing if I had more proofs, or if they were printed authors, only ones whose works were respected like Señor Don Quixote de la Mancha. Clearly, if the sermon deserved censure, they only had to produce it; and in the response they would know my proofs. Or they wanted to convict me without a hearing, as they did; or they wanted to give a censure, and they feared to risk it against the proofs that I might have (the dossier of printed authors, etc.). Also, the question was put to me if I knew Mexican, even though I had more right to ask if the censors knew it enough to judge a sermon all founded on numerous phrases of the language. Uribe says in his ruling that he did not speak it; but that he studied the grammar, and that his partner had been priest of various Indian villages. In other words, Uribe was like those nonsensical grammarians who have studied grammar in the classroom, and don't speak Latin, nor do they understand it. And Omaña knew some badly pronounced phrases, that is what many Priests know to ask Indian marriage couples their consent, and to take their rights. If he had known more, Uribe would not have used this circumlocution. But it assures that according to his grammar, all Borunda's phrases are well explained.

Having been asked about Borunda, in place of saying that he had instructed me in those phrases and ideas, I said I had taken them from his work, because even though I had not seen it, I knew what was contained in them. Seeing the forged beam, I wanted rather to receive the whole blow, than to make a family's unhappy father suffer, that if I had been surprised and deceived, it was with good intention. Borunda settled mine badly, because in Spain I saw in the court records a note to Uribe, by which he tried to throw the body out, when I had not even imagined in my life such a system, nor would I have dared to preach it without their insurmountable proofs. Even if one dares to call my sermon *rudis indigestaque moles* ("A rough and disordered mass") [2] when the censors confess that without the key of my sermon, which contains the quintessence of Borunda's work, it would have been impossible for them to penetrate his inextricable labyrinth. Perhaps because of his interpretation neither would I have found an exit; but he spoke better than he wrote, and my sermon was only an analysis of what I heard from him.

The ruling of Uribe for the most part is on the kind of challenge of Father Isla to the Surgeon; this is a continued joke, without saying an iota of substance. It is taken for granted that Borunda talked nonsense upon the point of American antiquities like Don Quixote on knighthood, and he deals with comparing various passages of his work with the adventures of the Knight of the Leones. It is necessary to take responsibility that the work of Borunda is no more than rough drafts. There is no doubt that there are passages very ridiculous, as there are also ridiculous etymologies in our game rules. This is a pension appended to the profession of etymologists and antiquaries, without this they stop making useful discoveries, or their mistakes of leading us to great truths. It is a condition of human understanding to always touch the extremes before opining to the middle. It seems to me that in all his ruling, Uribe also shows such blunders, that he could be compared with the Knight of the Mirrors. [3] [a]

I will put forth three examples, two in the serious genre, and one in the jocular. The first may be on Borunda saying that he adopts Paw's foolishness of a flood on our continent. It appears that Paw wrote his American investigations within the Polar Circle, according to his absolute ignorance of the things of America, and at the suggestion of a Spaniard he wrote against the Americans (as Carli says) with a pen stained in the blood of cannibals. He said that the whole America is a continent just come forth from the waters. By consequence, it was all full of swamps and stinky and fatal lagoons, incapable of ripening any fruit, and only capable of producing reeds, reptiles and thorns that from their corrupted ponds have sprung a cast of frogs called Indians, a species half-way between men and the orangutan monkeys. These are deliriums worthy of a cage. But that in the very violent earthquake of twenty-four hours that submerged the Atlantis Island, almost as large as Europe, the floods reaching to some lower parts or of our continent, this is very far from being nonsense. If Uribe had read Bailly's *Atlantis*, the letters on the same subject from the most erudite Count Carli, and had he seen the hydrographic letters from the English on the Atlantic Sea, considering the angles jutting forth and receding from the Antilles, which they match, and the direction of their rivers all towards the continent, he would have believed that they are nothing but the highest parts of the submerged land; the medallions of its flood.

When ours [Spanish] arrived at the Antilles, they found in them the tradition of having belonged to the continent; and Herbas proves it with an analogy of their languages with those of the neighboring coasts. Just as it proves with the languages of America the same that their monuments evidence, that it was populated by peoples from Asia on one hand; and on the other by peoples who rose from Atlantis. The word *atl* for saying water still survives in Mexican. What nation can the marble colonnades buried in the sandy beaches of Veracruz's coast be from? What can be the fourth of the four famous Mexican epochs?

But this does not have any connection with my sermon. The second example has some. Borunda to excuse the insult of Gradalupe's image, without prejudice of the miracle that he believed of the preservation, he imagined that perhaps it came from having the apostates insult her at the time of Huemac's persecution, it may allude to the fable of the flaying of the Mother of the Gods, or *Tetehuinan*, Ancient Queen of the Mexicans; because clearly this is an allegory.

Uribe begins by entirely mistaking the date of the epoch of the flaying of the *Tetehuinan*, and later says that even though it is certain that now already the image is not conserved, the colors are all cracked, and all the cloth more than a little damaged. It was not so in 1666. And from where does it appear? The painters and physicians of that time would have said it. Or they would not have said it, since Bartolache and his painters silenced it, even though in their inspections, which Uribe attended, he saw the damaged image. There is in all this fear of the common people, more trickery than what one thinks, unworthy of Christians on a matter of religion, in that the lie is not a slight sin. Just as Bartolache confesses that daring hands have, without doubt, been placed on the image, corrupting the divine original, and they subtracted (he says) traits, daubs, etc., so Father Florencia who attended the inspections of 1666, to excuse the abuse of the cloth, says that they told him that anciently in some imagined painting there was a trimming of angels surrounding the image that might keep her company, and smudging it like a human brush, the image stayed peeled, a satisfaction not requested, a manifest accusation. These accounts prove that the image was already damaged of old and wanted to do finishing touches to it. And it ought not to be a Borunda crime to at least seek in the land of fables some rubble with which to wall up the holes that everywhere undermine the pretended tradition.

The ruling of the physicians and painters of one thousand six hundred sixty-six was given more for enthusiasm, than for justice, in a time that they did not even know a good critique, or good physics. That of the painters is already condemned by those of Bartolache; and that of the physicians causes compassion. I don't tell of one hundred thirty-five, of the three hundred years they conserved in Mexico very many paintings intact, of those in Santo Domingo there are several, despite saline humidity of the air. Those physicians had heard the rooster crow on the miracle of the preservation of the bodies of the saints, but not even is this admitted as proof, except for later having proven the heroic virtues; nor is it given by a miracle, except the preservation of the mass of private parts, because the desiccation, says Benedict XIV, is a true corruption. Since they would first have to prove the painting was supernatural, and afterwards to prove something, to prove that in the image fresh colors were conserved. In the rest, what miracle had been proved with preservation of one hundred thirty-five years, if it is a painting of the Indians, whose colors convince one that they were indelible, and we see their paintings previous or coetaneous to the conquest, that they have worked abounding, even today with colors so bright that they astonish?

Third example: To interpret the Mexican hieroglyphics, one needs a profound knowledge of the language, and a large reading of the Indians' Teachers, the only ones who can teach us something, because the code has been lost, and Borunda has directed his efforts to provide a general code (if it is possible). Uribe who has neither that knowledge, nor this reading material, took it upon himself to refute with the arms of the ridiculous how Borunda deciphered the hieroglyphics. And for this like an echo from the common people he chose a passage in my sermon that had shocked him. Deciphering according to Borunda the hieroglyphics of the image, I said that it represented the Incarnation as indicated by the bulging belly of the image, and above it the waist knot, in Mexican called, *tlapi-li* that by its component parts means *the Principal of the Earth*. I don't know why it so shocked the common people. Hasn't the Virgin been pregnant? Never had she been more worthy of veneration than when she had the Son of God in her womb: from there come all her prerogatives, as she confessed it in her canticle: *Ex hoc beatam me dicent omnes generationes* (*"From henceforth all generations shall call me blessed"*). [4] And, they don't say that this painting conforms to the woman of the Apocalypses and even the Congregation of Rites has said *in ea fere specie* (*"almost in appearance"*). Since the woman of the Apocalypses is not as she wants, she is pregnant, but in labor. — *Siquum magnum apparuit in caelo: mulier amicta sole, et luna sub pedibus eius: et in capite eius corona stellarum duodecim: et utero habens, clamabat parturiens* (*"(T)here appeared a great wonder in heaven; a woman clothed with the sun, and the moon under her feet, and upon her head a crown of twelve stars: And she being with child cried, travailing in birth,"*). [5]

But what does Uribe say? That it would follow (because all the ruling is of consequences) that every Indian woman's sash that is worn with the knot above the belly, would be the Virgin Mother of God; which would be the heresy most heretical of the world. Really? With that one could not say that the crown that Uribe wears on the head indicates that he is a Priest of Jesus Christ, because it would follow that the priests of the idols, who also wore a crown, and for this the Council Iliberitano prohibited them to the Christian priests, were they priests of Jesus Christ? Neither can one say that imperial and royal crowns put on the images of the Virgin indicate that they are from the Mother of God, Empress, and Queen of the heavens and the earth, because it would follow that all empresses and queens were over the heavens and earth as Mothers of God. I am certainly not a Nahuatl expert; I believed that Borunda was one, because *peritis in arte credendum est* ("*Experts believe it is in the art.*"); from what I had read in Torquemada, Boturini, and Clavijero, the Boturndian mode of interpreting the hieroglyphics did not appear to me so irrational, and the Uribian method of refuting him appears much less rational to me. A picture of the Acolhuan or of Texcoco emperors is what he presents for an example. Of whom is this first figure? Of the Emperor *Xólotl*? Uribe would say no, because it would follow that any one-eyed person hunting alone is the Emperor *Xólotl*. Of whom is this other figure? Of the Emperor *Netzahuatlcoyotl*, because it has at the side the head of a coyote open-mouthed, that is like saying a hungry coyote, and this means *Netzahuatlcoyotl*. Not because it would follow that any coyote that comes to steal chickens because it is hungry is the Emperor *Netzahuatlcoyotl*. The Jesuit author of the true Quetzalcohuatl history says that he was able to see in the San Pedro and San Pablo College the pictures of the Mexican kings, and the last one was Cortés with his name also in Mexican hieroglyphic, and it was a small gourd with a handle, in Mexican *caoctl*, with a few small fishes inside, in Mexican *ahuatli*; in such a way that Cortés's naturalized name was *Cohuatli*. Not because it would follow that any Indian tray with *ahuautli,* is Hernan Cortés. Torquemada says that as the first missionaries taught the Indians the *Pater Noster* in Latin, to keep it in the memory they wrote in their way, and they painted a small banner that is *pantli* and a prickly pear that is *nochtl*. Not because it would follow that wherever there was a banner and prickly pear there is *Pater Noster*. Phrasing it like Uribe, is there folly more foolish than this mode of impugning the interpretation of the Mexican hieroglyphics?

But we come to the censure that directly affects me and divides into individual and general. He who heard the Archbishop preaching in his Edict, that according to the censors my sermon contained errors, blasphemies, and impieties, would believe that in effect they had found this coal mine. But already we heard them confess to have not found them in the rough draft, a thing worthy of scandal! Nor did they find anything in the sermon; and I even believe that by his influence the friars took the papers from my cell in search of spoiled meat upon which to nibble. Not finding it, they put to scratching in the mess of my rough drafts and small notes from Borunda that I handed over. In these they saw a proposition, to which they believed could be given a bad meaning, and another on a strip of paper, where I had put some three lines of maimed writings, inexact, and abandoned. Upon both, the two ravens put to scholastically fluttering about to satiate their hunger for corruption. This was the same as to want to prove that a man stinks, because some of his friends smell bad, or from the excrement that he left in the privy. Nevertheless, we see which the propositions and the censure are.

I already said that Borunda being with the black moon of the image, that thus the Indians painted for allusion to some mythological genesis, its color ingeniously converted into a hieroglyphic that symbolizes the eclipse of Christ's death; he adds in his notes that the Indians put it at the five days of the new moon. I omitted this erudition in my sermon, because it didn't make sense to me, because I did not how Borunda worked out this calculation, and because I had always heard said that the eclipse was on a full moon. The censure is that by putting it on the new moon, it would follow that it was not a miracle; and this is against the faith. What follows in truth from such censure are four defects in my censors; malice against me, maliciousness against Borunda, lack of physics, and lack of theology.

Malice against me, because they censured this as if it was found in my sermon; and it is not even found in the rough draft. Malice against Borunda, because he does not say the eclipse was at the five days of the new moon, but that thus the Indians put it, and this can be a holy truth. It is heresy to deny that Jesus is consubstantial to the Father; but it is a holy truth to say that Arrio denied it. A lack of physics, because according to the censure it does not follow that such an eclipse was not miraculous: the first thing, by universal accord, no eclipse of the sun can be naturally on the earth. It arises from the interposition of the moon between earth and the sun; and as the moon is smaller than the earth, it cannot entirely hide the light of the sun. The second thing, it lasted three hours; no eclipse of the sun can naturally exceed one quarter of an hour, for the rapidity with which one planet passes beneath another. The third thing, because to verify a natural eclipse, it is necessary that it be in what astronomically is called nodes; and it was necessary to prove that on the fifth day of the new moon of the month and year in which Christ died, those planets had met in their nodes in order that the eclipse could have been natural. Anyway, it lacks theology, because what the Scripture teaches was that there was darkness on the death of Christ; and the Popes of the Church explain them without turning to the eclipse, such as Saint Chrysostom who says that they came from opaque and thick clouds that hung-over Jerusalem, because not all the Popes opine that there was a universal darkness. By these sentences of the Popes and the arguments of the philosophers who object it would have been a general disturbance on the calendars of the nations, etc. Benedict XIV says that to save the Scripture, it is enough to say that the sun contracted its rays. The species of a true eclipse was made common in the Church, because in the early centuries they made common the works attributed to Saint Dionysius the Areopagite who says he saw it; today they are no longer taken as his.

But even a supposed true eclipse, where is it evident to Señor Uribe that it was in full moon? He will say that the Scripture ordered Easter celebrated then. We also ought to celebrate it at the full moon; and as in the time of the Nicene Council this converged on the Sunday following the 14th day of the March moon, it ordered that it be celebrated then. Moreover, separating a little the full moon of this day, we come to celebrate Easter many centuries so distant from the full moon that in one thousand five hundred eighty-six we celebrated it as many as ten days later, as it was suppressed in the Gregorian correction — all for lack of Astronomy. So, it is not enough that the Scripture orders Easter celebrated on the full moon. It was necessary that Uribe test that it is of faith that the Jews were good astronomers in order to take well the point of the full moon. They were not reliable, but very bad, according to the method that Camedi has published; and today the best theologians are convinced that the year of the death of Christ that they say was the 787th year of the foundation of Rome; they were wrong, since this year the full moon did not fall on Friday. So, the central and full eclipse is where it is in the theological knowledge of my censors.

I would want to see what they responded to the argument of the mythological color of the Guadalupano moon, because if they are not satisfied by it, the image must be removed according to the Second Mexican Council that prohibited images in which the Indians had mixed traits of their mythology. Or at least it is necessary to silver-plate it, or delete the moon, as was done by decree of the Fourth Mexican Council with the small dragon to the image de la Luz, because it could lead to an error. And they would do well even in changing the position of the moon, painting the horns down, because the theologians and exponents warn in Apocalypse

Chapter 12 that thus one sees the conjunction with the sun; and that thus it ought to be painted, in order that the woman that is upon the moon remains illuminated. It does not seem that the Angel painters concurred in this lack of physical perspective.

We follow up to see if my censors were better engaged on the other proposition that they censured. One finds on a small strip of paper three or four lines of writing incomplete and discarded for inaccuracies, as I already said: one does not find such a proposition in the sermon, or in the rough draft. It deals with the monuments excavated in the Plaza: and in assumption of containing the time of the Scripture, the rough draft said that they were a proof, the most irrefutable of the religion. This proposition, even if it had been found in the sermon, ought to be understood oratorically, it is to say, with a reduction, understanding that it was a big proof. Thus, we distinguish even in the writings of the Popes what they said oratorically or in a sermon, from what they said in their doctrinal works. But what Uribe wanted was to make me evil, so he takes the compass as if it were upon a geometric proposition and argues: "If he [Mier]wishes to say that it is more irrefutable than the revelation contained in the Divine Scriptures or the Apostolic Traditions, it is a blasphemy: if he wishes to say that it is more irrefutable than the miracles and doctrine of the Popes or the testimony of the martyrs, it is an error: if he wishes to say, etc." And if Señor Uribe does not wish to say any of this, or admit some Catholic sense; why not ask for the charity and the justice and even the criticism that they interpret in the best sense in the propositions of a Catholic Priest and Doctor? There is the wickedness of the theologians who we call consequential men, it is to say, literary men of the profession, whose role is to demonize whomever they fancy, and to stir up the Church, as they did in France with imaginary heresies until the Supreme Pontiff Innocent IX gave them peace, defining, as I already said, that even though they agree on principles from which they infer heretical consequences, they ought not attribute to that which denies them, however much they follow its principles.

The wise Jesuit Teófile Rayunda, to make seen the futility of similar qualifications began to censure the Creed, and he threw over his shoulder all the theological notes, from impious and heretical, up to rash and scandalous – the symbol of our faith. Yes, and there is not a false word in all the censure by the Jesuit. But why I will ask, can chemistry make a similar transformation? It is a piece of dung by an evil intentioned theologian. A proposition takes hold, they give it all the evil senses that they can give it, and in each it will qualify; but the good sense that it admits is silenced, and that maybe it is obvious and natural. The people, who ignore the traps of art, and hear such heresy, error, and impiety, etc., believe that a legion of demons has disembarked in the belly of that unhappy person, and strangled him, or applaud his theme, when he who deserves being reduced a hundred times to ashes is the damned hypothetical theologian, a man of consequence, a seducer of the people, and a calumniator of his fellowman. Clearly, the object that I had in mind when I wrote this proposition about the discovered monuments were the incredulous philosophers. These make fun of the revelations and of the Scriptures, of the Popes, of the martyrs, and the miracles, who they impugn in a thousand ways; but they are rational men who do not deny the visible monuments, nor can they, without entirely discrediting themselves, because all are in the state of judging from the evidence. The force of the evidence is respective. One does not argue the Gospel with a Jew, because he will not admit it, except with the Old Testament; nor to a Protestant with the Vulgate even though for us it is authentic, because it only gives credit to the original texts. Saint Thomas wrote his *Summa contra Gentiles* (*"Summary against Pagans"*) [6] at the petition of Saint Raymond of Pennafort against the Moors of Spain; and even though at the end of his articles he cites some texts of the Holy Scripture to show the consonance of the faith with reason, the nerve of his articles consists of philosophical reasons taken many times from Aristotle, Averroes, and Avicenna. —Señor Saint

Thomas, you prefer the authority of a Pagan and two Saracens to the Scripture, to the miracles, to the Popes, and Councils, etc. —It is that the Moors do not believe them. —Saint Paul, citing the Areopagus to give reason for his doctrine, began putting forth the inscription from a stone: *"To the unknown God: Whom therefore ye ignorantly worship, him declare I unto you."* [7] —Señor Saint Paul, you prefer a stone to the Prophets, to the miracles of Jesus Christ, etc. —It is that the Athenians do not believe them. —Ah, Saint Paul and Saint Thomas if in their time there had been Canons from Mexico, they would have gone to the fiery pit!

The Señores Canons knew very well that they were playing puppets to please their constituency, since later summarizing their ruling they assured that nothing had been reprehensible in the sermon if it had not denied the tradition of Guadalupe. Later they did not believe that there was nothing in it, this they were saying, because if there had been, it would always be very reprehensible even if I had not denied the tradition. But they are very reprehensible for having put to play puppets in front of persons from La Mancha exposed to becoming obsessed and taking them for reality, as happened to Don Quixote with the *totili mundi* (*"The whole world"*) of Master Pedro. To the sound of the Arabian kettledrums, Moors, Don Gaiferos, Melisendes, etc. [8] the man believed in the obligation of coming to the rescue in his capacity of a knight errant, he drew his sword and left on the altarpiece a puppet with no head, and if Master Pedro does not lower down his head, he would have been decapitated, as the writer of the Edict has cut off mine to curtail my honor. There is not to my faith in all the censure another thing to which the volley of errors, blasphemies, and impieties can allude that according to the censors (says the Archbishop) my sermon contains, but the two cited propositions, as innocent as the two herds of sheep that Don Quixote took for two armies of Moors. And so, honor is taken in a most grave matter from a Priest of Jesus Christ with such solemnity. *Obstupecite caeli super hoc* (*"Heaven is astounded over this"*)!

It is not fair the General Censure they gave to my sermon. It comes down to saying that in Spain a censure was given against the denial of the tradition of Our Lady of the Pillar, which Father Risco cites. It is thus that the Pillar and Guadalupe traditions are equal: it can then be applied to my sermon, in which they assume the Guadalupe tradition was denied. This syllogism walks on four legs, and every leg crippled. The first thing they assume is that I denied the Guadalupe tradition, and this assumption is false. I have already proved it. With what do they prove it? An admirable thing! This being the principal cause of my condemnation, and that was clamored so much in the pulpits, they don't bother to prove it, but they suppose it as clear and they go on at length, without taking charge that as the brightness is relative, and in a status of Doctors we are going to say nothing to their gratuitous circular affirmative answer, too much would be satisfied with a flat denial. Poor little fawning Canons! As they have dared to belie their Lord that it had already been preached in Mexico that I had denied the tradition. Thus, they assume I am guilty to justify the projected penalty.

The Canons also falsely assume that the tradition of Pillar and that of Guadalupe are equal. Well, the Congregation of Rites only says of this what they consider and say *fertur dicitur* (*"It carries the name."*), and of Pillar that it is considered an ancient and pious tradition, *pia et antiqua traditio fert* (*"It carries the pious and ancient tradition"*); and in this it appears to me that there is some difference. The more Uribe himself administers to me, since he says that the Jesuit Father López, postulant of the Guadalupe Prayer assured the Penitentiary Canon that having appealed to Benedict XIV; it served to grant that mention be made of the Apparition in the prayer of the official letter; he responded to him that too much had already been done for the Mexicans. Uribe tells this, believing to put a pike in Flanders; and it is his head that it has been put on her by his liturgical ignorance. Gravina, author of the primary vow on the subject says that it was not much needed for a hypothetical mention and relative to some event in the lessons of an official letter; but to relegate it to God face to face in the prayer by reason of conceding to us what we asked him, it is necessary to have a certainty, whatever fits rationally on the subject. Benedict XIV did not know of Guadalupe when he denied mentioning her in the prayer: and so, he did not know that having not conceded in the lessons except that *they tell, and they say* (a truth from Perogrullo, that we did not need that the Pope said it) it still seemed to him to have conceded too much to the Mexicans. Certainly, he did much, because he conceded the official letter without certificates had been lost. But I say: It is like this that the tradition of Pillar makes mention in the prayer of the official letter, then Guadalupe is not equal.

The two antecedent suppositions already falsified the censure given in Spain against the denial of Pillar is left inapplicable to my sermon. But there is more: said censure was a bundle of nonsense, politically pronounced by a stupid pen pusher, that the wise Doctor Ferreras, Priest of Madrid and celebrated historian of the nation, then reduced to dust.

He had said this in one of his works that they would desire better proofs of the tradition of the Pillar. This was enough so that some Zaragoza fanatics will agitate the people, declaring that Doctor Ferreras had denied the tradition: neither more nor less than others have done in Mexico with me. The people were driven crazy even burning Doctor Ferreras in effigy; and there was even a devotee assigned to go to piously kill him. A Royal order was taken out of the Court, that did no honor to what it gave nor to what was taken out to calm the masses; and in that it says that the denial of the Pillar is contrary to the piety, to the devotion of all Europe, injurious to the Holy See, and to the most serious Spanish and foreign authors; according to and as the Archbishop has copied in his Edict, by virtue of the Warrant given by my censors from what could be applied to my sermon. But Doctor Ferreras took the pen, pulverized those absurdities, and impugned on purpose the tradition of the Pillar, without any prejudice following him either on the first thing nor on the second thing, as has followed me.

I would have wanted to know from Uribe, what position the Royal Orders are arguing on Theology. I don't say that those who become a barbaric pen pusher, because one feels like it, or because an ignorant Minister ordered it; that many times laugh at the Magistrates; and many times, undo with a contradiction as easily as they facilitate one. The warrants, the same laws, the civil rights decisions are not a great argument for a theologian, because Jesus Christ did not commission the depository of his doctrine to the kings nor the tribunals. This is the alphabet of the Theology. As such, the Church when it goes beyond that depth of dogma and the morality confided to its custody and care it loses its infallibility, as when the magistrates go from the circle of legislation to Theology, to history, to medicine, etc. they merit no more faith than that of the experts whom they consult; and the other experts remain with the right of calling for a ruling revision by their companions, who are not infallible, and to reject it, upon better reasons. We examine the cited censure, and it does not contain more than curses and nonsense, by way of not saying superstition and fanaticism.

He [Uribe] says that to deny the tradition of the Pillar is contrary to piety. In what sense does it take away piety? Without doubt by worship owed to the Saints or their images. But the worship owed to images is only founded in that they are representatives of God or of his Saints; and as such they are the ghosts as well as those that are not. It can be said that ghosts are to make them more esteemed, but no worthier of religious worship. In heaven there are neither colors nor paintbrushes. *It would be contrary to the devotion of all Europe.* Here there is a curse and foolishness. The curse is on all of Europe, because from where I am writing, there are eight million Turks who comprise European Turkey, and some seventy million Protestants; in other words, almost half of Europe: and some others detest the images like so many other idols. This can be passed off to an ignorant pen pusher; but it is intolerable in an Archbishop and a Dean, much more theological. Foolishness, because devotion, strictly speaking, does not embrace images, then it is (according to Saint Thomas) a promptness of spirit to do whatever is pleasant to the person who embraces it, and the images are insensible paintings or statutes. To even have more devotion with one image than with another, as if the Virgin or God is more present there, or it may have one more virtue than another or it may put more confidence in one than in another, it is idolatry. If they do more miracles in a Sanctuary than in others, it is not because God hears better the memorials that they present before a portrait of him, than before another, like one catches fire more from a piece of wood or some paintbrush features than of others, which thing even in a human king would be crazy, but because one prays with more fervor in a sanctuary than in another, Muratori says in his arranged devotion approved by Benedict XIV like the true spirit of the Church. So, the appearance of an image not being reason for greater devotion with her, to deny it is not contrary to the devotion.

Injurious to the Apostolic See: a curse and nonsense. The Pope is not the Apostolic See, because as Saint Leon says *aluid est Sedes, et aliud Sedens* ("*The See is a lasting discharge, and another sitteth*"). The Apostolic Chair is the Pope in the middle of his Priests, who are the seated Cardinals also deliberating with him; and not a Congregation of theologians commissioned on rites, sometimes wise, and other times not so much; and there is a very large difference from the decrees of the See that we call the Ex-Cathedra, to a *motu proprio, etc.* [sic] [9] that is enough in the Church of France to make an abusive Bull. And the Pope and the Congregation of Rites are so far from taking offense that they refute with good reasons of the Breviary's historical points that they encourage, praise, and reward those who are occupied in these discussions. Later, I will speak on this with more extension. For now, I will only say that Benedict XIV roundly denies that of Pillar, like Natal Alejandro; and consequently, the Cardinals Baronio and Belarmino denied it, so in the Congregation under Clement VIII for the correction of the Breviary, they contradicted the preaching of James in Spain, and excluded from the Breviary the positive mention that was made of Pillar, with the approbation of the Pope.

Injurious to very serious Spanish and foreign authors: Also, there are very serious authors to the contrary: with those also it will be injurious to others. The pen pusher of the censure had heard bells, because there are works that are prohibited as injurious, or because they are libels, or they contain personal injuries, and insults, or because they censure with serious notes the doctrines of respectable authors, like the Señor Penpusher does with Dr. Ferreras, and the editor of the Archiepiscopal edict with me, who in the character of Priest and Doctor I am respectable, and it is what we call prohibiting a work *propter acerbitatem censurae* (*"Because of the severity of the censure"*). But it is foolishness to call injurious an author being opposed to the opinion of another, because there is no author who can agree with another on all things, and far from this being condemnable, when one believes that the other errs, it is very praiseworthy. *Contentio*, says Saint Thomas: *quanto est impugnation falsitatis cum debito acrimoniae, laudabilis est* (*"Dispute, the more it is a challenge of falsehood with proper irritating action, it is"*). We are lucid with what may be the injurious disputes of the schools. Clearly, this is to bray. But, it is to bray much louder applying this censure to the denial of Guadalupe, because here there are no more than four brochures, copies of the manuscript of an Indian, full of anachronisms, contradictions, and falsehoods: those same are plagued with these defects, for saying nothing of superstition nor even of idolatry. I will put forth an example: Father Florencia, who is the most voluminous and most read, cites an authority surely apocryphal of a Blessed Amadeo who I don't know who he is, because there are various and none of authority in the Church, in that he tells that the Virgin, going to heaven told the Apostles: "Even though I go, I stay in my images as in this painting and sculpture, and in them I will be present, "Principally where thou shall see miracles made: *Praecipue ubi miracula fieri videbitis.*" [10] From which, Florencia infers that having more miracles in the images of Guadalupe and Los Remedios, there she is more present, and we must occur with more confidence.

And, are such very serious authors named in a pastoral edict? The absurdity is passed on for having had images from the Apostolic Times, and principally of carvings, that were not known until the tenth century; but everything else is to teach idolatry; and it is a blasphemy to put such doctrine in the mouth of the Virgin. The Council of Trent orders that Priests and Bishops are to teach the people that in the images there is no virtue nor any divinity by which one is given to worship them, nor should they put confidence in them, like the idolaters do. And, who are the most serious foreign authors in favor of Guadalupe? Father Florencia is he who cites one or another Jesuit collector of miracles; who have made mention of hearsay: that Father Cuchicaco said to Father Cochinilla that Father Cochabamba Mexico's Attorney had told him that there was an image in his land; and on and on. These are not very serious authors, but verbiage middlemen in the Church of God, who merit as much faith as the *Golden Legend* of the blessed Archbishop Jacobus de Vorágine. We conclude that all the censure given in Spain against Ferreras is a string of foolishness and applied to my sermon very foolishly.

If it were valid to censure by compassion and similarity someone else, censures given in various times, few things even of the most well-established would escape today without very serious notes, and even of error and heresy. The first who would come out with the hands on his head was the Señor Archbishop of Mexico, because there is no doubt that the Pope solemnly condemned the Copernicus System, and Rome's Inquisition made a celebrated Astronomer recant that he was teaching it, by what Father Roselli even today defends in conclusion that it is reckless to defend it. And with everything the Señor Archbishop has ordered taught in his

Seminary nothing less than the Newton System, that is nothing, but Copernicus physically explained. All Spaniards read the works of the Nun de Agreda permitted in Spain by defense of the Bishop Samaniego and the Franciscan Fathers cite her even in the pulpits as Holy Father: and in everything, not only wise Bishops like Amort have contested them letter by letter, but that the Sorbonne after having condemned her forty-eight propositions, prohibited them all, at the request of the great Bossuet; and the Pope has done the same with the applause of the Bishops of Italy. In a word, we could not even say that we are in Mexico without being heretics and excommunicated, since Saint Augustin believed that it was against the faith to say that there were other lands within the ocean, distinct from the ancient continent, and the Pope Zachary emitted lightning from the Vatican against the Priest Virgilio who believed the Americas to exist. Let us not fool ourselves, all that he did against me, was no more than an intrigue and maneuver of iniquity.

Now Uribe goes on to prove the Guadalupe tradition, and he carries it out as well as in the censure. None of this is done against me, in that I have proved I did not deny it, but I will say something by honor of the truth and knock down the presumption of this censorial Canon. Because he says in it they concur with the proper scope the same conditions that the Church demands for the Apostolics, and Saint Vincent of Lérins encoded in that celebrated proverb *"quod ab omnibus, quod ubique, quod semper,* by everyone, everywhere, and always"* [11] this is what was believed. That of Guadalupe was believed by everyone: and everyone kept absolute silence about her for a hundred and seventeen years, and those who spoke like the Viceroy Enriquez, Sahagun, and Torquemada were to contradict it. Everywhere: and it was not known in the Sanctuary itself, as its Chaplain confessed in one thousand six hundred forty-eight. Always: and the Bishop of Tlaxcala did not know it three or four years later.

What proof is given against this? The reports that with hearsay witnesses they did a hundred and thirty-five years, after twenty years they proclaimed in their favor with printed works and sermons. There is no fable that cannot be proved with hearsay witnesses, if they were sought and picked out here and there, as was practiced here, and especially on pious materials in which so many people and especially commoners believe it to be a pious thing to lie, and they even take great care to proceed on this with rigorous criticism. What is left were examples of similar reports, such as those of the flowers of San Luis in Asturias, that examined afterwards with a little criticism were reproved.

One must not grow weary, witnesses prove nothing against the universal silence of some authors, and the positive testimonies of others. The only thing that they can prove at most, is some rumor or fame *tam ficti pravique tenax, quam nuncia veri ("As obstinately bent on falsehood and iniquity as on reporting truth")*. [12] In a thousand ways one can err with time, and I already have proved how, when and with what one errs.

I even fear that Uribe's great fame was not wrong, because continuing to support the tradition with the authority of the prayer, begins by saying that he does not intend to speak of that metaphysical certainty that the Church gives to the dogmas of the faith. An assistant clerk of theology would not say such a thing. Metaphysical certainty! The Church to give metaphysical certainty! This is evidence of reason, and the reason for an article of faith is to not have it, by which Saint Thomas says that the existence of God is not an article of faith, because one can demonstrate it with reason. The articles of faith are about it, and that's why Saint Paul defines the faith: *sperandarum substantia rerum, argumentum non apparentium ("is the substance of things hoped for, the evidence of things not seen")*. [13] Another mistake is to call the Church's authority that of the Pope or the Congregation of Rites. The Pope is the first of the Bishops, and the Congregation of Rites an Assembly of Theologians sometimes wise and other times not so much, who many times have erred in their decisions, since many times they have reformed them. But if the same universal Church, solely infallible of faith on dogma and moral matters, *credo sanctam ecclesiam catholicam* (" I believe the Holy Catholic Church"), [14] is not on points of a specific history, what authority do you want that the Congregation might appoint on a historical point like that of Guadalupe? Everything is reduced to a hypothetical mention of "they tell, and they say."

Anyway, Señor Uribe concludes his Guadalupian defense with a blow as an always consequential Master. If one were to deny the tradition, he says, after it has been preached to the people, like the rest of the religion, one would believe that neither was true. One cannot deny the inventiveness of Señor Uribe, because in so many disputes upon pious traditions and history like they stir up and have stirred up in Christianity, to no one has a similar reflection happened, because one already sees with this argument there would be no abuse that could not be shielded; and because it had worked sometimes evil, so it always has worked; and once some people were deceived, the deceived have to follow. Why so many Congregations for discussing historical points of the Breviary, whether entire services and lessons are removed, whether restored, whether corrected, as so many acts of the Saints, as so many dissertations that fill immense volumes? And the worst that [Antoine Augustin] Calmets says, praised by Benedict XIV, that the Church far from taking it to evil, praises and rewards the authors of the investigations, and when they discover the truth, they hurry up to adopt it and correct their Breviary. Does the Church not see that people would infer that the rest of the religion is false?

It is certain that the people so reason; but not for this has one to follow the multitude to do evil, The Holy Ghost says one must instruct himself.

It is certain that thus the philosophers have corrupted the people of France, making them see the abuses, the false miracles, and the feigned funny stories: and this is what proves a very serious fault in the priests that preach them as appertaining to the religion, not having anything to do with it. It does much damage to the religion, says Saint Thomas with Saint Augustine, to give as things appertaining to the Sacred religion and doctrine what does not pertain to it, because it is to make it ridiculous before the eyes of the incredulous who scoff at seeing things so flimsy. Since what the people, as the censors say, so badly argue, and from the nature of the fable it is what after all there is tobe discovered, what is inferred is that one ought to warn and say to people that the religion of Jesus Christ is based on the holy foundations of the Scriptures and the Apostolic traditions, not on popular traditions that will or will not be truths, according to the fundamentals on which they rely, and the religion disregards. That if it permits them it is hypocritical to the people, and because the object of the worship is always God, in which error does not fit in. That the Church as the daughter of the God of truth who abhors the lie and detests the fiction, also abhors them, and for this does all the diligence that he can by researching it on the points of a particular history, upon which his Divine Master did not concede any infallibility, because it was not necessary for the salvation of mankind, and if nevertheless his diligence sometimes is surprised, at the moment that the truth is discovered even in these indifferent points, its Breviary embraces and corrects it: That neither God nor his Mother are pleased except by the truth in all things; and to want to please them with lies of our invention, is to insult them and put the demons' incense into the Sanctuary's incense: That far from being obligated to subdue our understanding of things that are not of faith, we are obligated not to do it, in order to not confuse them with human opinions, but that we ought to examine them with rigor and criticism, to not attribute to God things that he has not done, because it would be a serious sin (says Saint Thomas), for more glorious than they seem to their Omnipotence, since not only does he not need our lies, but he has prohibited them. So even when the resurrection of Jesus Christ (he continues) would always be very glorious to his power, if it were not certain, says the Apostle, and we preached it, we would be false witnesses, and we would be giving a testimony against God. The title of piety is not to be mocked: this is a virtue, and falsity a sin, so nothing is pious, but what is true. Let us not make the religion consist of our fantasies. The wise person orders us to examine all things, and to retain what is good, and by consequence true, because these virtues are intimately connected.

Oh, well, as the mission sermons conclude with an act of contrition, the Canons conclude their ruling with an act of charity; and passing from counsels to public prosecutors, they ask for the publication of an edict, and they urge repeatedly that the issue go to the Inquisition. At a time that Dominicans and Franciscans are consumed in disputes, and no kind of munitions are scarce in the seraphic-cherubic field, a cocky person painted two dogs that symbolized them by their colors, being torn to pieces by bites, and at the foot he put these words of Saint Paul: *haec est charitas canonica* ("*This is charity (love) by canon*") [15] Couldn't one put at the foot of the Señores Canons throwing me to the fiery pit, *haec est charitas canonica*? To ask that the Pastoral authority intervene for a popular tale, very indifferent to the religion, and to invoke for the same thing the tribunal of faith! He responded with his accustomed judgement that this does not pertain to the faith. No, without a doubt, it pertains to the fanaticism, and to the love that he has for me. It was not enough to dishonor me with an edict, it was even necessary to defame me with an Inquisition process.

I will speak clearly: all this is no more than a comedy, with two acts and an interlude. Uribe knows that the Spaniards are always speaking against the Guadalupe tradition, which they do not believe; and knowing that the Archbishop stops at nothing to get what he wants since he hit against one of the Creoles, who are his sorcerers, villains, and scoundrels; using the occasion, he has jumped to throwing them a lock on the mouth with the weight of the Episcopal authority and the terror of the Inquisition; and he paid off the friar. The Europeans without believing the tradition of Guadalupe have shouted more loudly than the Creoles, to destroy the incidences of Saint Thomas's preaching, because they believe that it takes from them the glory of having brought the Gospel, and it makes them equal with the Indians regarding the image of Pillar. Unfortunately, a brilliant Creole has played the key; and His Illuminate has clasped with fury the shield to exterminate at once my honor and to leave me forever confused with the dust. This is the ordinary noise on the subject that has stirred the passions found on a point. That is why the rabble of my armed rivals, like so many other orangutan monkeys, from the sticks that have supplied them the envy, they have come upon the fallen one, who the friars have given to them in discretion with a gag in the mouth and feet and hands tied. To a dead Moor a great thrust of the spear. But what happened to Leon and to me weakened with old age and fever so that nothing was felt as much as the uprising of the brutes, as if the donkey had come to give him kicks as well.

Chapter 4, Notes

1. *Never used we flattering words, as ye know.* King James Bible, I Thessalonians 2:5,

"For neither at any time used we flattering words, as ye know, nor a cloke of covetousness; God is witness:".

2. *A rough and disordered mass,* (Ovid).

3. This is Fray Mier's Note. (a) "Señor Uribe, who in the funeral prayer of Don Bernardo de Galves, took Panzacola for an island. INSULAE PANZACOLAE being the capitol of west Florida on our continent, which could only happen to Sancho Panza; he ought not to pretend that we took him for an oracle upon antiquities of our America."

4. From the Canticle of Mary: *from henceforth all generations shall call me blessed.* King James Bible, St. Luke 1:48, "For he hath regarded the low estate of his handmaiden: for, behold, from henceforth all generations shall call me blessed."

5. The quoted translation is in italic letters. Fray Mier quotes from the Bible a description of the image of Mexico's Virgin of Guadalupe. King James Bible, Revelation 12:1-2: "And *there appeared a great wonder in heaven; a woman clothed with the sun, and the moon under her feet, and upon her head a crown of twelve stars: And she being with child cried, travailing in birth,* and pained to be delivered."

6. Saint Thomas Aquinas, *Summary against Pagans.*

7. King James Bible Acts 17:23.

8. Fray Mier is comparing officials of his inquisition to characters in the second part of **DON QUIJOTE DE LA MANCHA** by Miguel Cervantes Saavedra, titled: "Don Quijote

Attacks His Muslim Other: The Maese Pedro Episode of *Don Quijote.*"

9. Motu proprio: an edict issued by the Pope personally to the Roman Catholic Church.

10. Fray Mier precedes the Latin with a rare translation: "principally where thou shall see miracles made."

11. Fray Mier follows the Latin with his translation: "by everyone, everywhere, and always."

12. *As obstinately bent on falsehood and iniquity as on reporting truth:* Virgil's Aeneid.

13. Fray Mier quotes Hebrews11:1 in italics from King James Bible, "Now faith *Is the substance of things hoped for, the evidence of things not seen.*"

14. *I believe the Holy Catholic Church;* from the Apostles' Creed of the Roman Catholic Church.

15. *This is charity (love) by canon.* The more likely source is King James Bible, II Epistle of John 6, "This is love that we walk after his commandments."

Chapter 5

The Passions Defame Innocence with a Libel Called Episcopal Edict

It is not the Archbishop Haro whom I call a donkey, though I always had him so by ignorance, despite the credit that his countrymen and intimate friends gave him, because he never gave proof of deserving it. He was the first Archbishop who stopped arguing in the chapter acts of the religions, under the ridiculous pretext (according to what Maestro Leon, his consultant, told me) that making use of the scholastic license they could deny him any assumption, an intolerable thing for the universal Doctor of the Mexican Church. The same way as direct propositions could disown him without dishonor, assumptions could disown him, because arguing one does not speak his own mind. If they did not take to braying, without a doubt donkeys would be more imposing for their reliability and their ears.

What his flatterers were pestering us with in the dedications and harangues, during his long bishopric, was with having merited the recommendation of Benedict XIV. But this one, who even retained his Bologna Bishopric, gave more ignoramuses to his Spanish colleagues as a formula so that they came over from there to kiss his foot, and Cárlos III looked after them, because he boasted of being his friend. With Haro came equally recommended, one who for stupidity was made Canon of Covadonga and Tomé who was Archdeacon of Burgos for the same reason. This one used to say with grace that he did not believe the great wisdom of Benedict XIV, since in his recommendation he had said of him that he was adorned of wisdom and virtues, when he walked on two feet to the opprobrium of humanity. It was not much exaggerated, since to put some postscript in Latin, in his letters to Rome, he needed to go dictating letter by letter, and to advise him of the purpose of the word so that he could commence another. This was published in Burgos.

Haro's edicts either prove his ignorance, or they prove nothing, even though the flatterer of his funeral eulogy had compared his eloquence with that of Crisóstomo. One could ask His Illuminate the same famous question that the Poet Pirron asked a Bishop of France when he wondered how he was, "Well Monsignor, and You?" "Good, Have You read my pastoral letter?" "Not yet, Monsignor, and You?" Each of his edicts varied in style and genre of studies. While the Dominican Leon lived, theological and full texts were like the style of that monk. Later they were of a new canonist, as was Conejares, and later of a parasite, who was Bruno, who like a good native of La Mancha robbed from here and yonder some remnants and pieced them together with some stabs in the dark, because ignorance has always been hustling. This is the same Bruno Horse that when it was his turn to preach from the stage in the Cathedral, got a belly ache or twisted a foot and if at some time he preached in another location, it was a printed sermon, as I heard him on the Conception. The very same who being the Priest of Santa Catarina took in procession the Holy Sacrament against the aurora borealis that one saw toward the end of the past century in Mexico, and of which a sonnet of the time concludes:

. . How much goes, I said, how much?
What my Priest takes with fright
The baptismal font and the Holy Oil.

I have here the editor of the Edict in question, that they tell me someone else revised, Monteagudo by antiphrasis, of the Mancha flock that eats bread in the Archiepiscopal Palace, instead of giving it straw. The Edict itself will be his executioner. It can be divided into a narration of the events, the censure of the sermon, the proofs of the Guadalupe tradition, and the exhortation to the people, who become to be like the four legs of the donkey who gave a similar bray.

We make known, it begins, by charity for causing a second outcry at the three months of being already pacified the first that we rise: *"We make known,"* he said, two Episcopalian lies. First: *"That the Father Doctor Fray Servando de Mier of this Dominican Province of Mexico in the sermon that he preached in the Sanctuary the 12th day of December of last year 1794, denied the tradition of Our Lady of Guadalupe."* Second: *"Declaring it was on the cape of Saint Thomas.*

I have demonstrated that I did not deny the tradition, and to have only said that perhaps one could say, *even though with the least probability* that it was on the cape of the Apostle Saint Thomas of this Kingdom, it is not affirmed, but to have ventured a conjecture, warning that it was very weak. The edict writer omits with all care the specific detail that I spoke of Apostle Saint Thomas like he was of this Kingdom, so that the people do not fall for the account of the glory that I have given them, and of the true motive of the edict, however that in their ruling on this the censors had confessed. And one thus leaves the people mistaken who believed that I as a Dominican wanted to attribute to Saint Thomas Aquinas the stamp of the image of Guadalupe being painted on it.

It does not stop causing admiration that the Archbishop having made so much noise in the pulpits with the cape of Saint Thomas and now emphasizing this as if it were the sermon's principle point; Uribe did not give it as understood in his censure. He saw without doubt that it was a trifle very impertinent to the substance of the sermon and purely conjectural. But the Archbishop wrote it up, because it was the weakest point, he made me ridiculous suppressing the terms of a very weak conjecture, and sounding out the people in contradiction with the cape of their Juan Diego, it made him believe that the tradition had been completely denied, it disturbed him, it made him indignant against me, he concealed his unjust persecution under that cape, and he saw me as a Creole without any compassion for my fellow countrymen. Such edict is a master work of malice and iniquity.

He goes on to say that I affirmed *other errors*. We will see where the others are; so, what are these? Theological is supposed, because no one has a way of understanding that in an Episcopal Edict published with fury *inter missarum solemnia* (*"In solemn mass"*) throughout the Anáhuacan Church it dealt with printing errors, nor even of specific historic errors, because the universal Church not being infallible in them, they could be less a subject of condemnation in the pastoral letter of a Bishop as fallible in everything as me. But if to deny the Conception of Mary in grace is not an error, nor a theological scandal, nor even at least temerity or a mortal sin, and he who says that it is any of this, is excommunicated by the Bull of Sixtus IV renovated by the Council of Trent and other later Supreme Pontiffs, without Kings nor Universities having been able to move forward a span of ground on the issue, how was it to be that none of this denied the romance of the Indian Valeriano, or could it be a popular tradition, even destitute of every fundamental?

It is one of the conclusions of the wise Bishop Amort in his famous treatise *De Revelationibus*, [1] supported by many distinguished theologians whom he cites, that they can deny without temerity nor another note any revelations, apparitions, and vision even of canonized saints, like Santa Catarina, Santa Brígida, and Santa Gertrudis. So, on this, those are called the Church's approvals, and they are mere permissions to be able to read them, because they contain nothing contrary to the faith. It is a theological axiom that no private revelation builds faith in the Church. Those Saints could suffer an illusion of the demon transfigured into an angel of light, or from a very lively imagination in these women, warmed up in them by the continuous meditation, fasts, and penitence. A revelation of Santa Catarina refers to the Conception, diametrically opposite to another of Santa Brígida; and Serey proves that they are contrary to the many of the Nun of Agreda. The Church cannot certify specific acts of which there has not been a witness: it is permitted and nothing more. And one cannot deny without error, that it is the note next to heresy, a vision of the Indian Juan Diego, or to better say, a poetic–mythology fiction of the Indian Valeriano? An error is only what contradicts a thing so credible of faith that it only lacks the infallible decision of the universal Church, so that the contrary is heresy. And now, if such heresy is to deny that faith is what it is, like affirming that faith is what it is not, such a theological error will be to deny that it is an error what it is, as to affirm that it is an error what it is not. And surely these are not part of a particular history upon which I had uniquely spun my sermon. At the least to call one's denial an error, is an obvious superstition and fanaticism.

The edict writer proceeded to tell that I denied the apparitions of Our Lady of Los Remedios, of the Lord of Chalma, and other images of the Kingdom, saying that they were from the time of Saint Thomas. I swear *in verbo sacerdolis* (*"On the word of the priest"*) that I did not lie in the sermon on the Virgin of Los Remedios, for the brevity, and to not mix myself in another question that could shock so much, but I had it written in my rough draft, because thus Borunda dictated it to me, and I repeated it in the copy of the sermon that I had taken from my own memory.

And did the Archbishop believe those thousands of apparitions of images that are told in the Kingdom, and of which Father Oviedo has had the kindness of publishing a collection? It would be enough that there were things favorable to America for him not to believe them. Neither did he believe that of Guadalupe: Are there also some other of these that are named information and prayer? Therefore, what is the purpose of these tales to the people, of which I spoke not a word: To agitate them, to anger them against me, to scandalize them with a true, lively, scandal? Because according to the theologians such is what gives an opportunity to do spiritual ruin to the neighbor; and the Archbishop incited them to hate me and to curse me, what the common people could not do without the ruin of their soul.

The Edict is truly scandalous.

In Spain, they count so many and more appeared images than in America, and they usually happen four to five in one place, because the rabble in all parts is apparitions and superstitious. No man of reason believes them, and with reason because *qui cito credit, levis est corde* ("*He who believes straightway is the heart of the light*"), says the Holy Ghost. Some are usually persuaded that they are uncovered from those that the Christians buried or hid at the time of the Moors who hunted them down as idols. Thus, the famous Extremadura image of Guadalupe was found in a Cáceres's well. The ghosts of New Spain, recent the conquest, I have already said with Torquemada in general they came from what the Indians happened to paint, many that they carried and left in the churches where each day they appeared. Borunda seeing that the histories of some of the most famous were the same as those of the ancient images of the Indians which the missionaries substituted, and those which for his excessive piety he was not able to deny, he was also persuaded that they were images discovered from the time that there was Christianity among the Indians, who had hidden them from the persecution against Saint Tomé by Huémac, King of Tula. And this speaking in general, one absolutely cannot deny, since our first missionaries found images of Christ and of the Virgin in possession of the Indians, and they told them of others that they had hidden at the arrival of the Spaniards.

What I believe is God, He who says, "*I am God and I do not change: ego Deus et non mutor.* [2] And this God so jealous that the worship is not divided or mistaken that it is due to the first precept of the Decalogue that ordered there was to be no image or any likeness (Exodus 20:4); that because the altars of the idols were high and polished he ordered (ibid 24) that his were from the earth's fields, and in case of being of stones they were not carved nor were the altars to have steps; that for the same reason He prohibited He be worshiped on the heights and mounts where they usually had the false Gods; who gave them a particular name so that they were not to call him Royal or Sir, and that in Deuteronomy (4:15-16) He says to his people that He did not let them see Him in Horeb so that they did not make some image of Him in the figure of man or of woman; this God, I say, changed conduct so diametrically with the Indians, no less coarse and inclined to idolatry, than the Hebrews; and the same even when the blood of the victims and the incense of the demons was going up in smoke, and the Indians stubborn with their idols, He walked presenting to them at each step His images and those of His Mother on the same mounts and places where those had been, looking for the analogy with them in the name and in the history. The same God would have been the author of the idolatry, since this does not precisely consist of the object (so one can idolize an image of Jesus Christ, as one of Jupiter), except in the intention and manner, and this the Indians did not know, and no one could teach them, the conquest recent, for the ignorance of their language.

And as if all this is not enough, the Most Holy Virgin also walked presenting her images not only in the ancient dress of the idol that was previously in her place, not only with mythologies leading to error, but also in the favorite plant of the common vice of the Indians, which is drunkenness. The criminal code of a nation is the most authentic registry of their inclinations, and the laws of the Aztecs against drunkenness that can be seen in Herrera and Torquemada, were terrible. To the noble they tore down his house as unworthy of living in society, and they shaved his head, an insult so atrocious, as it was among the Goths of Spain. To the Indian peasants an episode of drunkenness cost him his life. Only to the aged and people of war were one or two cups of pulque [3] permitted. Lacking the bridle of these laws with the conquest and shocks with the disgraces that overcame them, they gave themselves up with such frenzy to drunkenness that an infinite number of them died; lucky that a Royal letter emanated ordering the tearing out of every maguey, and absolutely prohibiting pulque. This absolute remission in one blow caused another carnage, and it was necessary to rescind it with limitations and precautions such as the advertising of the pulque bars etc.; but if there is pulque it is the cause of the Indians' misery, of brawls, incest, and other sins, and disorders. And in the middle of the fury of their drunkenness, the conquest recent, the Virgin presented her image of Guadalupe figurative within the fleshy leaf of a maguey, as one can see by its decorative trimming, and in a maguey, clump appeared that of Los Remedios, as Bacchus in the vine tendrils, thus canonizing the favorite plant of the most criminal passion of the natives.

Now, it is necessary to speak clearly. The conquistadors and the first missionaries, taking away the idols, substituted the most famous, and in the same mountainous places images of Christianity, analogous in the names and the history, so that they could continue celebrating the ancient fiestas with the same analogy and concurrence, as we already hear Father Torquemada tell us. This practice was not only contrary to the conduct of God with his people in the Old Testament, but also in the New one of the Apostles with the newly converted Gentiles, and to those of the primitive Church that did not allow the images (as today all the wise men agree) until centuries passed even the memory of the idols ceased, and even almost all having been carved, still even today the Greek Church does not allow sculptured images, nor were they introduced into the Latin Church until the century of ignorance, the tenth. So, in America it turned out to be a practice so contrary, the opposite of that in the primitive Church. At this time the Gentiles called the Christians atheists, because they had no idols, and in America Torquemada tells that when he reproached the Indians for hiding their idols and not wanting to abandon them they responded: "Idols for idols, the Christians also have theirs; and ours we have experienced are good." They had reason; one form of idolatry was substituted for another, because neither conquistadors nor missionaries, for their substantial number and ignorance of the language, could instruct them in the manner of worshiping the images without idolatry. Nor did prudence dictate, even when it could, throwing in the huge danger of idolatry with neophytes so crude, the images so indifferent to the religion.

From there it is that they could not use the arguments with which the Popes of the Church attacked idolatry. Because when they argue to them that they worship sticks and stones, they responded, like Maxiscatzin, Captain General of Tlaxcala to Cortés, that they knew well that their images were of this kind, but that they did not worship them itself, except for being representations of the immortal beings who inhabited the heavens. And when one answered back to them that they worshiped men, they responded that they knelt only before the pure spirited Omnipotent God, and if they venerated some portraits of men like *Quetzalcohuatl*, it was because in them there had shined something of God. Torquemada brings forth these responses that they used to silence the conquistadors.

Oh, well obliged to venerate our images, they struggled with worship, or they divide it between the God of Israel and the calves of Jeroboam, as the Archbishop Dávila Padilla testifies of it, who tells that even beneath the crosses they buried little idols so they could participate in their intention of worship; and a few years before my noisy sermon, wanting to renovate the major altarpiece of Xochimilco, idols were found hung at the back, and I would bring forth many other examples. Anyway, the Indians attributed to the new images the same virtues as to the ancient ones, and even the same apparitions and histories in accounts written in their language, that falling later into the hands of the Creoles, ignorant of their antiquities, they have published them translated for the glory of the native land, as truths, and of the new images.

Such are those of Guadalupe, of Los Remedios, and of the Lord of Chalma, specifically the Archbishop who censured me has denied, and of which I will speak of the same. Of course, I have already proved that the history of Our Lady of Guadalupe in its depth is no more than the history of the ancient *Tonantzin* who the Indians venerated in Tepeyac, and to whom Torquemada says the missionaries substituted the image of Our Lady of Guadalupe. He follows speaking of Our Lady of Los Remedios.

What is its history? It gave birth to it in a few linked and bombastic novenas by the same Sanchez, author of that of Guadalupe. In a small place to the west of Mexico City, a distance I believe of three leagues, previously called Otancapulco, and today Los Remedios, an Indian Chief called Don Juan de la Águila or *Quauhtzin*, occasionally spotted at night, the conquest recent, some lights in that field that one falsely supposes deserted. Passing by it during the day, he also saw in a maguey a girl and a boy, who it was believed to be Saint Joseph, who kept her company. I do not know why the Indian did not pay attention to this, and perhaps for the inclination that leads us to favor the fair sex, he decided to grab the girl and take her to his house; and believing her a little Spanish girl he gave her his atole and corn tortillas. Is it credible that a noble and reasonable Indian, accustomed to seeing their images and ours, would believe that a tiny image like a doll of half a stick was a Spanish girl, who does not even have a human figure except to the waist? These are tales for lulling children to sleep.

The girl escaped from him and went to the maguey; the Indian returned to bring her back, and to her grief he even locked her up in a box; by luck in the fight and stubbornness, he lost his nose lost by the lid of the box that in vain he had tried to restore to her. Anyway, the Indian vexed by her ingratitude abandoned her to the maguey. But going to the Sanctuary of Our Lady of Guadalupe, this one reproached him to come to her house, for having thrown her from his. Then he knew that she was the same, he bent the ears, and he made to her as he could the Little Temple that she has. The Virgin in repayment threw him from on high a leather belt that is kept as a relic in the Sanctuary.

And from where would the image in the Temple of Otancapulco come? It is believed that it is the same that the

Spaniards brought with them, and with license from Montezuma they were put among the idols in the main temple of Mexico, like the Philistines put the ark of God in the temple of Dagon. And they also say that it is the same lady conquistador, before whom Cortés praying with his holy soldiers, received a miraculous rain that Herrera tells, the Indians having complained to him of the drought that destroyed the corn fields, for his having prohibited their sacrifices. And so, at the foot of their images an Indian is painted presenting a stalk of dry corn. But Torquemada says that the image that the conquistadors carried with them, and called her the lady conquistador, is Our Lady of the Macana, who is venerated in San Francisco.

And if the lady conquistador is Los Remedios, when or how did she escape from them? No, with the haste of the flight from Mexico, on the famous Sorrowful Night, toward Otancapulco, they must have left her lying in those fields. And from where would she come before, by Spanish hands? It is said that a soldier brought her from Spain in the sleeve of his cloak. What a sleeve so wide! And from whence did the soldier get it? Becerra, (Mexico's coat of arms) now tries to prove that it is the same that Don Pelagius carried eleven centuries ago in the war against the Moors. Is there patience to listen to so much foolishness like the Archbishop Haro presumed us to believe? It was not he who ought to accuse me and Borunda of deliriums.

Acosta and Torquemada say that the Spaniards defeated on the night of their flight on the road from Tacuba, took refuge in the temple of the Goddess of the Waters that was in Otancapulco; and later attributing it in favor of the Virgin Mary, they rebuilt the temple of the Goddess of the Waters, that they had destroyed during the siege of Mexico, like the one of Tepeyac and those of all the surrounding area, and they put in it an image of Our Lady that at the beginning they called Las Victorias according to Torquemada, or of the Socorro according to Acosta because of the help they had received there, until they fixed on the title of Our Lady of Los

Remedios, another famous Sanctuary of Extremadura, of whose image they were so devoted that at their first settlement (getting close to Anáhuac) on Cozumel, they called her Our Lady of Los Remedios, and with this title it was their Bishop Garcés who transferred it to Tlaxcala, and he was the first consecrated Bishop of New Spain, from which the Bishops of Puebla came to be Delegates of the Apostolic See. While the council of Mexico's conquistadors made the temple of Los Remedios, Cremeño fabricated another titled of Los Mártires, in the place where the soldiers of Cortés, who did not want to lighten themselves of the gold stolen from Montezuma, drowned on the same Sorrowful Night. As the title of Martyrs is not suitable to such thieves, this amusing Sanctuary did not last; but yes, that of the Virgin who protected the monks of San Francisco, did.

The image put there, the Indians continued worshiping it like what they had previously as Patroness of the Rains, like they worshiped Our Lady of Guadalupe as Patroness of the Cornfields, a title that they also had for the ancient Tonantzin, and for this they called her *Centeotl* according to Torquemada, even though both were of others, because they were all the Tlaloque Gods and Goddesses who were in the hills and mountains. As for the apparition of Our Lady of Guadalupe to the little shepherd in one thousand five hundred fifty-six, it inflamed the devotion and a temple was built to her as was the devotion to Los Remedios. The Mexico City Council demanded the patronage of the Church, a dispute was put forth to the Franciscan Fathers, to which Florencia refers, the temple was taken from them, and since one thousand five hundred sixty-two a chaplain who is from the City was put there, and in accordance with the Indians' devotion, she is worshiped like a special Patroness of the Rains in Mexico City, no more nor less than for the same devotion of the Indians, Mexico's peasants have a special fiesta to Our Lady of Guadalupe.

This is the true history. The rest is a romance of an Indian to prove that one and another image in their paganism were now like the only Mother of the true God. In the beginning, says Torquemada, the missionaries thought that the Goddesses of the Waters and the Cornfields that were worshiped in the hills were different, but later it was known that they were nothing but the same under different names. And this is what the Indian author wished to say when he tells that Don Juan *Quáuhtzin* having gone to see Our Lady of Guadalupe, he complained that he came to see her, having her thrown from his house. He tells that she appeared in a maguey, because Our Lady of Guadalupe is painted on the fleshy leaf of a maguey, and the Indian to whom she appeared is called, *Quáuhtzin* because *Quauhtli* in Mexican is Juan, as I already previously proved, and he is the same Juan Diego, and not Chief Don Juan, because the reverential term *Tzin* that has led to believe this Don and Chief dignity, is also given to Juan Diego calling him *Quauhtlatoatzin*, even though he was a commoner. And there is no more difference, except that in the history of Guadalupe, because he speaks as an Ambassador, it is Juan who speaks, or *Quauhtlato*; and here who does not speak, it is simply Juan or *Quauhtli*. The *Tzin* is added to him for respect to his virtue or his commission. In the place of origin of both images, I believe that both came from the paint shop that was set up for the Indians behind the back of San Francisco Fray Pedro de Gante, since there they made, Torquemada says, all the images there were up to his time on the altarpieces of New Spain, and as well as it of Guadalupe has the defects connected to the Indians' brush, that of Los Remedios is so similar to those of the bad carving that they had in their santocallis,[4] that is known to be by the same hand. Or they were not so skillful in the sculpture, as in the painting; or it was their mania for hieroglyph, as our authors note, to make their images of ugly sculpture and even horrendous that they might inspire fear and respect. It is a foolishness, therefore, to call one a female Creole, and another a female Spaniard; and when the Spaniards have made her a female General Los Remedios, in competition with what the Americans have raised her to that of Guadalupe as a banner, it is a superstition. The images by themselves are nothing, and the Mother of God is as Saint Peter said of God, *in veritate comperi quia non est personarum acceptor Deus; sed in omni gente que timet Deum et operatur justitiam, acceptus est illi* ("*Of a truth I perceive that God is no respecter of persons: But in every nation he that feareth him, and worketh righteousnees is accepted with him.*"). [5] These also among the Old Christians are remains of the paganism that believed with passion in their Gods and Goddesses, fighting in favor of their biases, and who relied on their respective images, where they believed that they were present, or they conferred upon them virtue to help them.

I have not read the history of the Holy Christ of Chalma, but neither do I need it. Already one supposes that he appeared to an Indian, the conquest recent, and they say he was in the cave where he is. To find out its true origin and history, it is enough for me to know what the Indians still practice today when they go to this pilgrimage. Borunda who was very practical with them, and observed them, I have also heard it from other persons. Before arriving, they gathered a portion of filth, in Mexican *tlazolli;* they wallow in it, and then they burn it, believing that thus their sins are destroyed. With this, I already know the idol that they worshiped there before the conquest. It was the God *Tlazolteotl* or God of Filth, of whom Torquemada, calling him erroneously goddess, says that the dishonest persons were very devoted to obtaining the pardon of their sins. The monks searching according to their custom an analogous image to replace in the cave saw that a God who pardoned their sins corresponded to the image of Jesus Christ, and they switched it. I bet my ears that this is the true history of the Lord of Chalma.

By this tone go the histories of the images found in the kingdom. One, of Borunda's silly Things, was that Saint John the Baptist came and preached in America. My refuting this foolishness, he responded to me with text of Saint John: *hic venit in testimonium, ut testimonium perhiberet de lumine, ut omnes crederent per illum* ("*The same came for a witness, to bear witness of the Light, that all men through him might believe.*"). [6]

But his foundation were the accounts of the Indians about Saint John the Baptist of Tianguismanaleo where Torquemada says that the missionaries replaced his statue with that of the God *Telpuchtli*, that means to say young. And, it is that the Indians, according to their custom, have applied to Saint John the Baptist the ancient history of the God *Telpuchtli*, with so much stupidity like that of the missionaries in replacing him with the image of Saint John, because *Telpuchtli* was not a young man, but Omnipotent God under the attribute of Eternal; and for this always young. The same Torquemada explains it thus expounding elsewhere that they gave names to God for his attributes. If I continued to speak of all the images found in the Kingdom, maybe I would have to unwrap all the Mexican mythology. Was it from an Archbishop in a solemn pastoral to begin canonizing these mythological fables because of his complaints against me, these remains of superstition and of entire idolatry, caused and permanent by the mistaken conduct of the first missionaries? For these were at the beginning excesses with regard to the images, that the three Mexican Councils of the XVI Century were occupied in suppressing them, by either prohibiting the images in which the Indians had mixed traces of their mythology, like the first and the second, or explaining with all clarity the worship that is owed to them, and condemning as idolatry the rest that was noticeable in the devotion of the Indians. If some of these things are capable of some excuse and composition, it would only be in the gallant system of Borunda, Esq.

The Archbishop proceeds his narration saying that I delivered at the beginning a few points of the sermon and then the sermon. I have already told the truth, and what I delivered at the beginning was the sermon in a complete rough draft that was the only thing that I had. And he continues to relate that I voluntarily retracted, confessing that I had erred, humbly asking for pardon, offering complete satisfaction, and even that of composing and printing at my cost a work contrary to my sermon. *Ex ore tuo te judico, serve nequam* ("*Out of thy own mouth I judge thee, thou wicked servant.*").

If I did all this, that is more than what could and should be ordered in a point of fact, particularly, unconnected with the dogma, and indifferent to the religion, how is it that you applied to me a sentence that the exorbitant tribunal of the Inquisition would only apply to a heretic convinced of such? How did you condemn me in the edict with my name, surname, grade, profession, and province? The Church of Jesus Christ has never done such with the heretics even in obstinate years, and already convinced in councils, while they promised that they would subject one to the justice of the Church. Gilberto Porretano was already convinced in councils it was Alberto de Bruis. Luther had been disturbing the Church with his heresies for years, and the Church kept quiet their names,like that of the Abbot Joaquin, in his condemnations, while they promised, as I said, that they would subject themselves to his judgement. To the judgement of the Church, I say that it is infallible on points of dogma: how much more ought a Bishop, so fallible in all as I, to imitate it, and on a point of fact, on which nor is the Church infallible, my having voluntarily retracted without any convincing, etc.! The Church knows very well that nobody ought to be discredited without necessity, and that charity ordains, as Saint Augustine says, "Love the person, kill the errors: *Diligite homine, interficite errores.*" Much less should a Bishop dishonor so solemnly his brother Priest! Constantine the Great said that if he saw a priest sin, he would cover him with his imperial cloak so that the public does not see him, and for the same reason the Church never subjected the priests to public penitence.

But, why did I have to ask Haro for moderation and charity, when all what he was saying and doing, was a lie, a calumny, and a maneuver of the passions in rage? In his reserved reports to the King he tells him that he condemned me, despite my retraction, because it had not been sincere. And from where did he know it, if I was incommunicado, and he notified me of my sentence the day following the edict, in which I was assured that I voluntarily retracted myself? He knew very well that everything had been violence, intrigue, and deceit. And in the edict, he said that my retraction had been voluntary, because it well suited him to excuse before the people the visible lack of a hearing. And to the King he wrote that I had not been sincere, to excuse the barbaric excess of the sentence; as if for all parts without this it was not unjust, atrocious, and null.

The censure of the sermon that he published in his edict was no less wicked. After skillfully managing the qualifications of the two Canons whom he chose to his taste as censors, to win more respect for the censure, as if the qualifications are always valued by what they are pronounced; he declares that according to them the sermon contains errors, blasphemies, and impieties, fables and deliriums, without reason nor a shadow of veracity. And from there, upon the so-called denial of the Guadalupe tradition, the censure from the idiot clerk completely and truthfully sets me up against Doctor Ferreras on the denial also of the so-called Pillar tradition, as I previously referred to and refuted.

Nothing worked me up more since I read the edict, than the tale of the errors, blasphemies and impieties; and I was in a supreme curiosity to see since they had been approved to find such notes, that neither Doctor Alcalá, nor other theologians with whom I had consulted on the sermon, nor the Chapter of the Collegiate Church, nor with me being a theologian, and not peripatetic, we had been careful. So, when the Council of the Indies passed the sentences on me in Madrid, I first read with anxiety the ruling of the censors. Seeing with surprise that neither had they encountered any of this in my sermon, in which summarizing their ruling after some scholastic excursions to forage material for the censors, they are assured that there was nothing reprehensible besides the denial of Guadalupe that they suppose and do not prove, because they were not capable of proving it, I imagined that I could find in the work of Borunda some of what the edict said.

It could be that had I then met with him on the censure, to excuse him if I demanded, loading him with the heavier part of the burden. Consequently, I put myself to reading Borunda's work that were also passed along with the court records, and that had not been seen in Mexico. They were a few rough drafts, and in the copy, they collected a thin volume in folio.

Of course, I never thought to find *formal* errors, impieties, and blaspheme, even though Haro's lack of charity does not name him, because Borunda was a very pious man; but perhaps *materials*, for his theological ignorance. But I only found disparities, silliness, and even deliriums among some grains of gold. In his work nor in my sermon did the censors find anything worthy of the censure that the edict attributes them to have imparted. It is then as calumnious against them as against us. In a word, it is an inflammatory, superstitious, and scandalous libel worthy of the public flames, which our certificate laws condemn. And those of Roman rights are no less terrible against their authors.

The Ecclesiastics are scared. Our national Iliberitano Council, so ancient and so famous in the Church, prohibits giving the communion even in the hour of death to those who publish libels in the Church, the same as to those who will falsely attribute crimes to priests. And for this very serious communion, theologians understand the sacramental absolution. What would deserve bringing both offenses together, it might be added having done all this with the seal of episcopal authority, in the middle of the sacred mysteries, on a festival day in all the Churches of America, separately reprinting his defamatory pastoral, and even inserting it in the civil gazette? The hell in its deepest caverns, if I were to die without the honor restored, because as Saint Augustine says *non- remittitur peccatum nisi restituatur ablatum* ("*There is no remission without restitution.*"). The Archbishop not only did not restore it, but he added new calumnies in confidential reports, and spent the income of the Bishopric, which is the blood of the poor, to bribe and to block me from the channels of justice, and to prevent restoring this honor to me. It has been lost to me forever. I doubt much for his salvation, and even that of his accomplices.

Benedict XIV in his Bull *Sollicita ac provida* (*"The Meticulous and Insightful"*)orders that no work is prohibited, without having heard its author or someone who acts in his stead, in the case of a long absence and without being able to notify him. And, that if they find in it notable things, notes so serious like an error or heresy, the censure is deferred to the justice of the Apostolic See. And, with reason because even in their Provincial and Diocesan Councils, it is forbidden that Bishops meddle or decide questions of faith. The very most important heresies have had Bishops for authors, and many, almost all, by important instigators. The secret assemblies, in which they have prevaricated, are so numerous and almost as many as the Councils. On every page of the ecclesiastic history one encounters the proof of all this. Even when the pair of theologians that the Archbishop chose at his pleasure, had erroneously, blasphemously, and impiously judged my sermon, not for this ought His Illuminate to announce this censure to the people as a truth. I do not say the ruling of two vulgar ecclesiastics, who for another part were very disqualified in law: the ruling of a University as famous as was that of Paris, judging a proposition contrary to the faith, it could only have been temerity, as it is to prefer their own justice to that of so many wise men. The professors of theology mutually qualify erroneous and heretical doctrines contrary to their schools, and not for what they are. Only the judgement of the universal Church that is infallible of faith, can obligate us to look without doubt as erroneous or heretical some proposition, and only on dogma and morality material. Why annoy me more? The Christian people take no utility from general censures and vagaries that do not determine what one ought to believe on each point. They are only directed, when they are given by necessity, to discredit some printed work, so that the people abstain from drinking from a suspicious fountain. But when it does not exist, or no work has been published, to censure it so bitterly and with the name of the author, only leads to discrediting his persona, which is totally illicit and criminal.

Now follow the proofs of the Guadalupe tradition, or better said, a weave of the most foolish plagiarisms, obvious nonsense, vulgarities, and pompous lies, to hallucinate and heat up the imbecile populace, the neighing of the Bruno Horse to stir up the herd of mares.

It begins with Florencia's already cited plagiarism, saying: "That in 1666 inquiries were made of Our Lady of Guadalupe with more than twenty witnesses of whom, some knew and dealt with the same ones who had taken part in the miracle." I now leave proven that in this plagiarism there are as many lies as words.

It is said that Our Lady of Guadalupe is worshiped with devotion in Spain, Italy, France, Russia, Prussia-Saxony, Holland, England etc. Had the editor of the edict traveled all of this? It is a literal plagiarism of the account of the foundation of the Congregation of Our Lady of Guadalupe in Madrid, anonymously printed among the brief treatises pertinent to Guadalupe, printed (like I already said) at the expense of the Torres Canons. Our compatriot, most blessed clergyman, Don Teobaldo seeing the misery and helplessness that the Americans suffered in Madrid, thought to set up for them a house of charity and a congregation that could sustain them, with the title of Our Lady of Guadalupe. To heat up the imaginations, and to squeeze in effect the pocketbooks, especially of the Americans of one and another America, he wrote this account of a mindless plaintiff, in which he gathered all the brilliant species that he could adopt or imagine.

So, count among other falsehoods that the image of Guadalupe was painted with the roses that Juan Diego carried in his cape, in which opening it in front of the Bishop, they stayed stuck, forming with the green leaves the mantle, and with the hood, the tunic, and the rest of the image. When we now see that according to the original manuscript of Lazo

Esq., Chaplin of the Sanctuary, and Becerra Tanco the Virgin was already painted when it was brought to the Bishop, and even Sanchez the first historian who printed copies of Alva's paraphrases, says that the bundles of flowers that Juan Diego carried fell to the floor in front of the Bishop.

Don Teobaldo also dreams that when the current Sanctuary began, a rose-colored stone pot appeared and disappeared the day that it was finished, without one stone left. With that will we not only have to believe the apparitions of the Virgin, of the image, and the flowers, and the disappearance of Juan Diego, but also the apparition and disappearance of the rose-colored pot? I confess that I cannot swallow it. One cannot deny that the imagination of my fellow countrymen is very flowery; but certainly, it is not less impious to stop believing the miraculous truths, than to fake them.

What an author! What criticism! What a text for an Archbishop in a dogmatic edict! And Don Teobalde to assure the devotion of Guadalupe in all of Europe had he traveled to it? He never left Madrid. What happened was that celebrating in Madrid the General Chapter of the Order of San Francisco, Don Teobaldo printed a triduum, [7] in which he jumbled the history of Guadalupe, and took it to the Chapter's Monks, begging them to take charge of promoting the devotion in their respective posts. What were the Monks to respond to such a demand, if by chance they understood Castilian, but that they would try it? And as if this accomplishment proves the fact, and in effect the devotion spread everywhere, he counted the countries to which said monks belonged, and showed all of them as deeply rooted in the devotion of Guadalupe. Don Teobalde did not know that most were Protestant countries where they abhor images as idols; but an Archbishop ought not to ignore it. And how could the absurdities of Don Teobaldo have been so neatly written, if he had known that the Archbishop elect of Manila died, to bewilder the populace, which is pleased by names and titles? But the miters they suppose do not give wisdom, and a sharp-pointed cap does not better a head of its unhappy nature. The venerable and wise Gerson says the ruling of a layman instructed in Sacred Letters is worth more than that of an ignorant Pope.

What will the Protestant Ministers say to their sheep if Señor Haro's edict should fall into their hands? "See here how the Catholic Bishops deceived their people. See how the Roman Catholic religion is not sustained except by force of frauds." This is how with these exaggerations and lies, that far from being needed, our religion detests them, and it does an immense prejudice to itself.

Our Archbishop proceeds to tell that the history of Guadalupe was brought to light in 1648 by Br. Sanchez who took it from the papers of an Indian, as they say of an evangelist. And the Mexican Councils do not even want his sworn testimony accepted. *Moreover*, the Indian was anonymous to the Archbishop and to the Grandiloquent Sanchez. It is admirable, the contrast between the first Bishop of Mexico and the last one of my time. That one burned all the Indians' manuscripts and libraries as witchcraft and demons, and this one wishes that he had them as texts of Scripture.

Our Archbishop says that the image was moved the year 1533 to a provisional hermitage that Zumárraga built. Ill-treated by the stroke of a pen on earth, all the praised witnesses of 1666 and all the Guadalupano authors just called the most serious, because one and another affirmed that the image was moved the year 1531, fifteen days after the appearance. It is true that the Archbishop with reason took this from Cabrera's "Mexico's Coat of Arms" that alleges for this reason an ancient Mexican inscription that is there in the Sanctuary; and certainly, in fifteen days a hermitage of earth could not sufficiently dry to put there such a precious treasure. But it is also true that Zumárrago spent the entire year 1533 in Spain, and by consequence neither is it true that he moved the image. And Haro remains without any proof of when the hermitage was built, because it is not evident except from the saying of those authors and witnesses who refute the other half of the incident. In conclusion, two years after the apparition of the image is too much time to make a provisional hermitage of adobe when in two years the Indians fabricated twenty-four thousand stone houses in Mexico City. I already said, also, that Zumárraga before going to Spain built from stone his palace and the Love of God Hospital, and the Santiago College the year 1534 that he returned to Mexico, and that the construction then cost no more than an order. All of which proves that neither before nor after his return, did he make a case of the image, which is impossible if the apparition had been true.

He proceeds to say that the reports of Guadalupe were examined two times by the Sacred Congregation of Rites for the granting of the prayer. A lie, because the second time in Father López's time they had already lost it, and the first time it is only evidenced by the testimony of Nicoselli, which they presented. Also, a donkey turns up in a theater, and no one will say for this that it is examined and approved.

But where the editor displays his eloquence is on the prayer, because it resounded (he says) from the Vatican's High Throne that *non fecit taliter omni nationi* ("*He hath not Dealt so with any nation*"). [8] In this way the plebe is bewildered. Bruno ought to know that when one speaks of the Pope, he does not speak about the throne, but about Authority, and unfortunately, the brief was not issued from the Vatican Mount's Guadalupano Office, but from the *Horse* Mount, because if wrong, I do not remember it is noted *apud Sanctam MariamMajorem* ("*Before the Most Holy Mary*"). The Pope appears to write the first thing in the Basilica, even though it sits a quarter of a league away, like Saint Mary the Superior from the Palace of the Horse Mount. But this name sounded so ugly and Bruno loved to deceive the populace that he bedazzles them with names. More also, Vatican translated to Castilian means nothing but Mount of Poets or Fortune-tellers. And what did the Pope say from the Mount of the Prophets of Doom? *That he did not do a similar thing with another nation.*

Father Florencia says that a devout person fancied putting this half a verse at the foot of the image. And the composer of the prayer later did the antiphony of the *Benedictus*, which was tossed to the same postulate, if he has the talent for it, or another to whom he paid for his work. Bruno who had heard, and who afterwards examines the prayer, believed that this verse had also been examined from the High Throne of the Vatican; but the lessons, responses, etc. are not examined when they are from Scripture, because they put their texts wherever one wishes, they do not have nor can they have another literal sense than what they have in the place from where they were taken. The middle verse in question is the last of Psalms 147, *Lauda Jerusalem Dominum* (*"Praise the Lord, O Jerusalem"*),[9] where the Prophet exhorts the Israelites to praise God for having chosen them among all the nations of the world to give them his law and to manifest to them his mysteries. Who announces, "He says to them, His word to Jacob, His justices and trials to Israel. He did not do a similar thing with another nation and did not declare to another His precepts." The second part of the last verse is the explanation of the first, because in Hebrew poetry each verse contains a precept under two phrases, of which the one is explained by the other. And the Prophet did not dream to speak of the Mexicans, nor of the Virgin of Guadalupe. It happened to Bruno the same as the Nun Agreda, who hearing in the festivals of the Virgin by way of the Proverb Epistle Chapter 8 *Dominus possedit me*(*"The Lord possessed me"*) etc. [10] It literally applied to them. But this is punctually one of the forty-eight propositions that the Sorbonne censured, and the flame nothing less than erroneous, because it says that this chapter only ought to be literally understood as increated Wisdom.

The texts of the Scripture are applied to the prayers in the mystic sense, for which certain allusions and general relations are enough. In the same Guadalupe Office, Bruno had the proof. In an antiphon or verse is put that of the songs *Flores apparuerunt interra nostra* (*"The flowers appear on the earth"*), [11] with which the editor of the prayer intended to allude without a doubt to Guadalupe's flowers; but if the literal meaning was understood, neither would the flowers be a miracle, nor could the apparition have been in December, because the entire text says: "For, lo the winter is past, the rain is over and gone; the flowers appear on the earth." Apocalypse, Chapter 12, also applies to the Virgin of Guadalupe, of the woman who *appeared in the heaven crowned by twelve stars and the moon beneath her feet*; and neither is the Virgin of Guadalupe crowned by stars, nor can that chapter be understood as the literal meaning of the Virgin without denying her virginity in the birth, because it says that the woman being made pregnant, who Saint John saw, gave screams from the pains of birth. *Et in utero habens, clamabat parturiens, et cruciabatur ut pariat ("And she being with child cried, travailing in birth, and pained to be delivered")*. [12] The literal meaning is the Church with its twelve Apostles at the head, whogave birth to the Christians with the pains of martyrdom and persecution. If in the literal meaning, as Bruno understands them, they had to take the texts of the Scripture applied in the Breviary to the festivals of the Saints, this would be the registry of the heresies, the foolishness, and the absurdities.

And would this not be clear foolishness to believe that the Virgin had not done a greater favor than that of Guadalupe to some nation? Would a favor at the end of the centuries be a comparison, after having abandoned us sixteen centuries to the eternal perdition, with the Virgin having gone in mortal flesh to Zaragoza [Spain], and to leave there her image for a reward that would never fail the religion in Spain? With the same house where Most Holy Mary grew up and incarnated the Word, having come by air from Nazareth to Loreto [Italy}? With having written in her own handwriting to those of Messina, promising them her protection, if all these things were true? What remains in the old women's histories of Spain and other nations, are images that appeared to shepherds, monks, hermits, etc. from which in America have been taken many copies.

How would Bruno think that this hemistich was a grandiose thing, because in the Cathedral to sing a great tinkling round of all the instruments is made, and the people run to this lure like partridges? Not all what the Canons do is good. Also, one comes around to them for the canonical hour, to receive the contribution, the attendance to the bull fights, and it is a spectacle so indecent to the ecclesiastical gentleness and charity, that it was even forbidden to the clergy with excommunication, and a Pope having raised it for the secular clergy at the request of our court, has not made it more decent. American imbeciles, the Archbishop's Europeans made fun of us, and far from believing that the Virgin has made ye more favored with Guadalupe than they with the Pillar, one of the motives of my persecution was that I secured for you an equal favor, and I equaled you with them.

The edict's exhortation, in short, is reduced to two points: the first is to exhort the people that it must believe the Guadalupe tradition, and to the ecclesiastics that they must sustain it with as many reasons as they can, in order that if with time her falseness is discovered (and they always come to discover the fables), the priests may be seen as impostors, and the populace reasoning like Uribe makes it reason, infers that the rest of the religion by which he has confounded them, is equally false, when it has nothing to do with these traditions, or popular tales, to which one ought not to lend more faith than the fundamentals on which they are based deserve. Nothing is added to the Virgin with our inventions, nor does it need false incenses. *Falso non eget honore virgo regia veris cumulata honorum titulis* ("*A false honor to the royal Virgin, which she does not need.*"), says Saint Bernard. [13] The true doctrine that a Bishop ought to give is what I finally gave in the refutation of the ruling of the censors. It would make me happy to have in hand the Pastoral already cited, on images, from the Bishop of Avila, King Fernando's Minister, then a Prince, and there I would see a doctrine diametrically opposed to that of Haro, and supported in the Trent Council, the III Mexican Council, and the confessional of the most learned Bishop Tostado.

The second point which the Archbishop exhorts is that the Mexicans are not to speak of the origins of the American Church like the Borunda, Esq. Which is, he prohibits that we speak of the ancient Christianity of our native land, and the preaching of Saint Tomé in it. And he does not mention me, even though this was the basis of my entire sermon, so that the people could not notice what I preached, and the thing could receive some credit, with mine, or so that it could not be understood that this was the true cause of so much scandal and of my persecution. It cannot be explained more clearly, that in the end this mess could not be revealed, and for the respect of the censors' rulings.

And what authority did the Archbishop have to order that we not speak of a thing so glorious to our native land defended by most serious authors even Bishops, Archbishops, and Cardinals, most in accordance with Scripture, and the Popes, most worthy of the mercy of God, the most proper to suppress the blasphemies of the incredulous against the religion, and supported in unimpeachable documents? It is incredible the despotism with which some Bishops wish to dominate even the most indifferent opinions. *Multum erigimini filii Levi* (*"Ye take too much upon you, ye sons of Levi"*). [14] And it is very strange that even though, the Bishops of Europe pry into all antiquity to find in their laws some trace of origin in the Apostolic times, those of America not only refuse this honor that comes to their hands, but rather they prohibit it be given, and they pursue with rage the one who procures them. The affair is that America may not have any glory, that the heaven also assembled the hate that they profess toward it, and the honor that can come to them does not matter though so contrary to their laws.

Haro only loved the peso coins of America, to enrich his family. It was necessary with a Royal order to take the niece from his side, for trusting to the greed of her husband the administrator of the Love of God Hospital, the wealthiest of

Mexico, he lost this; and it was necessary, to maintain its relics, to move them to San Andres, to subject all the nuns to the monopoly of a pharmacy, and destroying the harmony of the tobacco dealers, subjecting them to being hidden in their illnesses within the new hospital. His clerical nephew left for Spain with sixty-two thousand Chaplain money. And there, Don Juan Bautista Muñoz who managed his household interests, told me; I have evidence that the Archbishop does not give, but that he pours the money on his family. In Mexico it was also said publicly that other Sacraments were not given in the Archbishopric, except those that were worth money, because orders were never lacking, and the whole Archbishopric was years and years without a confirmation, as if it were a sacrament of execution. Still the altars became scarce, because their consecration is bothersome, and they would have been missed if the Bishops that consecrate them in Mexico, had not made good.

And such Bishop affected a furious zeal for a point of history in favor of America! It was I who did the favor to my native land, and for this to discredit and ruin me this favor was managed with the appearance of religious fervor. In front of a Bishop who usually did not preach except at the most a sermon every twelve years, a brilliant American could not preach something that does not entirely square up with his ideas, except that at the moment he tries throw out a trip-up to ruin you, as he did with me, and sought to do so, with the Archdeacon Zerruto at a cost of a thousand scandals.

The edicts, whose printing by custom are tolerated by the Bishops, were a resource to arouse the populace, and to subjugate everyone, by fear of the discredit and the scandal. With the name of edicts, usurped in America to the decrees of the civil authority, because the edicts were always from the Caesars and Praetors, and the rabble of La Mancha had forgotten, the fool and abuse that surround him, that the Bishop's Pastorals ought not be a blindman's sticks, nor vomits of anger, but exhortations full of charity and sweetness, according to that which the Divine Master

exhorted to his Apostles to learn from him that he was meek
and lowly of heart; he chastised them that to want him to
bring down fire upon Samaria as contrary to the spirit that
should animate them, because he did not come to lose men,
but to save them, that like a good shepherd he carried upon
his loving shoulders the sheep that had gone astray, to bring
it back to the fold, he did not give it a beating, nor did he
throw it to the dogs, nor disturb the flock. But almost every
Pastoral of Haro shook up his own people, and secular and
regular clergy, and this principally, to which he has an
aversion, because he did not respect persons or bodies,
apostolic privileges or immemorial customs. Especially
tempestuous in this genre was the Viceroyalty of the Count of
Revillagigedo, because this Señor for the most part, and for
another distressed with the French Revolution, asked the
Archbishop for reforms on some points, that he could only
remedy with the lance of edicts, of which there was then a
violent downpour.

I will cite for example only three for their celebrity:

1st ⁻A soldier on the Palace Bridge trampled on the
bookseller Clergy Jauregui, and this one dressed in black, but
short, rose up to complain to the Viceroy. This one insinuated
to the Archbishop that to build respect for the clergy is why
he should wear his distinctive wardrobe. Well the Archbishop
could have responded that black clothing with collar and
open crown as in Rome is quite enough, and that it was
already the immemorial custom in America. But already that
at the end of twenty-four years of a Bishopric, in which he had
not spoken a word on the wardrobe, he should order the
clergy to get dressed in length, and he ought to control their
pastoral, and not to have it published in the pulpits before the
people, that in place of edifying them, he scandalized them
about the defects of the ecclesiastics. And did not stop only on
ecclesiastic clothes, but he also ordered that they wear a
shovel hat and a chamber pot crown, an unheard-of thing in
the American clergy, except for the Jesuits and Filipenses. The
clergies asked him, who would suggest to the Archbishop

that his ignorance, or that of the editor who knows no more than to copy, will tarnish us? It is almost to the letter a Pastoral from Señor Beltran, Bishop of Salamanca, and he made us wear it, as if here there was no need to respect any of the clergy's customs. He was fortunate that he did not deal with some French or Italian Bishop's pastoral, where the clergy wear curls, powders, and grease; our clergy would have had to walk after the wigmakers.

2nd-A tailor, very much a friend of the Church folk, obtained at five on an afternoon a general ringing at the turning of a handbell, by fame of the Royal Order that was granted a coachmen's gathering in The Martyr Saint Catherine Parish. The Viceroy complained to the Archbishop of this disorder, and one already imagines the edict to the singing, plagiarized out of Lambertini's Pastorals. It is well that the excess and the abuses on the ringing of the bells are corrected; but the Archbishop always exceeds his powers, and he dealt with everything by the same measure, without remembering that the bells of the Regulars are exempt like their Churches, and that of Saint Dominic is a Royal Church, exempt even for only this from his jurisdiction. And he ordered that they could not ring the bells at the turning of a handbell except on the royal fiestas, this is when the King has granted to some brotherhood, even though it may be of shoemakers, who call him Elder Brother; pious things which one never denies; when the Archbishop went to some Church, or two, or three, secularized monks from Saint Chrodegang or from Saint Augustine (the Canons are not another thing) with the reputation of a chapter house that they still preserve. And by which Canons is this rule enacted? And where do they speak of bells at the turning of a handbell? And must the convent's tower bells toll unabated for those reasons, and do they not have the power to ring in the fiestas of their patriarchs, especially of Saint Dominic, Saint Francis, and Saint Augustine, which until the other day were a fiesta, and with reason because they are true patriarchs of America, since their sons founded this Church with their sweat and their blood? In all the Church, one always deems founded by the Masters what their disciples founded; and for Saint Mark a disciple of Saint Peter having founded the Church of Alexandria, it was superior to all those of the East, and even that of Antioch, whose Chair Saint Peter occupied in person. And, on his order, neither could they ring at the turning of a hand bell on the principal patronage fiesta of the Virgin, in the same manner as that of the Rosary, the Mercy, the Carmen, nor the Dominicans' day of Saint Thomas, which is the glory of their order etc.?

But still it was the biggest audacity to accuse out of ignorance the ringing of some bell the Holy Friday, a reprehension directed at the Dominicans who rang a bell at one o'clock to call the people to the celebration of the burial of Christ, to which the City Council concurs with all the guilds. And the Saint Dominic Prelate cowards gave in by agreements. But the ring of this bell, like the procession, of this day, was a remnant of the most celebrated Congregation of the Magdalene, contemporary to the conquest. Not being able to summon at the beginning another sort, the immense multitude of the Jews, Gentiles, Neophytes, and Catechumens to celebrate the burial of Christ, where the City Council concurs, it was needful to ring a bell, and to call ignorant a custom introduced with such a legitimate reason, and continued for three hundred years without protest from the celebrated Councils in Mexico, nor of the Bishops, including Haro in twenty-two years, is true ignorance. If forty years of a legitimate custom is enough to prescribe against an ecclesiastical law, how has an immemorial not been enough? The Regulars in America make use of predictions without Bulls, because when these came (as Torquemada says), they already judged them as not necessary, for having prescribed the law with the custom. In the Mexican Council IV this point agitated them, and they did not dare condemn it. On fast day all the people for the same reason use pork lard. How much less ought an ignorant one from La Mancha condemn another? In Spain, the Basilian Nuns in Toledo and the

Franciscans in Avila ring a bell on Holy Friday. In Rome the carriages travel around, and the shops are open.

3rd-The pious Dominican and Carmelite women, etc. keep the face covered with their cloak. It seemed to Revillagigedo that some French revolutionary could hide under it, and he asked the Archbishop for an alternative. By appealing this only to the Prelates of the Orders, it was all resolved without any scandal. But it was not the gentleness in the genius of our Knight of La Mancha; noise, trampling underfoot, and excessiveness were necessary. Therefore, the Archbishop ordered in a suitable edict, not only that they uncover their faces, but that any soldier who encountered these poor virtuous women in the streets, was to force them to uncover themselves. And he added that they take off the wimples that they wore, because they were confused with the Virgins consecrated to God in the convents. Who has confused a locked-up Nun with a pious woman who goes through the streets? Besides the wimples are very different from those of the nuns, even novices, or lay sisters, because those of the professed are black, and those of the pious women white. More identical are the clothes, and they do not take them off, because they are the true religious ones consecrated to God; nor can they take off their wimples, because they are approved in their constitutions by the Apostolic See; and the pious women wear them everywhere, and in Spain all the married women laborers of Castile, unlike the maidens. If I had been a Saint Dominic Prelate, I would have made them dress as they must be and as they are in Italy, where they call them *Mantellettas*, because they wear the long cloak, and with a large veil over the wimples, very much like that of the Nuns, and then yes, they would seem to be them. And what does it matter? The Nuns have not always been locked up, and there are Nuns locked-up in the Kingdom of Naples, and Nuns that they call from home, who go through the streets identically dressed; and far from being trampled on, a preferential place in the Churches is given to them that was always given in the Church to the Virgins consecrated to God.

The Prelates of the Religious Orders did not give up meeting on the matter of the pious women, nor did the Saint Dominic Council Fathers on the bells, principally those of the Holy Friday. It matters little, they said after all, to ring a bell, or that the pious women wear wimples, but it matters much to avoid the anger of the Archbishop. If this Prelate finds out, or hears reasons, they might complain to him, but beginning by edicts that already publicly compromise his authority, is a signal that he wants to be obeyed, and he must consider resistance a crime that will come by a thousand means. These responses were not doing honor to the Archbishop.

He well knows that he exceeds his authority; but he also knew the power of his agents in Spain, and he understood the key of the Council of the Indies. Thus, to have his unjust orders obeyed, he sent his edicts to the Council to say to the government hall that they, there call Of-the-Neckties, because it is composed in its majority of gentlemen of cape and sword. *I passed over to the Public Prosecutor*: this goes without saying. The Public Prosecutor, or venal, or ignorant, or he who cannot be instructed in all the discipline especially local, and that for another part is overwhelmed by the weight of all North America, seeing that nobody claimed, because one does not dare, the Bishop believed in order, and later there came a royal order running over the Apostolic Bulls, the privileges of the Regulars, and the immemorial customs of the Churches.

Some are surprised to see the clergy in New Spain at the front of the insurrection, when in all parts he is the one who yokes the peoples to the coach of the Kings. Haro is the one who has raised it. A Viceroy, asked why he had not constructed castles and fortresses in New Spain, responded to the King that here the best fortresses were the Churches and the Convents, and our clergy was always the best value of the Spanish dominion in the Americas. But Haro worked incessantly, for twenty-nine years, in demolishing it with contempt, postponement, and persecution. All the weak and persecuted gather like the bushes intertwining themselves to withstand the storm, a spirit is forming, and a repressed spirit shakes even the earth.

The laws of the Indies on the Kings' onerous pacts with our fathers give preference for all jobs to those born in the Indies. But excluded almost entirely from the civil, military, and political ones, by political intrigue or chance, they have taken refuge in the Church with the correspondent studies, because they not only have to their favor the laws of the Indies for their jobs, but the pacts of the first Bishops with the Kings, and the Canons which exclude those who are not natives of the Dioceses. But Haro had not only exclusively populated his Palace with successive colonies of Europeans, but they fill the Cathedral, the University, and the nuns' stewardships; and to occupy the parishes he was creating a large colony in the Seminary, against the nature of its institution. And the Europeans also having little commerce that is permitted to them what is left to the sons of these same European employees and merchants is a noose to hang them? And is prosperity expected, when the most distinguished part of the nation is reduced to desperation, the most instructed in their rights and of major influence? Given the chance they must leave like the winds chained in the caverns of Aeolus. [15] *Qua data porta ruunt, immare ac murmure perflant* ("*With what was given to rush the gate, and a roaring blow through an abyss.*"). Haro, therefore, prepared all the fuel for the insurrection of America, when that of the Peninsula fixed the wick to the mine.

Torquemada already wrote in his time that the things of America had no remedy for being so removed from the eyes of their King. Therefore, chancelleries have been made of all America's Courts, when in Spain there are only those of Valladolid and Granada: and to the Viceroys their Deputies, when in Spain it is only that of Navarre. The Vice-patronage is not to rule the Church, but to protect it. And why, when the Bishops abuse the custom that tolerates them printing their edicts for publicizing libels, was there no way of removing or restricting them? A Bishop is no more than a Council; and neither can the Diocesan print without the consent of the

Viceroy and Court, nor the Provincial without that of the Council of the Indies. He is not more than the Pope; and since these commenced to abuse their Pastorals or Bulls, all the nations provide themselves with the *Royal Exequatur*. Let us go back to take the thread around my persecution and let us speak now of the public prosecutor's indictment.

Chapter 5, Notes

1. *De Revelationibus, Visionibus Et Apparitionibus Privatis Regulæ Tutæ Ex Scriptura, Conciliis, Ss. Patribus, Aliisque Optimis Authoribus Collectæ, Explicatæ Et Exemplis Illustrat*, published by Bishop Eusebius Amort, in Spain 1744, currently available in Latin.

2. *I am the Lord, I change not:* Spanish and Latin text is from the Bible Malachi 4:6.

3. Pulque is a Mexican alcoholic drink made by fermenting sap from the maguey, an agave plant.

4. The origin of "santocalli" is a combination of Spanish "santo," holy, and Aztec "calli," house. Santocallis were private oratories in Mexican homes that were kept as places of worship before and even after the conquest.

5. King James Bible Acts 10:34-35: *Of a truth I perceive that God is no respecter of persons: But in every nation he that feareth him, and worketh righteousnees is accepted with him.*

6. The quote is from Latin Vulgate Bible, John 1:7; King James Bible John 1:6 -7: "There was a man sent from God, whose name was John. *The same came for a witness, to bear witness of the Light, that all men through him might believe.*"

7. A three-day period of prayer preceding the Catholic observance of Easter.

8. King James Bible, Psalms 147:20: *He hath not dealt so with any*

nation. A quote attributed to Miguel Cabrera (1695-1768), printed on Guadalupe medallions and paintings.

9. King James Bible; Psalms 147:12; *Praise the Lord, O Jerusalem.*

10. King James Bible, Proverbs 8:22; *The Lord possessed me.*

11. King James Bible, The Song of Solomon 2:12; *The flowers appear on the earth.*

12. King James Bible, Revelation 12:2; *And she being with child cried, travailing in birth, and pained to be delivered.* The preceding italic phrase of the woman who appeared abbreviates Revelation 12:1.

13. Saint Bernard of Clairvaux (1090-1153): *A false honor to the royal Virgin, which she does not need.*

14. King James Bible, Numbers 16:7; *Ye take too much upon you, ye sons of Levi.*

15. Aeolus is a Greek divine keeper of the winds and king of the mythical, on the island of Aeolia. He kept the winds inside the cavernous interior of his isle, releasing them only at the command of the greatest gods to wreak devastation upon the world.

Chapter 6

The Passions Incriminate Innocence with a Public Prosecutor's Indictment that the Same was Nothing but a Horrific Crime. And They Condemned It with a Sentence Worthy of Such a Tribunal; but with the Cruel Derision of Calling the Most Absurd and Atrocious Penalty, Piety and Clemency

This is what follows to prove in the order of the events, because it is said that on another day after the Edict's publication, it arrived announcing the sentence to me, at the hour that the Royal Court had entered Holy Week vacations. For taking time in the meantime, the appeal or its effects frustrated me, if I were interposing it. With the sentence, the public prosecutor's indictment, upon which it was based, was read to me.

The Archbishop had purposely named as the public prosecutor of my cause the Priest Larragoiti, for being a good one-eyed, and known for his little delicacy of conscience in serving the intrigues of the Ecclesiastical Palace. Promptly, he said that he had obtained the Parish Sacrarium for the violation of the canonical forms in the election of the University's Secretary that relapsed despite the Doctors and at a cost of a thousand scandals and violations by a European relative of the Archbishop. Now Larragoiti would expect a Canonry for the complete prostitution of his soul.

He therefore asked, "bearing in mind that I had voluntarily retracted; humbly asked forgiveness, offered all satisfaction, even of composing and printing at my cost a work contrary to my sermon; and with respect to the long imprisonment that I had suffered, His Illuminate for piety and clemency exiled me to Spain, to be a prisoner for ten years in the Convent of the Caldas that is in a desert near Santander, so that I might learn humility; with perpetual ineligibility for all public teaching on authority, pulpit, and confessional!!!"

. . . . lumine laesus, Rem magnam praestas, Zoile, si bonus es. (". . . . .Wounded in the eye, you furnish something great, Zoilius, if thou art good.") [1]

The one-eyed public prosecutor was obliged to justify his petition, to prove three things:

1st, that the Archbishop had jurisdiction over a Regular exempt from it.

2nd, that he had it for exiling him and punishing him at two thousand leagues from his Archbishopric, and—

3rd, to establish a sentence so exorbitant and barbaric; because to say that having humbly asked forgiveness, etc. he exiled me so that I might learn humility, is as if he said, in that this child reads very well, I ask that he be sent to school so that he may learn to read.

The proof that the Archbishop had jurisdiction over me, was only this, to the letter, "that the Council of Trent, *Reformation Session 25*: orders that the Bishops proceed in a form of law, as Delegates of the Apostolic See, against the preacher who preaches errors or scandals, even though he may be exempt, with general or special privilege."

The one-eyed lied and sacrilegiously corrupted the Council of Trent, joining the beginning with the end of the afore mentioned decree, and suppressing the means, to have it say precisely contrary to what it says. I have here the decree to the letter from the *Reformation Session 25*. "If some preacher disseminates errors or scandals to the people, even though he preaches in a monastery of his order or of another, the Bishop may ban the preaching. But if, what God does not permit is allowed, heresies will disseminate. The Bishop as a Delegate of the Apostolic See may proceed according to the form of law against him, even though he understands that he is exempt with a general or special privilege. Nevertheless, the Bishops are on guard pursuing such preachers, under the pretext of heresies or errors."

This last closure, since the public prosecutor did not see right, he left it aside. But who does not see that this bad man without being able to accuse me of having preached heresies, applied what the Council says in this case, to that of having preached errors or scandals? The worst for him is that neither was I found in this last case, because the Council speaks of theological errors and scandals, not of errors on points of specific facts, because on these neither is the universal Church infallible. Neither of scandals inappropriately called such, or disturbances of the ignorant and superstitious populace, or deliberately seduced; pharisaic or passive scandals, received ·and not given; because these preachings of Jesus Christ and that of his Apostles also caused them. The very wise Bishop Melchor Cano, dealing with theological notes, teaches that disturbances of the populace ought not be reputed to theological scandals that in touching their little images and superstitions, the shouts rise to heaven. The same cites the case of excommunication that is for him who will say that to deny the Conception of Mary in grace is an error, scandal, impiety, temerity, or mortal sin. How since there was nothing of this to deny, if I had denied it, a popular chair tradition that only the Congregation of Rites holds a hypothetical approval, of the very lowest rank, *they say, and they tell*; a mere permission agreed upon false reports and manifest fraud, as I have already demonstrated it?

Now let us see how the one-eyed public prosecutor proves that the Archbishop had the power to exile me and punish me at two thousand leagues away, a case of me being subject to him. His only proof is, "that the Laws 49 and 50 of the Indies (I do not remember of what title), and others, order that the monks who cause a scandal may be sent to Spain with the agreement of the Bishops."

The one-eyed lied: the first law says; "that in consideration that there are in the Philippines some monks who having left their habits, live scandalously, send them to Mexico." It does not speak a word of Bishops; and even if he spoke, it is about apostates of a scandalous life, that like the vagrants are subject to the Bishops. And it speaks of sending them to Mexico, not to Spain. What did this have to do with me or my case?

The second law that he quotes says: "That in consideration of the various monks who have come from Spain without license, and lazy persons travel through the Indies, where their Orders have no convents, causing scandals in the villages, the Viceroys ship them to Spain with the agreement of the Bishops." What had any of this to do with me, because I am Creole and a son of Mexico's Saint Dominic, where I peaceably taught?

It is a constant law of the Indies, that all who come from Spain, without a license, ought to be imprisoned, their goods confiscated if they have any, and sent to Spain to be punished. Here it is added that it be with the agreement of the Bishops, because it speaks of vagrant monks and such, according to the Council of Trent, who are subject to the Bishops. To even take a Negro from the house of his master, and to send him to a prison, justice takes to this one the authorization, without which it follows that the master has the same power as the justice to send the Negro to prison, as the Public Prosecutor wished to here infer, since it was not the Viceroy who wished to send me to Spain with the agreement of the Archbishop, but this one with the agreement of the Viceroy.

The rogue Public Prosecutor says that there are other laws. Why did he not cite them? If the ones that he specified, without doubt for being the best to his purpose, were such, which ones would be global? If any were, the public prosecutor would say that they were temporary laws, given the recent conquest for uprooting from among the fledgling or neophyte Indians the ministers of scandalous customs.

Speaking of monks, because this was the clergy of then, and of sending them to Spain because they were from there, and their convents were there, as well as the law that the public prosecutor first cited, he speaks of sending the apostate monks of a scandalous life from the Philippines to Mexico, because they were from here, the conquest of that island being recent, and here they had their convents.

Such laws, having come to their end for the variation of times and circumstances, have fallen of their own weight. Otherwise, this would be worse for the condition of the regulars than the secular clergies, due to their sweats and their blood in return for the foundation of the American and Philippine Church. And it would be an absurdity that when the clergies of a scandalous life are sent to the convents for their correction, they had their monks taken from them to send them to Spain, taxing the convents with the cost of their transport and of the maintenance in Spain of useless members.

This is so far from the spirit of the laws that the same vagrants that the second law quoted orders returned to Spain, and so it calls them, and commands them returned because their Orders had no convents in the Indies. In a word, to have seen Larragoiti obligated to attribute to his Archbishop jurisdiction over me by such means as to corrupt a General Council, to falsify some laws of the Indies, and to imagine others non-existent, is to have fully confessed that he did not have any.

In the past the Laws of the Indies entirely condemn the power that was usurped upon me. "We order," says a law, "and we command, that the regulars keep their privileges according to the Council of Trent, and the Viceroys and Courts keep vigil on this." So, according to the Council of Trent, only a Bishop can proceed in law against an exempt preacher in the case of having preached heresies, of which I was not accused, nor was it possible to accuse me. Therefore, the sentence and all the procedures of the Archbishop against me were against the Laws of the Indies and the Royal

Patronage. And it was also the help he got from the Viceroy that according to the law, it was to me to whom the Royal protection should have been awarded.

And on what, did Larragoiti finally base such an atrocious and exorbitant sentence? On nothing. How was it possible to find such an absurdity? Because, what greater absurdity than a Bishop, whose power is spiritual and circumscribed to his Diocese, to claim for himself the power of exiling to two thousand leagues the vassals of his Sovereign and the immediate subjects of the Supreme Pontiff, that in moving from Diocese, they change domicile, and now they have nothing to do with the previous Diocesan? What greater absurdity for the same, than to want to have me suspended and forever from all public teaching in the cathedral, pulpit, and confessional to two thousand leagues, it is to say, a foreign citizen, in a foreign Diocese, and more being a public Doctor that I have the authority to teach everywhere, by the Pope and by the King, superiors of the Archbishop, and of which he could not deprive me nor my University, except in a case not only of heresy, but of obstinacy and contempt on it? What greater absurdity than to want to have me a recluse for ten years in a convent of my Order at two thousand leagues; as if he were the General of the Order, and the Dominicans where ever they may be found, and their convents, were they under the thumb of Mexico's Archbishop? What greater absurdity than after publicizing that I voluntarily retracted, I asked humbly for pardon, I offered all satisfaction, and even that of composing and printing at my cost a work contrary to my sermon, to come to me applying a penalty that scarcely the exorbitant Tribunal of the Inquisition would apply to a heretic convicted of such? And this after having ruined my honor, falsely attributing errors, blasphemies, and impieties to me in an edict published on a festive day *inter missarum solemnia* ("*In solemn mass*") in all the Churches of America, reprinted for its sale, and inserted into the civil gazette. And this after having solicited that the Inquisition take knowledge of the matter (a step that by itself already defames), and for that my University erases me from the list of their Doctors. And still the public prosecutor says that this is for piety and clemency. With which for having erred without obstinacy, if it is that I erred on a point of specific history, undeniably disconnected, and indifferent to the religion, what I deserved was the gallows, because only this was missing. And only this would have satisfied the charity of the Archbishop, because not content with confirming the public prosecutor's indictment, he abolished my title of Doctor by virtue of his sentence, as if he could, and the University had not denied his request. If the Archbishop had believed the Guadalupe tradition, this would have been the fanaticism in rage. But as he did not believe it, it was anti-Americanism in delirium, hatred in fury, that this bad Bishop had his sheep precisely because they were his, since if they were not Mexicans, he would not be Archbishop of Mexico. This epitaph applied to him is not given in vain.

Si mei non fuissent dominati . . . . . .Tunc emundaret á delicto máximo. (*"If I had not been dominant . . . . . .Then amend the greatest sin."*)

What good did this Prelate do?
His family was enriched
From the fleece that he sheared,
Even though he loathed the flock.
His countryman was his beloved,
The creole his enchanter
Whom he pursued with fury;
Where would Don Quixote go?
To Spain? To hell at a trot:
Where does a bad Shepherd go?

What the Archbishop most admires is the determination with which all his protégés and sidekicks invented each one thinking up something with which to incriminate and color me, if it were possible, the atrocity of their Patron. As the

179

censors had gotten to the public prosecutors, the public prosecutor the same as the editor of the edict also got to do the job of censor, and to the charges that those did to me, added their own stamp that I condemned myself for having denied that the image of Guadalupe was of the Conception.

What sin was this? What authority has defined it? The image of the Conception has a crown of twelve stars, that of Guadalupe has a royal crown, and only on the cloak has she not twelve but forty-six stars. That one has the cloak blue and the tunic white, this one the cloak green and the tunic pink; that one is on the back of a silvery moon, and this one within the horns of a black moon; that one steps on a serpent, and this one steps on an angel; that one has wings and this one does not; this one has a cross around the neck, and that one does not; this one is within the fleshy leaf of a maguey, and that one not so. The only thing, in which they look alike, is in having beams around about. Also, that of the Assumption has them, and it is to us of the Conception. In a word, it is not called the image of the Conception, but of Guadalupe. Is it not a thing of laughter that the Council of Auch prohibits the dedication of the images, because it says that they do not control them, they only entitle them to take alms, and Larragoiti makes me a criminal for denying Guadalupe the title of Conception?

But, where did I deny such a thing? There is absolutely nothing in the whole sermon, to which this charge could allude to, except that explaining according to the ideas of Borunda the image of Guadalupe as a composed Mexican hieroglyphic, I said that it represented the Incarnation. This was not to deny that the image may be that of the Conception, since this also represents it, according to what they say it is like the woman of the Apocalypse, who was not only pregnant, but in labor. What miseries to incriminate me!

The one-eyed public prosecutor brought ignorance to the malignance. The Virgin of Guadalupe is painted like the Virgin Mary is always painted. All her images attributed to Saint Luke are like this. It is ordered by an Eastern Council that they paint them like this, and the Virgin of Guadalupe of the Extremadura Choir is like this, of which that of Mexico is an exact copy; and it was put there since the 15th Century, before there were images of the Conception. These had originated from a vision of the Nun of Agreda in the 16th Century. And from there it came that the Franciscans of the Indies changed to blue their brown habit, since those who came to Mexico were Minor Conventuals from the Extremadura Province of San Gabriel who had accepted some reform chapters from Saint Peter of Alcántara. And in Europe they are not imitated except the head of the Valencians who have dressed themselves in sky blue. From there also came the conceived nuns who in the 16th Century founded a Portuguese convent in Toledo and spread themselves into America. That is the reason for the blue cloak of the Order of Charles III, at the suggestion of the Dieguino Fray Gil. The Franciscan Fathers are even accustomed to calling their Agreda Mother, the second Bible; are owners of believing what fancies them; but I also am owner of rather believing the Sorbonne and the Apostolic See that have prohibited their works, and even much more owner of saying with ample reason that Larragoiti was a scoundrel.

Has the purpose of this false, ridiculous, and strange charge been understood? I had heard that the Dominicans have suffered great persecutions in Spain on the point of the Conception, especially when Franciscans have occupied the Kings' confessionals. And this man wishes to say that I as a Dominican have denied that Guadalupe was an image of the Conception, to have this way a pretext in the Court of continuing my persecution. Has a similar evil been seen, when the species that I preached was from Borunda, and as a Doctor of the University I had taken an oath of defending the Concepcion?

I have demonstrated the injustice, atrocity, and nullity of the sentence, according to the Laws of the Indies, and the current or modern discipline of the Church. I am going to demonstrate also the nullity, according to the ancient discipline, because there are many who think like the lawyer who I consulted, that the regulars are or ought to be subjects to the Bishops as successors of the Apostles. These believe it in such a way that they cannot support nor, can one speak of the privileges of the regulars, whom they look upon as usurpations of the Court of Rome upon their rights *de jure divino* (*"By divine right"*).

But of course, they are not successors of the Apostles in the faculty of imprisoning, shackling, nor exiling, because they and their primitive successor Bishops did not know jails, shackles, nor exiles other than those suffered by Jesus Christ. Thus, he declared that *his kingdom was not of this world; nor had he the power to be Judge, and to divide an estate between two brothers*. It is to say that all the power of his mission was only spiritual, and this alone is what he communicated to his Apostles and Vicars. The data of the coactive power of the Bishops exists in the Code of the Emperors, and in that of our Gothic Kings with respect to Spain. So, he who could give it to them, could take it away from them; and much more, to restrict it from them. And, in respect to the regulars, they were effectively restricted from it by the Laws of the Indies.

In that the Bishops are successors of the Apostles, there is no doubt; but neither is there in that, so we are the Priests. To some Father the allegory occurred to him that the Bishops are successors of the twelve Apostles, and the Priests of the seventy-two disciples; and there the scholars have settled, as if in another sense that the literal Scripture offers a solid argument on theology. Saint Augustine says, *Quis audeat sensum in allegoria positum pro se interpretari* (*"Who dares to interpret the meaning of the allegory is set for himself"*)? How are we the Priests to be the successors of a few laymen? At the least, it does not appear that the seventy-two disciples were priests. The Deacon Saint Philip was one of them, and he was no more than a Deacon. "To you belongs," says the Bishop to the Priests in their ordination, "to preside, to teach, to preach, to baptize, etc." And are not these the principal functions of the Apostleship? Since we are also successors of the Apostles, although not in the Bishops' meeting of powers, nor they in all the plenitude of the apostolic powers.

In the primitive Church the name of Bishops was common, (to the letter, *Superintendents*) and to some and another of the Priests or Elders, and more often one finds in the Scriptures it is given to the Priests than the other way around. When Saint Paul said: *Attendite vobis et universo gregi, in quo vos Spiritus Sactus possuit Episcopos regere ecclesiam Dei* (*"Take heed to yourselves and to the whole flock, wherein the Holy Ghost hath placed you bishops, to rule the Church of God."*), [2] he spoke with Priests of Ephesus, *vocavit majores natu ecclesiae* (*"and called the elders of the church"*); [3] and clearly in the Church there were not many Bishops. When he wrote to Timothy and to Titus of the obligations and powers of the Bishops, he spoke of the Priests, and does not distinguish them, since immediately he follows, *similiter Diaconos* (*"likewise, must the deacons"*). [4] Upon this same Saint Jerome says: "The Priests, so that there was order, chose one of them who presides, and this is he who we call Bishop." And what does this one, do except for ordering what the Priest cannot do? And true it has not always been reserved to them in the Church, except for the ordination of Priests and Deacons, on whom we also impose the hands. [Juan Francisco] Masdeu proves that in the ancient Church of Spain the Priests gave the rest of the ordinations, and the confirmation, and they consecrated the head. In the General Council of Chalcedon composed of 630 Bishops, having to punish one of them, one proposed that he be set aside as Bishop, and remain as Priest. Why the Council exclaimed, after Bishop he must remain as a Priest, if it is the same thing? What mode of thinking so distant from that of our scholars! Therefore, you will tell me, is there no difference? Saint Chryostom says: *Paululum differt episcopatus a presbiterat* (*"The Priest differs little from the Bishop"*) about the cited epistles of Saint Paul. It is true that the Bishops are superiors to the Priests; but the Council of Trent refused to take a stance that they were by divine right. There is of the faith no other ordination sacrament in the Church, other than the Priesthood.

From where then comes this arrogance of the Bishops, before whom the Priests today do not dare to present themselves without trembling, like the slaves before their master? Many causes could be pointed out; but two have been the principal ones. First, the coactive power that the Kings have given them, especially in Europe, where they granted them fiefdoms and dominions to help them domesticate the barbarians of the North. And the second, the false decretals that were introduced like a plague in the Church the middle of the 8th Century, ruining all their ancient and holy discipline according to their true and legitimate Canons, and upon which ruinous fundamental noted by the Monk Graciano with scholastic subtlety, supposed Councils, and apocryphal works of the Popes, raised the whole edifice of the modern canon law.

The author of this pernicious slander was surely the Archbishop of Mainz, toward the middle of the 8th Century, who took care of having his colleagues in the Bishopric almost go unpunished for the difficulty of Rome's resources etc. And since then consequently, the Bishops were letting go the cables that tied the ship of their power up to throwing it to full sails over their presbytery, against the mandate of the Apostle *of not dominating the clergy. Ab initio autem non fuit sic* (*"But from the beginning it was not so."*). [5] I am not the only one who complains: One must read the celebrated Councils from that time, and they will see repeated and heartfelt complaints in the Canons against the cruelty and arrogance with which the Bishops oppress, trample, and persecute the Priests. *Ab initio autem non fuit sic (*"But from the beginning it was not so."*).
5

The Bishops complaint that Rome has usurped their jurisdiction, exempting the Regulars from it, well in the beautiful days of the Church they have always been subject to them. But the religious orders began to diminish at least in the 4th Century with the formalities of today, and it appears by the testimony of Saint Cyprian that in this century all the nuns of Africa were subjects only to the Primate of Carthage. The Council of Agde in the 5th Century already granted or recognized the privileges of the monks of Lerins and Saint Gregory the Great exempted many monasteries in the 6th Century. In those 7th and 8th Centuries in Ireland and Scotland, it was almost the same to say "Abbots" as Bishops, because all the Abbots were so and consequently their monasteries were not subject to the Bishops of the territory. Neither would there be a great disadvantage in that the monasteries or monks' convents might be subject to the Bishops, even though these are usually their enemies, and not understanding anything of the monastic discipline, because after all each monastery composes a Province. But how could they be subjects to the Bishops, without the greatest disadvantages, the Mendicants of a single Province of one hundred fifty friars like that of the Dominicans of Mexico usually occupy a kingdom as is all New Spain (except for the Bishoprics of Puebla and Oaxaca), extending also seven hundred leagues into California? What would a Bishop get with a tenement house of seven friars, without novitiate, nor house of study, where they are recruited, disciplined, and instructed? How would they minister to the missions in the adjacent Gentile countries? How then would they run the Gentile and foreign nations, to introduce in them the religion, or support it as the Protestants do theirs? This would be to destroy all its usefulness, that the General Council II of Leon calls a clear regard of the Preachers and Minor Orders by a label of jurisdiction, and to cause the religion and the Church an immense prejudice. The mendicant orders are the light infantry battalions of the Church of God, and necessarily they have need of another tactic for their evolutions, different than that of the line troops, or of the heavy cavalry. It does not appear that the Bishops must give God a very tight account of each of his subjects, according to the determination that they show for spreading his jurisdiction.

Certainly, when they complain about the usurpations of Rome, they do not remember that they have retaliated upon their presbytery. And what happens, some Kings of Europe who having suppressed the Courts of the nations, believe theirs the rights that only they are suitable for presiding over the assemblies of the nation. We go back, noble Bishops, to the ancient discipline, therefore the spurious fundamentals of the modern discipline are discovered; but we go back completely like God orders, not invoking from the ancient one only those that favor them, without wishing to abandon nothing of what they have grabbed in the new one under the apocryphal titles, and leaving only to the Priests the tip of the funnel in one and another. No: This would be to play with two decks of cards, a thing so detestable to the eyes of men, as to those of God, who abhors two weights and two measurements.

We go back (and we will see who weighs) those ancient and true Canons that ruled the Church of God until the middle of the 8th Century. Canons that Saint Leo called: *Spiritu Dei conditos, et totius orbis reverentia consecratos: qui nulla possunt auctoritate convelli, nulla temporum praescriptione deleri* (*"The Spirit of God created that and hallowed by the respect of the entire world: he that cannot be torn asunder by the authority that cannot by prescription be blotted out of the times."*). Then one will see that Jesus Christ did not establish monarchs for Bishops: *Principes gentium dominantur earum; vos autem non-sic* (*"The Princes of the Gentiles exercise dominion over them, but ye shall not be so."*). One will see that the Bishops are no more than a few company chiefs. You should be told of something and more than for terrifying you with edicts, the Christian plebs who compose the Church as defined by Saint Cyprian *Sacerdote plegs adunata* (*"The People make one a Priest."*). An account would be given of everything such as Saint Cyprian and Saint Augustine gave it, because it is the Court to which Jesus Christ sent the Apostles themselves: *Dic ecclesiae; si ecclesiam non audierit sit tibi sicut ethnicus et publicanus* (*"Tell it unto the church: but if he neglects to hear the church, let him be unto thee as a heathen man and a publican."*) [6] It will choose its Bishops in the company of the clergy, and none will have to regret their Bishop.

A Senate would be recognized in each Church. Not the Senate of false decrees of the Popes, or the Body of the Religious or Regulars, which is to say Canons, today secularized by Saint Chrodegang or by Saint Augustine, who since the 10th Century raised them with the rights of a legitimate Senate, tithings have been known to maintain the forehead of the Bishops. No: the true Senate is the Presbytery made up of the Priests and Deacons of each Church. And as the Mendicant regulars are true clergy and not Monks, they would start to make up the Presbytery, and would not need the privileges of Rome, because according to the true Canons every determination of the Bishop, without the deliberation and consent of their Presbytery, is null and void. They make up with the Bishop what one calls the *See* that is not only the Bishop, because as Saint Leo says: *aliud est Sedes et aliud Sedens* (*"Seat is one thing and the other sitteth."*). They would have two Councils each year, and in them the Bishops would be judged and deposed without the need of resorting to the Courts of Rome and Madrid, long and difficult appeals, where risking the pawning and the money, the remedy is tardy or nothing, and the arrogance grows with the impunity. We, the Priests, would not have in the Councils the advisory vote recently invented, but deliberative, like we have had it in the same General Councils, because we are true judges of the faith inside and outside of the Councils. Anyway, one would not judge a Priest but in a Council of twelve Bishops. With that according to this, the sentence of the Archbishop of Mexico against me was also void according to the ancient, holy, and legitimate discipline of the Church.

Haro knows very well the whole offense that he committed against me; and after having used here for deception and violence, holding me with a padlock to my mouth, he resorted to preventing the spirits and to blocking me from the channels of justice in Spain, to the recourse of all the powerful when they commit a shocking injustice, which is to slander their victim with confidential reports. I am going to give notice of them and undo the veil to this new iniquity.

Chapter 6, Notes

1. Marcus Valerius Martialis (about 38-104 A.D.), Epigrams 12.54: *Wounded in the eye, you furnish something great, Zoilius, if thou art good.*

2. Douay-Rheims Bible Acts 20:28; *Take heed to yourselves and to the whole flock, Wherein the Holy Ghost hath placed you bishops, to rule the Church of God.*

3. King James Bible Acts 20:17; *and called the elders of the church.*

4. King James Bible, First Timothy 3:8; *likewise, must the deacons.*

5. King James Bible, Matthew 19:8; *But from the beginning it was not so.*

6. King James Bible, Matthew 18:17; *Tell it unto the church: but if he neglects to hear the church let him be unto thee as a heathen man and a publican.*

Chapter 7

Confidential Reports Sent to the King, to the General of my Order, and to the Prior of Las Caldas

Since the conquest is a maxim in the mouth of the Mandarins of America, "God is very high, the King in Madrid, and I here. That if something were to arrive in Spain, confidential reports and gold coins are trump cards." But if God orders in Deuteronomy, chapter 19, verse 15, *Non stabit unus testis contra aliquem quid-quid illud peccati et facinoris fuerit; sed in ore duorum aut trium stabit omne verbun* ("*One witness shall not rise up against a man for any iniquity, or for any sin, in any sin that he sinneth: at the mouth of two witnesses, or at the mouth of three witnesses, shall the matter be established.*"): [1] what would only one be worth, against whom does one appeal as unjust? In the same act of sending reports without anyone asking for them, it is already suspicious, because redress asked for no manifest accusation. The same name of confidential is a proof that they are slanders that are entrusted to secrecy because in public they could not be proved.

The disgrace is that our Court lives in continuous alarm over America and every denunciation against Americans, far from punishing them, if one is not rewarded, one is grateful as an effect of zeal; and in any case Lazarus always suffers. Thus, the cunning of the accuser for assuring his effect is in mixing something that smells at the cost of the State. Above all, the gold gives value to what by itself is worth nothing, and what the corrupt Pen-pushers and Counsels want, are some pretexts with which to cover up the victory of the sovereign bribery upon their soul. And that a pretext so apparent as the reports of a Bishop! It is true that the catalogue of the bad

Bishops is immense in the annals of the Church; but this is so contrary to the idea that gives us the name of Bishops who in love of neighbor must be embraced, and to the sanctity that they swear in their consecration that they must serve their flock to a model of perfection (*imitatores mei estote fratres, sicut est ego Christi*)(" *Be ye followers of me, even as I also am of Christ.*"), [2] that their reports generally infer a very strong vanity.

No one would believe that a Bishop has trampled the Canons, the Laws, the Patronage of his Sovereign, and all the rules of equality and justice, to dishonoring, exiling, and burying at two thousand leagues one of his consecrated clergy, without the need to punish an incorrigible demon in him. At the least if it is not, it is necessary that the Bishop must have a very bad opinion of the Court and of its tribunals, to send to the fountain of power and justice the same oppressed priest, and who did not hold his tongue at all.

This was done promptly; and the Archbishop sent me to Spain, relying on the intrigues and the influence of his agents who would not let me arrive at the Court, providing in those reports pretexts by which they concealed their violations and taking from corrupt documents some miserable and ridiculous slanders suggested by the Saint Dominic Vizier in some fermentation of fresh wine.

So, the first thing the Archbishop said was that I was prone to flight. And in what jails had I been, before his persecution, to know this propensity? He had no more grounds for such an assertion than to have said that I wanted to take asylum in a convent against his oppression and to appeal to the Royal Court, as a friar corrected since an early age by the Holy Office because of his inconsistency, concubinary, and a poisoner. What testimony so respectable for a Bishop to report about him to his Sovereign! What the Archbishop intended with his slander, was to excuse the most unjust prison in which he had me, without any power over me, and to furnish pretexts to keep me in chains in Europe. And, he got it.

The second thing he said was that he had convicted me because my retraction had not been sincere. I said before, where did he learned it, if he convicted me the next day of having published his edict, and in this he assured me that I had voluntarily retracted? I had nothing to retract, since neither, did I deny the tradition, nor was there in my sermon a thing worthy of censure. The Archbishop knew that all had been violence, intrigue, and deceit: and as I said before, also in the edict he said that I retracted voluntarily to palliate before the public the visible lack of a public hearing, and to the King he reported that my retraction had not been sincere, to excuse the atrocity of the sentence, as if throughout it were not barbarous, absurd, and void.

The third thing he said was that I was arrogant. The friars of such low extraction, as was Gandarias born of an unhappy family from Yuste, they call "arrogance" a point of honor of a well-born soul, who they are not capable of feeling or knowing. Raised from among the bottom mire to the monastic prelacy people, they swell like frogs with these scraps, and they cannot tolerate that some monk of distinguished birth, who by account of errors falls into the pigsty, may be left to grovel at his feet with a thousand flatteries and vile deeds, like other vermin of his class, and they have the major determination and delight in shaming him, humiliating him, and insulting him. How have I been arrogant; if I have never known either ambition or envy, inseparable companions of pride? What I have, despite my apparent liveliness, is an immense candor, the fountain of the misfortunes of my life. And with it, it appears to me that all that is good, just, and true; one can say, defend and execute. And as the despots do not care, except that one must blindly do their will, even if it may be the most one-eyed. My frank disapproval they called arrogance, and it was only theirs. I must have some like all the sons of Adam, since we are sinners, and the Apostle says *initium omnis peccati est superbira* ("*For pride is the beginning of sin.*"), [3] from which the Spanish are crossed out in the entire world. But neither are the passions grave sins, except when some commandment of God is broken by them, nor does it concern any Judge of the world to judge the interior effects, nor are there laws that punish them. What one can assure the Archbishop, was that in his heart, where he nestled an implacable hatred and an inexorable revenge, there was concealed the monster of arrogance.

The last charge is the one that sounds most grave and is worth the least, even though my enemies make a big mystery; and for the same I must expand more on it. Since, he said that I had been prosecuted by two Viceroys and he did not specify more, to inflate even more the pregnancy. But what does "prosecuted" mean? Because Jesus Christ was, his Apostles were, twelve million martyrs and the major part of the saints and of the great men, since for a lawsuit one needs no more than the slander of a ráscal, and this always bites where there is something to envy. The success is he who can say something and if I turned out bad, how come the Viceroys have not punished me? And if good, of what did the Archbishop accuse me? I am going to tell what these lawsuits were.

The first lawsuit: The entire world knows that the Count Revillagigedo received anonymous letters in a tiny box placed at the entrance of his palace, and that he removed his successor for being contrary to the laws and to public tranquility. In effect it is to give a free passport to the malicious ones for causing prejudice without fear of receiving it. If the thing is true, they lose one: if not, they are always defamed. The first, because in these secret inquiries the life of one is investigated, and as few are saints, on the other hand some are harmed. The second, because men are always inclined to judge badly the neighbor, the saying of someone is enough for them, at the least to suspect; and if they are enemies they make use of the accusation and of the lawsuit (like the Saint Dominic Provincial and the Archbishop against me) whatever may have been the success.

In this reign of the anonymous letters, an anonymous letter was made up by a low-class, ignorant, envious friar of

Saint Dominic, who must be an author of anonymous letters, and who in the order they named, *Cold Tooth*, for his good mordacity. He seriously accused the virtuous Doctor Arana and the same to Provincial Gandarias. Both fully satisfied the Viceroy almost on the same day that they were reprimanded, because the accusations were manifest slanders. Then he accused me of having suggested to the Tobacconists by means of someone who I knew, the innocent appeal shouting *Long Live the King*, they formed a corps before that Viceroy against his administrator, and at the same time he vomited all the blackness of his envy, so importune and impudent against me, that the Doctor Enriquez being Provincial had to publicly reproach him in the choir. Soon afterwards the Porta Coeli College brought to his breast this viper, I breathed in Saint Dominic, because day and night he did not stop persecuting me, even thought, like a vile man, always a betrayal.

The Tobacconists did not need for their appeal another motive than the immense prejudice that followed them for their Administrator having taken from them the paper for the cigarettes that they were in possession of to take to their house and to furrow it with the help of their family, being well advanced for the next day half of their work. Nor did they have need of another inductive reason, other than their own example, since they had made another equal appeal before Count de Galves, who received them laughing, because he knew the customs of America. The Indians gathered themselves to ask for something, like we gather all the saints in a day, *ut multiplicatis intercessoribus largiaris* (*"That as our intercessors are multiplied."*). And they even believe that they honor with this homage the person before whom they go to beg. But Count Revillagigedo whose nature was suspicious and harsh, was offended by it, and even though he granted their petition, the Tobacconists returned to their tobacco store, as they had come, disarmed and shouting, "Long live the King," he made the troops beat up a few. The same Count, my telling him in Madrid that it had been an innocent appeal, responded to me that it was true; but he was offended by it, for the circumstances which Europe was in with the French Revolution.

The anonymous letter received from the friar against me, a secret commissioner who was Señor Valenzuela was appointed to investigate, according to the custom in the case of their anonymous letters. This fired up all those Tobacconists who showed up to have influenced in the appeal. They took their declarations, and no one mentioned me, because it could occur to no one what had not happened. Thus, the anonymous letter was rejected, as it always should have been rejected, and neither did it speak a word; and the Viceroy left for Spain. If this investigation is a lawsuit, and this lawsuit a crime, I would receive it from the Viceroy; against the laws the anonymous letter and from the infamous friar who made use of means so illicit and vile to slander his own habit. Now that Revillagigedo received them, turning out to be slanderous he must have delivered them to the fire, and not to archive these evil things that might serve as the basis of other new ones, as did happen.

I had already been informed from Mexico City at San Juan de Ulúa that the Archbishop wanted to bind to his reports what had gone on in the Viceroyalty; but it was in Burgos where I positively knew that in effect he had used it informing the Prior of Las Caldas. I wrote to the Count in Madrid, begging him to send me a letter on this, capable of being presented in a court. He sent it to me certifying that nothing had happened regarding me during his Viceroyalty; but rather he had always had good notices of my talent and literature. And later he wrote me another letter saying my agent presented himself to him to receive some help for me, that giving him thanks I did not want to receive. And I sent this letter with the same agent to Don Francisco Antonio Leon, a board clerk of Mexico, to whom he delivered it.

The second lawsuit: Happened to Revillagigado, Branciforte, Italian, accused, and prosecuted before the Council for having robbed the Canary Island's Treasury; a dispute that only came out because of his marriage with

Godoy's sister; and the unhappy treasurer was a prisoner until another day. He was Viceroy of Mexico for the same marriage, (although as a foreigner according to the law he could not be one), so that his house could be built, it is said that he sent someone to steal, and in effect he was a true crook. He was very desirous of doing some service to ingratiate himself with the Court, where for the dispute before the Council he was discredited. And he credited, or he believed that some unfaithful Frenchmen, domiciled here, wanted to wage some revolution; he trampled and apprehended them, informing the Court that he had liberated Mexico. And he sent them to Spain, although the most married, and were found entirely innocent by the courts. Before this scoundrel, the Pharmacist Cervantes accused me of what I had said on the Boulevard that I would rather be a Turkish soldier than of Spain, as if speaking seriously a priest could belong to either one. He was not able to prove the accusation, because the two witnesses that he cited said that they did not remember such an expression, and he added one of them a European (who was the physician Warmis) that if perhaps I had said it that it would be in the same tone, by which to set my blood on fire, since they were blaspheming the Creoles as some great big cowards. This circumstance had silenced the charitable informer. Who had to say to me that while this one was scratching the belly enriching himself in Mexico with his monopoly pharmacy, and Branciforte served Joseph Napoleon, I had to be voluntarily risking my life in continuous combats for four years, by defending Spain and the rights of Fernando VII? So, for trifles the rascals lost the most loyal hearts.

Another donkey added to this accusation about an argument that I raised in the University about the conquest. I call him a donkey, because it is necessary to be one for not knowing that he who argues plays a comedy role, in which he represents the Heretics, Deists, Atheists, and the same demons as demanded by the contradiction that must be made at the conclusion. This is like a military army, where a few soldiers appear to the enemy to see if it would be able to defend itself from their true attack.

Branciforte added to these gossips the friar's anonymous letter and reported secretly upon these big legal actions sent to the Saint Dominic Provincial. This one, even though he was my enemy, replied that he had no reason by my conduct to mistrust me—that if I had said the denounced proposition, it would be some rashness: and as to the argument of the University, it had been a foolishness to accuse me, since arguing one does not speak properly. The Viceroy passed everything by the royal agreement, who advised that nothing was proved against me. And even more, His Excellency could warn that not even arguing should he speak on the conquest, because already one sees that one must not mention the noose in the house of the hanged man.

The Viceroy told me it with much secrecy and telling my Provincial (who was with me) that looking to preach of Hernan Cortés, there I could say things that might belie the species. The Viceroy added that in effect it was a beautiful occasion, and it would be well to praise the Kings, principally the current ones, for what has transpired in public, even though for the honor of the habit he had treated everything with stealth. The Saint Dominic Provincial did not keep it, as if he was my enemy, and nor does wine keep a secret. I did in the funeral prayer of Hernan Cortés what the Viceroy ordered me; but before I performed another diligence.

I had been amazed to see the case that had been made at a snap of the fingers against a man who had preached two complete sermons with the greatest enthusiasm in favor of the King. One was on Holy Sunday before the most Noble City, the day of the Mayor's election, the year that Castañeda came out elected, at the beginning of the French Revolution, impugning with every kind of arguments the famous declaration of the Assembly, or the Rousseau System. And the other, Easter Sunday of the Holy Spirit in the Cathedral the day after the news having arrived of the French Regicide, against he who I declaimed, taking as a theme that the obedience to the Kings was an essential obligation of Christianity. As this sermon was cheekier and was highly applauded, contributing much to the generosity of the donations that were made for the war against the French Republic, I took this and carried it to the Archdeacon Serruto, then Bishop elect of Durango. He certified that by the enthusiasm with which I said it, and by what he knew of me, he could assure that they were expressions from my heart.

Then I presented it to the Viceroy with a document in which I asked that he hear me, because nothing would turn my conscience against me, and upon similar themes did I agree to not leave even a stain. The Viceroy called me, and after telling me that the sermon was excellent, he assured me that there was no need to hear me; that I had come off perfectly innocent, if not, he would have punished me, so that by what occurred I had nothing to fear. With what soul then, with what conscience could Archbishop Haro accuse me before the King of those lawsuits, giving them for a motive as having trampled on his patronage, the canons, and the laws? Would he not precisely believe that I had come with some crime Against Majesty? Thus, it was that I was always treated as a defendant of the State, and after all I was accused as such, without any more basis nor proof than the said charged report from the Archbishop, and he almost made me die in a horrid prison, where if I survived life, I lost a sense of hearing, I left grey-haired, and every appearance of youth destroyed.

Oh Bishops, Bishops! Thou saith that thou art successors of the Apostles, and oh to God thou mightiest be always of their virtues, without that none proposeth for a model the wicked Apostle Judas Iscariot. The miter and the power that thou giveth the incomes, the poor of each Bishopric who extract a moderate support belong to rigorous justice they do not have to accompany thee beyond the tomb, except to make thee accept *a very hard judgement. Judicium durissimum his qui praesunt, fiet. Exiguo enim coceditur misericordia; potentes autem potenter tormenta sustinebunt. Non enim subtrahet personam cuiusquam Deus, nec verebitur magnitudinem cuiusquam;*

quoniam pusillum et magnum ipse fecit, et aequaliter est illi cura de omnibus. Fortioribus autem fortior instat cruciatio ("*But mighty men shall be mightily tormented. For he which is Lord over all shall fear no man's person, neither shall he stand in awe of any man's greatness: for he hath made the small and the great, and careth for all alike. But a sore trial shall come upon the mighty.*"). (Wisdom Ch. VI, verses 7, 8, and 9) [sic] [4]

And had I offended this Prelate in something? Never in my life, by thought, word, nor deed. From him, I had received newly professed the confirmation in his Oratory, and all the orders. Neither had he heard me, nor did he know me except in those occasions, of sight and in a crowd. But to be hated by this man in his anger to whom God had permitted to be our Pastor, it was enough to be a *gourd*, as he called us, this is, to be of his native sheep; and if this gourd shined for his talent, the abhorrence declined in fury, and the brilliant performance was made an object of his vengeance.

I have now announced the infernal machine that his hate constructed for my perdition. It remains to be told how his agents, enabled with his letters, caused it to explode, to obstruct, to corrupt the channels of justice, to stops me from its achievement, and to complete my ruin.

Chapter 7, Notes

1. King James Bible, Deuteronomy 19:15; *One witness shall not rise up against a man for any iniquity, or for any sin, in any sin that he sinneth: at the mouth of two witnesses, or at the mouth of three witnesses, shall the matter be established.*

2. King James Bible, I Corinthians 1:1; *Be ye followers of me, even as I also am of Christ.*

3. King James Bible, Apocrypha, Ecclesiasticus 10:13; *For pride is the beginning of sin.*

4. King James Bible, Apocrypha, Wisdom of Solomon 6: 6-8; *But mighty men shall be mightily tormented. For he which is Lord over all shall fear no man's person, neither shall he stand in awe of any man's greatness: for he hath made the small and the great, and careth for all alike. But a sore trial shall come upon the mighty.*

SECTION II

PORTUGAL, SPAIN, ENGLAND, AND AMERICA: DR. MIER'S ROAD TO HONOR

What thing is an Inquisition?
One crucifix, two candlesticks
And three big idiots
This is its definition.

by Fray Servando Teresa de Mier

.. (A)nd he came in this time to be the most popular man in
Mexico. (1821-1827)

Biography of Fray Servando Teresa de Mier Noriega y
Guerra, by José Eleuterio González

Introduction

Chapters 8, 9, 10, and 11 are translated from *Biografía del benemérito mexicano D. Servando Teresa de Mier Noriega y Guerra,* ("Biography of the Distinguished Mexican Don Servando Teresa de Mier Noriega y Guerra"), by José Eleuterio González, Monterey, Mexico 1876. Facsimile of the Original 1876 *Biografía* was published by the State of Nuevo Leon, Mexico, and the Autonomous University of Nuevo Leon upon the Sesquicentennial of the death of Father Mier 1827-1977.

González served as Governor of the State of Nuevo Leon: 1870, 1872-1873, and 1874. Governor González's biography of the last third of Fray Mier's life, 1805 to 1827, including Fray Mier'speeches and writings are not found in any prior English translation. Governor González gives credence to Fray Mier's *Apologia,* in defense of his Inquisition and prosecution, and adds a stamp of credibility to Fray Mier's December 12, 1794 sermon. Fray Mier is respected for his contribution to Mexico's liberty by a small circle of scholars— Mexican Catholic Clergy and Mexican Government Officials— even while he is so shrouded by a veil of secrecy that most Mexicans know nothing of their Mexican hero, Fray Servando Teresa de Mier.

Here is a summary of SECTION II, "Portugal, Spain, England, and America: Dr. Mier's Road to Honor." Chapter 8 translates writings of Governor González with quotes he attributes to other sources including Dr. Mier. Chapter 9 and 10 are speeches Dr. Mier delivers as an elected member of Mexico's First and Second Constituent Congresses. Governor González introduces his biographical writings on "Dr. Mier in Portugal, Spain, England, and America" with this note: "Dr. Mier concluded here the Memoirs of his life. It is to be regretted that something more will not go on, since nothing else is lacking except for twenty-two years of happenings to complete his interesting biography. In the following brief treatise, what one will see such an interesting subject that I could not have gathered without magnificent work."

Chapter 8

Dr. Mier Fights for Liberty and Equality

Poor and destitute, in truth, but content and satisfied for being far from the Toribios's house and in full enjoyment of his natural liberty, Doctor Mier finds himself in the Kingdom of Portugal, where he stays most of three years. For whatever reason the ancient ones had for formulating that celebrated maxim: *For the journey one must prepare those provisions that float with the shipwrecked person.* The talents and the knowledge of the famous Doctor were barely known when he encountered the remedy for his needs: Señor Lugo, Consul General of Spain, for whom Mier wrote a short outline in which are recorded the general rules of the consulates, appointed him to be his secretary. So, he could now live comfortably in Lisbon. Remembering his first vocation, which was to join the order of preachers to propagate the Catholic faith, and being in a country such as Portugal where there is an abundance of Jews, he dedicated himself to the teaching of Christianity's sublime dogmas, and with these laudable works he was able to convert to the faith of Christ and to baptize two renowned Rabbis with their families, for which the Supreme Pontiff Pius VII promoted him to be a Domestic Prelate, which appointment he received from the hand of Portugal's Papal Nuncio.

Meanwhile, the glorious Spanish revolution against the French erupted in May 1808. General Junot, who by order of Napoleon occupied the Kingdom of Portugal, disarmed and sent to prisons the Spanish troops that he had captured. Father Mier. sympathetic to the miserable luck and the shortages and tasks of those poor prisoners, lent them whatever services there were within his reach, serving them, helping them, and consoling them in whatever manner he could. Junot was defeated and forced to leave, by he who later became the Duke of Wellington. General Don Gregorio Laguna came to Portugal to recover the Spanish prisoners and knowing how much of a gift Father Mier had been to these poor men, he offered him a position in the army that was being organized in Spain to repel the French. Fray Mier accepted the offer. He went over to the Spanish provinces with General Laguna and was placed in the position of chaplain and army priest of Valencia's Battalion of volunteers.

Here Doctor Mier is already in campaign fighting against the terrible Napoleon; indeed, there could not have been anything more to his pleasure than to fight despots and tyrants, of whom he later said in the Mexican Constitutional Congress, that he would be able to die, but not to obey them. He carried out, indeed, very well his dangerous role of army priest. He found himself in many and terrible battles; he thrust himself into all the most hard-fought battles, helping and consoling the wounded, until in the battle of Belchite he fell prisoner in the hands of the French. He was carried off to Zaragoza, where for the influence of some officials he had known and dealt with in Paris, he came to be set free. But as he was of a very compassionate and naturally sensitive heart, and since he knew very well what prisons and tasks were, of course he gave himself to protecting and helping with all his strength his unfortunate companions, who still groaned in chains, for which the French, fearing the he might facilitate the escape of their prisoners, again put him in jail.

Some months later he managed to escape, and he went to where he found General Black to whom he presented himself, and this gentleman sent him to Seville very well recommended and asked the Central Assembly that in reward for the good services that Father Mier had given to the First Army, that he should be rewarded with a canonical position in Mexico City's Cathedral. Most had barely become aware of this affair when the Central Assembly dissolved itself leaving the Government of Spain to the Regency that was in Cádiz. There Señor Mier returned to following his aspirations.

Which he did in this city—as to how he happened to go to England and of his return to the Americas, his biographers, as well as the many that have written on the glorious expedition of General Mina, speak with much variety, all tell of the very diverse manner of things, in terms that have been impossible for me to reconcile. Fortunately, Doctor Mier himself, in the first discourse that he pronounced in the Congress, tells, although very briefly, what then happened. Thus, it is what I will be guided by that to which he himself refers, and of his cited discourse I will take what I am going to say in the paragraphs that follows.

In the year 1811, Doctor Mier presented himself before the Regency of Spain, asking that in reward for the services that he had given the First Army, that he might be granted a pension; the Regency acceded and assigned him three thousand pesos annually from the income of Mexico's Archbishopric; after no more than a few days, the Courts prohibited the pensions. The Regency, in order to substitute that which it had conceded to Father Mier, ordered that the Council of the Indies should nominate him for a Mexico City Cathedral canonical position. At this time, there was only one Prebendary vacancy, or half-ration, which was offered to him and he could not accept, because of the requirement that he preside over the choir in his capacity as the Pope's Domestic Prelate, but this was incompatible with being a Prebendary; and moreover, he decided to wait until another higher position might be vacated.

Meanwhile, the businesses of Spain had become much worst and the French positioned themselves to bombard Cádiz; and as Doctor Mier already had notice of the glorious uprising of the Priest Hidalgo and of the war that had begun in Mexico, he decided to go to London to defend through the press the rights of his native land. He stayed in England five years, and in those years wrote and gave to the London press his two writings: *Cartas de un americano al español en Londres* (*"Letters from an American in London to the Spanish"*), and his *Revolución de Anáhuac*, (*"Anáhuac Revolution"*). Additionally, he reprinted some short works of Father Las Casas.

In 1814 he returned to France and after some few months he returned to England. In London he met Mina and he agreed to join with him together with the Mexican Independents. To achieve this, they agreed to a treaty with some delegates of the United States, whose government was disposed to declare war on Spain in favor of the independence of Mexico. Mina and Mier came to Washington; but as the Attorney Herrera, Mexican Independent Minister, had not arrived, the United States Government did nothing and was limited to recommending them to Baltimore's commerce. There they were trying to raise a good expedition, when Don José Alvares de Toledo spread the notice of the Tehuacan Congress having been dissolved, which discouraged the businessmen and ruined the enterprise. Not without work, Señor Mier obtained one hundred twenty thousand pesos that his friend Mr. Daniel Smith loaned him, with which they were able to organize the small expedition that came to the coasts of Mexico.

Some authors put much weight on the extreme poverty of Doctor Mier in England; but the truth is, that he did things there that could not have been done without relying upon moderate resources, since it is evident that he had dedicated those years to writing, and he made many copious editions of the works that he then wrote. Of these important productions, perhaps the most celebrated is his *Historia de la revolucion de Anáhuac* (*"History of the Revolution of Anáhuac"*), which earned him the title of Member of the National Institute of France, which reading caused Fernando VII to remove Venegas from Viceroyalty and to name Calleja in his place. Don Cárlos María Bustamante says, the reading of this work also converted Iturbide from a Royalist into an Independent: this interesting work is very little known among us, because having bought almost the entire edition that was very copious, the Envoys of Buenos Aires took them to their country. It is sad that a reprint of this interesting history has not been made in Mexico, of which there are very few copies in this nation; in Philadelphia Doctor Mier printed *Memoria política instructiva* (*"Instructive Political Memoir"*), addressed to the Independent Leaders of Anáhuac, of which he sent six thousand copies, which were distributed in the nation with Mina's Manifesto. Coming to the Mexican coasts this General gave Doctor Mier the commission of going to survey Boquilla de Piedras, to seek for and put himself in communication with Victoria or some other independent leader; but the Doctor stayed in New Orleans because of the many strong storms and ordered the captain of the frigate in which he sailed to carry out the reconnaissance. It was verified that Boquilla de Piedras was occupied by Royalist troops. Knowing that Mina was in Galveston, Doctor Mier went to join up with him.

The first notice that Monterrey had of the Mina expedition is that contained in the following report. These original reports exist in the Government archive and because it appears to me to be of some interest, I insert it here.

The current 8th I left from Brazo de Santiago by way of the beach on course to the north to the Island of Corpus Christi, and at little more than two leagues I encountered a rowboat or harbor boat with a sail composed of pieces of calico and four oars inside, a very new and well-made English work, I was astonished to see it, because I believed these were the Táncahues Indians, and shouting: Who goes there? There came from those sand dunes three Blacks, and one Spaniard crying out to God for something to eat and giving thanks to the Most Holy Virgin because I had come upon them in that waste land, without knowing where they were, dying of hunger, that surely by the dawn of the 10th they would have been cadavers; asking them from where did they come they responded to me, that they had sailed from the island of Galveston on the night of January 13th for the love of their families, and that they were prisoners of Mr. Orí pirate or owner of corsairs who pursued the coast of Veracruz. The three Blacks were sailors from Bombarda and the White Captain pilot and owner of the Schooner, San Antonio Alian Buen Amigo, captured near Veracruz, some in August and the other in September. These same say that on that island there are two parties, the one Constitutional and the other of the Mexican Independence. Don Javier Mina defends the first, who has four hundred staff officers, a large train of artillery, mules and horses, rifles, etc., and he expects fifteen troop ships in that port. In this same party comes Don Servando Mier and they treat him as Bishop, his camp is in the middle of that of Mina, and the Colonel and the officers are from Navarra, Vizcaya, England, and other nations. By virtue of Mier's letter, they sent all provisions from Jamaica to the afore-mentioned Mina. The other is the Governor of that island, they made the payments by paper, even though they have much money and provisions from what they have stolen.

Mina treats this like a thief and pirate; but he tolerates it all because his troops have not arrived, and until now they keep up a friendly appearance; but they do not mingle with one another; this gives Orí so much fear he does not leave his barracks while Mina walks where ever he wants; this gentleman is much the politician. The infamous Gutierrez is of the Independence Party and is on the border of Sabinas or on its outskirts with one hundred or two hundred men. Orí supplies him provisions from the robberies that his privateers do. Captain Menchaca is of this same party and a few days ago he came upon that island with twenty men, all fugitive rebels form the Medina action. There are many others known whose names I do not recall; a short while ago these tyrants grabbed the frigate of a Señora from Veracruz who came loaded with indigo and other fruits for Spain, she carried twenty-seven thousand Royal pesos and they took her captive. On all the island there are no more than eight women including this Señora, no lodging, all are barracks; and men of both parties will be a little more than a thousand. The rebel

Orí intends to populate with the convicts that he has, he has much provisions, wines; liquor, codfish, ham, olives, chili peppers, goods, etc. He lacks nothing and all those on it are given rations; they do not dare leave for any reason, they are ignorant of where they will try their unloading.

I found the four individuals and I strengthened them by dint of hot water, meat, and necessities that I carried, caring for them the best that I could, since they were at the point of dying of hunger. They stayed alive with watercress without knowing where they were, until I led them to the Refugio, from where Captain Solis gave an account to the Government. The captain or owner of the Schooner says that it was easy to make a landing on the other side of these pirates' camp and to grab them, the island is seven leagues long. This individual is named Don José María Pose, a native son of Campeche, and the three Blacks from the same coast. It is what they have told me, and according to the reliability of this Captain all ought to be true and much more that I do not recall. — Cadereyta, Mexico, February 25, 1817 — Andres de Muguerza.

This Orí who is spoken of in the previous part was the Commodore Aury who met Mina in Galveston, ready to support the Independents; but he did not want to join them, and only gave him some aid for his intended expedition. There Mina organized his troops the best that he could and headed for Soto la Marina by counsel of a young man named Anselmo Hinojosa, a native of that villa, who assured them that from there they could easily communicate with the Independents; but this young man was in New Orleans since the age of ten and really did not know how things worked in his country. On April 15, 1817, they landed at the mouth of the Santander River and headed for the Soto la Marina villa, which is eighteen leagues up the river. Here General Mina ordered a fort built, to the east of the villa, at the edge of the river, to deposit in it his supplies and ammunition. The fort was built under the direction of Engineer Rigal and they put four canons from the ships, the campaign pieces, the howitzers, two mortars and all the armaments and munitions of muzzle and war that he could. Mina advanced, as is well known, toward San Luis through the Valle del Maíz to tempt fortune, leaving in the fort a hundred men at the command of Major Don José Sardá, with the order to resist until the end, promising them to return quickly to their relief if the enemy arrived at the site. Staying with Sardá in the fort were Dr. Don Joaquin Infante, from Havana, who filled the position of War Auditor, and Dr. Mier, who brought a printing press, on which he printed various papers to propel the revolution and among them a Papal Encyclical, which was principally directed to his kinsmen the Guerras, Garzas, and Treviños, designed to prove that in no way was Independence opposed to religion. A few days after the departure of Mina, Lieutenant Colonel Myers and Commissioner Bianchi had a falling out with Sardá and they left the fort with a few soldiers who wished to follow them. At another time the Italian Captain Andreas left with a party to look for wheat, and when he returned with twenty-seven loaded mules the party was attacked and destroyed by a party of Royalists, so that no one returned to the fort, leaving Andreas at the service of the King's troops. With these losses and with some more soldiers that had deserted, the fort's garrison was reduced to less than half of its beginning force.

The attack and surrender of the Soto la Marina Fort are spoken of with many variations by historians, but that which I prefer is what Don Manuel Cespedes, an eyewitness, says in his report of the campaigns of Arredondo to whom he was an Adjutant. So, he reports:

In April 1817 Arredondo knew that in Soto la Marina, the place of his General Command, Don Francisco Javier Mina had made a landing with an expedition. It was already known for some time before that the coasts of this his provinces were threatened. He ordered to attack it, but with so such pause in preparations and in his march, as one infers from the delay in arriving at the Marina, that there are no more than eighty leagues. The Viceroy Apodaca was exasperated: orders came and went to him, all more demanding that he flared up; but Arredondo on the pretext of having brought cavalry troops from the fortresses, did not hasten his pace. Finally, he left from Monterrey the beginning of May on the way to Linares, Real de Borbon, Padilla, and Santillana. Colonel Don Benito Armiño came with his regiment through Altamira: another party of cavalry from San Luis came to the Cojo Hacienda, and Fernando VII's line battalion came through Aguayo. With all the help of this superabundance of people: Mina with barely two hundred fifty foreign men with no knowledge of the country, outwitted all; he left the colony, passing the Sierra Madre and linked up probably with Mexicans of the northern plateaus. Arredondo did not pursue him and just headed to La Marina to take the fort constructed by Mina, who had already left with a very small garrison of troops with all their fleet and train of artillery.

Arredondo's division arrived at La Marina with the help of Fernando VII's Battalion that joined them in Padilla, and he put a kind of blockade around the fort, which Don José Sarda commanded by order of Mina. It grew stronger in four or five days with a battery of eight pieces that he managed to put within the firing range of a rifle on the night of June 14, and the following day because of fires and of all the troops that were approaching the fort from all directions, the assault was imminent. The fort surrendered about two in the afternoon by agreement. After a few days, the prisoners were dispatched to Altamira and from there to Veracruz. Doctor Mier was found in the fort accompanying the expedition, despite the agreement and the pardon promulgated days before by Arredondo himself, and made surety in his favor. Dr. Mier was remitted to Mexico with a pair of shackles, because it was said that he had wanted to corrupt a soldier assigned as sentry.

Don Lucas Alaman says that Arredondo attacked the fort with six hundred sixty-six infantry soldiers, one hundred-nine artillerymen and eight hundred-fifty horse cavalries, and there were thirty-seven who surrendered by agreement, a thing that much amazed Arredondo himself, but not even for this did he fulfill what was stipulated in the agreement.

While Doctor Mier was confined to prison, they ransacked his luggage and gathered all his books and papers, as well as his press. This as a useless thing, since no one there knew how to use it, and very many could not even imagine for what it could be used, and thus it was left in safekeeping for six years, until, as the selfsame Doctor Mier says in his first letter to Doctor Cantú, he commissioned Don Felipe de la Garza to bring it to Monterrey. In effect, he brought it and handed it over to the Government, to which it was of much service, for having been the first press that it had, since that which Arredondo brought in the year 1813, found among the booty gathered after the battle of Medina, was so small the it could barely print a quarter plate of paper. Doctor Mier's press exists even today in the printing office of the Government of Nuevo Leon, and it still works. The current director of the printing office, Accountant Viviano Florez, knows it well; and it would be very appropriate to mark it and conserve it as a historical monument of importance.

As soon as Doctor Mier's imprisonment was known in Monterrey and then by the ecclesiastical council, or rather Doctor Don José Leon Lobo who as Council Vicar governed the Bishopric in the vacant See, gave a mandate to Fray Don Joaquin Guzman, Priest of the small town of Cruillas, in order that he might proceed to gather an information summary on the conduct of Fray Servando Mier. Captain Andreas, an official surnamed Maxtinik, and a Franciscan Friar named Fray Manuel María Marin de Peñalosa testified as witnesses in this summary, the first two deserters from the Independent troops converted to Royalists and the last one carried out the service as Soto la Marina's priest.

Don Manuel Payno, who assures having had in sight this original summary, says that from it the following curious charges resulted: That Doctor Mier dressed in purple clothes;

that he heard the confession of a man named Máximo García who Mina had ordered executed by firing squad; that he preached a sermon in the Church saying, among other things, that the kings are the creation of men and not of God; that he granted indulgences; that he was of the family of His Holiness; that he conferred or omitted many words from the Mass' sacred music, doing part of the ceremonies of the Greek Church; that he wished that the Priest Fray Manuel Marin will celebrate with Castilian liquor for lack of wine; that he said that the Theology was a joining of absurdities with which children were deceived; that he expressed himself strongly against King Fernando, against tyranny, and in favor of independence and of liberty. "Therefore, this was the true offense, exclaimed Señor Payno, and the others were no more than supposed faults."

This curious summary concluded, Doctor Mier was sent with it to Mexico City by way of Huaxteca shackled and upon a horse with saddle and harness. His custody was entrusted to an escort of twenty-five men commanded by a Spanish official named Félix Cevallos, a very cruel man who treated the unhappy prisoner with great barbarity.

Mr. Payno gives an honest impression of that which the unfortunate Father Mier then suffered, and cites two interesting documents, from which I will here copy the following passage of his work cited in the prologue:

The brutal and barbaric mode with which the prisoners and defeated are always treated by the cruel military, is perfectly evident in the narrative done by the Doctor himself.

He says a bit, they put a pair of shackles on me and at eleven in the night they took me upon a horse with saddle and harness and an escort of twenty-five men. I leave to your consideration what I will have suffered with similar equipment and at an advanced age, in the intensity of the heat and the rains, even worst on pack mules, and passing a long time in the plaza of each town exposed to public shame. Human weakness prevailed, and I was very ill from fevers in

Huejulta.

This was a warning to my driver that being ill, with shackles, and being continuous fast-flowing, volatile, and abysses of the Sierra's rivers, I could not stop to break down or to die. Miraculously, as we say it, in six falls I received no personal harm; but in the seventh my right arm was horribly broken, and nevertheless, five days went by when without my getting better for lack of a doctor, I carry on isolated and locked up with shackles.

From Atotonilco el Grande the Doctor addressed a representation to the Viceroy, and from this document it appears that Doctor Mier was invited by Mina in London to make the voyage aboard his ship, that he accepted with the desire to return to his homeland, that both in New Orleans as in Texas and Soto la Marina, he had no other object but to communicate with his home. As one can guess none of this was true, but the Doctor coming into the claws of his enemies, had no other means to save his life than to ask for the grace of forgiveness and deny or apologize for having done damage.

Sick with fever, badly treated and with his arm broken, he suffered a thousand torments and pains, he continued on the way and on July 26 we find him in Pachuca, from where he wrote a letter to Doctor Pomposo, Fray of San Salvador, that we candidly copy because it completes the picture that he has proposed to draw.

Pachuca, July 26, 1817—Señor Don Agustin Pomposo— My dear and sweet friend: You are all my solace and my hope: from Huejtla in Huaxteca I wrote to you with a thousand anxieties and risks, because Captain Cevallos who led me was a hard-hearted man. In Atotonilco, another captain who is more charitable arrived from Mexico City to lead me, and this one has brought me up here, but the right arm broken, for which I cannot write; and to send a representation to the Lord Viceroy I have had to avail myself of a friend for being in solitary confinement. The petition or representation is full of blemishes. Good that it is going into your hands that will correct it, and by mail or your own hand you will deliver it to

His Excellence as soon as possible. Take notice that in this petition is all my hope against the storm that I await at any instance. Eight days ago, Captain Cevallos left for Mexico City loaded with papers and accusations against me. I fear some explosion before continuing the journey, and that since they keep me here. I fear they will take me to die in a prison cell in San Juan de Ulúa like the Fathers Subastegui and Talmantes. God free me from falling into these claws: already the commandant here has ordered that they keep me well locked up as I am, and I believe that only public opinion restrains them. Make many copies of my petition and distribute them so that they might be restrained from giving me a *Pax Cristi* (*"Peace of Christ"*). Give copies to my cousin Don Alejandro Treviño, to the City Councilors, and primarily to Rivero y Azcárate, to Father Pichardo, to Doctor Alcocer, to the Guadalupe Magistrate, Cisneros, to the Marchioness of Aguayo, and to Mother; they must make active inquiries and put up much outcry; in you I confide as my most dear and faithful friend. I am yours and I will always be, remembering to dear Mother and children. Even though you already know I cannot sign what I write you.

—Servando Teresa de Mier—

Doctor Don Agustin Pomoso Fernandez of San Salvador, who was always a loyal friend of Doctor Mier, did as many inquiries as were possible, helped by the rest of the illustrious prisoner's friends and relatives; but, despite all of this, as soon as Doctor Mier arrived in Mexico City, he was ordered imprisoned by the Inquisition. Even though the Inquisitors did not formulate a cause, they made him appear before the Tribunal and Doctor Tirado began by inquiring if he had a rosary, if he knew the Christian doctrine, and finally, he ordered that he say the Lord's Prayer. Father Mier answered him with fortitude: "These are asked of children I am a Doctor of Theology." Fortunately, at this time, the Holy Office was not now what it had been anciently, its primitive severity had been very much reduced, it was discredited and was now feared very little or not at all, now it had no brazier, now it did not use tortures, and it was more occupied in politics than in religion. With this our Doctor was slightly less wronged than what he could have been at other times: he was permitted to have some conveniences, to write, to provide him some books and to even have some communication with those outside. He was a prisoner there three years, and in them he wrote his *Apologia*, some other brief treatises and reproduced the literary correspondence that many years before he had had in Spain with the Chronicler Muñoz.

I remember having heard many times the late Don Manuel María de Llano telling the following anecdote, true or not is uncertain, but it does not lack humor. The first time that Doctor Mier asked permission to write in his prison, the jailkeeper brought him a sheet of paper and a very short pencil, telling him that the Holy Tribunal would allow him to write on that sheet, with the condition that what he wrote had to be reviewed and if it was appropriate it would be returned to him and if not, no. The Doctor took the paper and immediately wrote the following quatrain:

> *What thing is an Inquisition?*
> *One crucifix, two candlesticks*
> *And three big idiots*
> *This is its definition.*

Right away he signed and returned the paper to the jail keeper so that he could take it to the revision.

Reestablished in 1820, the Constitution dissolved the Inquisition Tribunal of the year 1812. Without waiting that an order be given to do so, ordered the prisoners that it had in the Court's jail and archive be passed to the Archbishopric.

A tribunal had been formed to judge Dr. Mier, as he said, *Hermaphrodite,* composed of the Viceroy and Don Félix Alatorre, Vicar of the Archbishop. While the Doctor was in the Inquisition, these gentlemen left the affair to sleep; moreover coming now to the Court's jail they wanted in some way to end their task, and without any form of justice and without hearing the accused, considering him pardoned since the agreement of Soto la Marina, they order him to be taken to San Juan de Ulúa, in order that there they could ship him and he could go to enjoy his pardon in Spain. The 18th day of July of the same year 1820 he left for Veracruz; as soon as he arrived, he was taken to Ulúa, and from there at the first chance that present itself, they shipped him to Cádiz. In Havana, he had the fortune of being able to escape and later he crossed over to the United States.

He stayed about a year enjoying his free will in the classic country of liberty, studying the republican system put into practice and the customs of one of the freest people of the world. Occupied in these studies, he found notice of the Independence of Mexico having been consummated by the triumph of the Plan of Iguala [1] and the entrance of the Triguarantor Army to the capital of Anáhuac. Since then, he now could not think of anything but his return to the homeland. And at the first opportunity that he had, he embarked for Veracruz, where he arrived February 1822. But he had barely stepped on the land so dear and so desired when the Commandant Don José Dávila apprehended him and led him prisoner to Ulúa Castle that was still in the domain of the Spanish.

Chapter 8, Notes

1. The Plan of Iguala established: Mexico's independence, primacy of Catholicism, and social equality.

Chapter 9

Dr. Mier's Speech the Day He Takes His Seat in the Chamber of Deputies in Mexico's First Constituent Congress, July 15, 1822 [3]

Mexico installed the first Constituent Congress February 24th, anniversary of the glorious pronouncement of Iturbide at Iguala; and Doctor Mier was elected Deputy to this august Assembly by the Province of Nuevo Reyno de Leon. The Congress energetically asked for its Deputy and did so with such force to get him out [of prison] that, in the end, Commandant Dávila turned him over. Don Francisco de Paula Arrangoiz says that it was then suspected that if Dávila put him free it was because he was considered as a new and powerful element against Iturbide, as in effect he was. In any case, now set free, Doctor Mier immediately departed for Mexico City. Iturbide had been crowned June 21st, and he arrived by the middle of the following July. Before presenting himself to Congress, he obtained an Emperor's Hearing in San Agustin de las Cuevas. In the July 15, 1822 session, Doctor Mier presented himself before Congress to take his seat, his credentials having been previously approved, and after the customary oath of office he delivered the following speech.

Señor.--I give thanks to Heaven for my having been restored to the bosom of the homeland at the end of 27 years of a most atrocious persecution and of immense labors: I give thanks to Nuevo Reyno de Leon, [2] where I was born, for having elevated me to the high honor of occupying a seat in this august Congress: I give thanks to Your Majesty for the generous efforts that you did to get me out of the claws of the

Ulúa tyrant; [3] and I give thanks to all my dear compatriots for the attentions and the applause with which you have received me and I am far from deserving. I would be overjoyed to have the talent and the instruction that are attributed to me to meet your concept and your expectations. What I certainly hold is an untarnished patriotism; my writings give testimony, and my broken right hand is irrefutable proof. And still, *si Pergama dextra defendi possent, etiam hac defensa fuissent* ("*If Pergama* [the fortress of Troy] *could be defended by a right hand, indeed it would have been defended by this.*").[4] I fear to have arrived late and that the remedies may be as difficult as the evils are grave. Nevertheless, the Emperor has done the favor of listening to me for two and a half hours and has promised that he will cooperate with all his effort to whatever means that may be proposed to him for the good of our homeland. I was alarmed by the existence of the national representation; but the Emperor assured me that everything said against it was slander, and that he was determined to sustain Congress as the best anchor of the Empire. I could not hide my feelings, obvious in my writings, and of that government that best suits us was the republican, under which all of South America is constituted and the rest of the North [America], but I also told him, that I could not nor would I want to oppose that which was already done, as long as we preserve the representative government and it may rule us with moderation and equality. Otherwise, he would lose, and I would be his irreconcilable enemy, because it is not in my hand to stop being against despots and tyrants. I would know how to die; but not how to obey them.

We should pray to God that He may inspire us to support, not only independence but also liberty. Turkey is independent, Barbary is independent, but their inhabitants are slaves. We do not want independence for independence, but independence for liberty. One ounce of gold is a very precious thing, but if he who gives it to me prohibits the use of it for necessary things, far from being a gift, it is an insult. We have not been eleven years staining the fields of Anáhuac with our blood to obtain a useless independence: liberty is what we want—and if it is not fulfilled, the war is still not concluded: all the heroes have not died, and defenders of the native land will not be lacking. [And, he added giving himself a blow to the chest.]

"Si fractus illabatur orbis,
Impavidum ferient ruinœ."[5]
("Should the whole frame of Nature round him break,
in ruin and confusion hurled.")

Today I will limit myself, Señor, to asking only for the restitution of my books, papers, maps, and doctoral insignias. The Mexicans in the year 1794 filled me with curses, believing that in a sermon I had negated the tradition of Our Lady of Guadalupe. They deceived them—such could not have crossed my imagination: I expressly protest that I preached to defend her and to highlight her.

What I preached was, that America, no more a sinner that the rest of the world, entered also into the plan of redemption of mankind, and that Jesus Christ, having sent his Apostles to announce it to every creature which is under heaven, in the whole world, unto the uttermost part of the earth,[6] expressions all from the Gospel. Precisely one ought to come even if to half the globe, to the large part of the world which is where we live; and since he who came to the Indians was called Saint Tomé, I said he was the Apostle Saint Thomas. This same has been the opinion of many very serious authors, even Archbishops, Bishops, and Cardinals, as I have demonstrated in my writings.

Consequently, I said that the Most Holy Virgin did not wait for one thousand six-hundred years to pass to be our Lady and Mother, but that she was since she began to be to all the Christians. The same Virgin in her first message, spoke thus to Juan Diego: *Thou shall say to the Bishop that the Mother of the true God sends thee, and that I desire that a temple shall be build unto me in this place, from where the Mother's ancient*

affections are shown that I conserve for the people of thy lineage.
What were the Mother's ancient affections that she conserved
to the linage of the Indians, if she had been watching them
brought down to sixteen centuries of hell, without throwing
them a glance of compassion until the apostles of the sword
came to kill them and to enslave them?"

At the end of my preaching, the Guadalupe Canons asked
me for the sermon to archive it as an erudite piece that did
honor to the Americas; but the City Counselors told me not to
give it to them because it would be printed. This was Friday,
and neither then, nor on Saturday was there any scandal or
new development. Moreover, the Spanish began to say that I
had intended to take from them the glory of their having
brought us the gospel: as if this glory was theirs and not ours.
Well, it was from our fathers: *gloria filiorum patres eorum* ("*The
glory of children are their fathers.*").[7] Also, the Spanish accused
me of thus ruining the rights of the King of Spain in the
Americas, founded on the preaching of the Gospel, as if the
Gospel of Peace and Liberty could be a title of dominion. With
this Señor Haro, who God had allowed, passes himself off in
his rage with the title of Pastor to our America, entirely on his
own without God or the devil, without my having been heard
or any charge made against me, he sent a decree to the
Churches that the preachers on the Sunday of the Festival of
Guadalupe must preach against me for having denied the
tradition.

> "... *Ex templo it fama per urbem,*
> *Fama malum, quo non velocius ullum*
> *Movilitate viget, viresque acquirit cundo*" [sic].[8]
> ("*Straightway throughout... the cities fly rumors;*
> *– the report of evil things than which nothing is swifter;*
> *it flourishes by its very activity and gains new strength by its*
> *movements...*")

The *mitote* fits the solemnity of the *teponaxtle*,[9] and the ulterior procedures were in accordance with the slander spread about. Fray Domingo Gandarias, Santo Domingo Provincial, was such a sworn enemy of the Americans, the same as the Archbishop: *Principes convenerunt in unum ("The rulers take counsel together.")*,[10] thus I was imprisoned against the privileges of the regular clergy. Because I asked to be heard, they took from me ink, paper, books, and communication. No more could have been done in Constantinople's bath. The Archbishop had printed an edict Sunday in *pasione* ("Palm Sunday") [11] of 1795, clandestinely so that it did not come to my attention. Nevertheless, it came around; I asked for a judgement to interpose an appeal of force on the Royal Court and it was denied to me. The edict was published the following day and it notified me of a sentence of ten years exile to the Peninsula, in seclusion the entire time in the Caldas Convent, which is in the desert, and perpetual disablement of all public teaching in cathedral, pulpit and confessional. The Inquisition, this monster of frying-pans and grills, could not have imposed a greater penalty upon a heretic convicted of such. They confiscated my goods, my library, and even the insignias of Doctor. Never has been seen a more complete stripping of liberty, honor, homeland, and goods: all was taken from me. Madrid's Royal Academy of History had to read this sentence up to five times because they could never come to believe its exorbitance; but not only was it excessive but unjust for lack of legal procedures, and null for the incompetence of the Archbishop about a common exemption, to one who is not accused of heresy. He found himself awaiting his confirmation of the two appeals that the Viceroys had made on my behalf, because I desired the liberty of my homeland. Patriotism in me is not a new thing, and all the clamor that drives it, and the sentence the Archbishop gave, was no more than anti-Americanism in its delirium and rage.

I turned to the King, who ordered the Council of the Indies to hear me, and it consulted with the Royal Academy of History, that was then perhaps the wisest body of the nation, and which examined the subject eight months, almost exclusively. Finally, it responded that I had not negated the tradition of Guadalupe, nor in my sermon had there been anything worthy of censor or of a theological note: that all the proceedings in Mexico were illegal and unjust, and all a work of envy and other passions. That the Archbishop had exceeded all his powers, and his edict was an inflammatory foolish fanatical libel, most unworthy of a prelate, therefore he ought to retire, the orator to be indemnified as asked in honor, homeland, and goods, and put under the shield of the laws against his persecutors.

The Council's Most Distinguished Public Prosecutor consequently asked that the Archbishop be reprimanded, that he be fined, his edict be recalled that he should return me to the homeland with all honor at the expense of the Public Treasury. He should reinstate to me all my honors and goods, indemnifying me of all my damages and sufferings at the expense of my persecutors.

My triumph was complete; but because of the death of the Archbishop and other incidents the sentence was not carried out. I demanded before the Regency of Spain in the year 1811 asking for a pension, it set up for me three thousand pesos out of Mexico's Office of the Archbishop. But as later the Courts prohibited the pension, the Regency ordered the Chamber of the Indies to consider putting me first in line as a Canon or Dignitary of Mexico City's Cathedral; General Black in agreement had already asked this of the Central Council by reason of my services done since the beginning of the war in the First Army. There had not been a vacancy except for a half–prebendary that was offered to me, and I could not accept, because having to preside over the choir as Domestic Prelate of the Supreme Pontiff, was not compatible with being a half-prebendary.

While a major plaza was vacated, Spain ends up losing; Cadiz was to be bombarded; the Shout of Liberty had resonated in my homeland, and in order to defend it, I withdrew to London; I wrote and printed the first and second *Carta de un americano al español en Londres* (*"Letter from an American to the Spanish in London"*); [13] I did the first reprint of Casas, which I later repeated in Philadelphia with a more extensive prologue, and gave birth in two volumes, 4th the *Historia de la revolucion de Anáhuac ó Nueva España* (*"History of the Anáhuac or New Spain Revolution"*). [sic] [14]

General Mina and I came from London after a treaty made with representatives of the United States Government that had resulted in declaring war on Spain in favor of Mexico's independence. It had not been verified when we arrived in North America, because Mexico's Minister had not presented himself in Washington. But the Government recommended us to Baltimore's commerce, and we were raising a brilliant expedition, that since then would have given liberty to the homeland, when the notice spread by Toledo of the Congress of Tehuacan having dissolved, completely ruined us. Only from my friend Master Daniel Smith could I obtain the loan of a hundred twenty thousand pesos, and with this we engaged the small expedition with which Mina and I disembarked at Soto La Marina. I wish to God that that young man of 26 years, as educated to be generous and valiant, would have followed my counsels! The homeland would have been free from that time, and he would not have died at the side of so many illustrious young men who accompanied us. Mexican gratitude will not permit his laurels be kept buried."

We who remained in the Soto la Marina Fort, having defended ourselves until no more could be done, surrendered with very much honor, and one of the conditions was the conservation intrigue of our baggage. Nothing came true to us; and Arredondo's military guard stole my valuable baggage: he could not load three chests of my books and Arredondo carried them away, from whom I grabbed them earning me the Inquisition. For this I was led away in shackles and an escort of twenty-five men, by the path of birds over the Sierra, a Caribe European named Felix Cevallos, who appears to have had an order to kill me by force of insults, affronts, and maltreatments. At every turn he threatened to shoot me, according to his instructions, and he wanted to do it on Las Presas only because I told him that it was not an affront to suffer for the homeland. It is great that I could have escaped from this tiger with only a broken arm. But Your Majesty should know that this European, nevertheless, for having opposed Independence, is our disgrace, a Grenadier Captain in Saltillo, and he has posted on his sheet of service, by one insignia, to have conducted a prisoner, the apostate Mier, to Mexico City.

The Government had no shame to raise me in their gazettes, this apostasy after 17 years of being secularized, the same Supreme Pontiff being my benevolent investigating official. Hypocrites, without shame, discredit the defenders of the homeland. Who has now removed this apostasy from a representative of the Nation?

Señor, in the Inquisition, where I was trapped three years, I wrote of my life, I believe on a hundred sheets, beginning since my 1794 sermon until my 1805 entry into Portugal: I reproduced the literary correspondence that I had since Burgos with Don Juan Bautista Muñoz, Royal Chronicler of the Indies, and I wrote various other treatises. All this with my three chests of books and various documents that I presented to the Inquisition when I entered that were passed on to the Archbishop when it was put to an end.

As many will desire to know the true cause for which I was in the Santa de la Vela Verde dungeons, Your Majesty has permitted me the reading at the least a bit of the letter that the Inquisitors wrote to their accomplice Apodaca the 26th day of May 1820; it is to say, when the Minotaur was giving unrepentant last gasps. The piece is authentic, public, and was printed in the *Noticioso* of Havana the 17th day of September of the same year.

Fray Servando, (says the dean, because he treated me as an apostate friar to please Apodaca, even though in their own prison they treated me as Monsignor, according to who I am), is the most harmful and fearful man of this Kingdom of the many they have known, he is of a haughty, arrogant and presumptuous character: he possesses a vast education in evil literature, he is of a hard temper, lively and audacious, his uncommon talent moreover gives him a great facility to foment action. His heart is so corrupted, that far from having manifested in the time of his imprisonment some variation of ideas, we have received nothing but proofs of a shameful obstinacy. He still retains an inflexible vitality and a tranquil spirit, superior to his misfortunes. In a word, his force and dominant passion is revolutionary independence that disgracefully he has inspired and fomented in both Americas, by means of his writings filled with poison and venom. The adjunct work in two volumes, (The History of the Revolution of New Spain) that with other documents accompany Your Excellency, and the reading of which the Tribunal has seen fit to deprive even to those who have permission to read prohibited books, will of course give to Your Excellency the most exact idea of the character of this man, and that of most interest is the security of his persona for the public tranquility, the good of the religion, and of the State. All of which I put to the superior knowledge of Your Excellency by order of this Tribunal. — Antonio Peredo.

Behold that which occupied what was called the Holy Tribunal of Faith—to punish us because we wanted the independence of our homeland. I have read this letter so that you may see what my offense was, and you should not believe that I was there for some religious offense. I have defended it against the incredulous, Jews, and heretics. For having challenged Volney, who denied the existence of Jesus Christ, I was given the Paris Parish of Saint Thomas. For having converted two celebrated Rabbis with their families, the Supreme Pontiff promoted me to be his domestic prelate. I was already a Prothonotary Apostolic.

What I most admire is, how the Inquisitors had the nerve to prohibit the aforementioned history, without my having heard an authorized vow, not only a law of Cárlos III, but also

Benedict XIV's Bull *Si licita et provida* [sic].[15] When they told me that their officials had found my history injurious to the Inquisition and to Alejandro Borja, I responded they were two monsters against whom libel could not fit; and I asked for a copy of the censure in order to contest it.

The most amusing is, that Fernando VII having read such history and ordered the malicious [Juan López] Cancelada, held as prisoner (that by my count was two-and-a-half years) sent by means of his Ambassador in London to buy at whatever price several copies to distribute in his Court. The same history was the motive for the celebrated Bishop Gregoire, Baron de Humboldt supporting it, putting me forth as a member of the National Institute of France; the supreme literary honor in Europe.

We must disillusion ourselves Señores, the Inquisition was no more than a police tribunal, and the Inquisitors a few pimps of despotism. The term is not noble; but it was no more than a vile and anti-evangelical depository of political gossip, accusations, and espionage, all hypocritically covered with the secret oath and sacred veil of religion. They were a few Freemasons of bad lineage as I told you.

The night of July 18, 1820, that I left Mexico City for Veracruz, I reclaimed my books, my papers, and documents that the Inquisition had passed on to the Archbishop: the Viceroy officially informed the Archbishop, and his Vicar Don Felix Alatorre responded that my documents and papers were necessary for my case. However, of the books, a few were prohibited even for those that have a license to read them, others needed to be expunged, and the rest were exempt from delivery. The list was passed on to Doctor Carrasco of the Santo Domingo Convent for him to sweat over.

As for the first thing, I responded to Señor Alatorre from San Juan de Ulúa that my case was purely political, and that having been united said Vicar General to the Viceroy in a hermaphrodite Tribunal and of his creation against the Constitution. In order to send me off without hearing me to

Spain to enjoy my pardon, I did not even know what the Archbishop had to do with me; especially my not being subject except to the Supreme Pontiff, as a prelate of his household, And as to my books, I asked if the barbarous expurgatory of the extinct Inquisition still rules, how with some evil books has it prohibited many excellent ones, and buried the Nation in ignorance? The Courts of Spain in similar proceedings have reprimanded ecclesiastic vicars of Spain and ordered that books could not be prohibited except those that might have been by the same Courts. My documents evidence that I have a license from the Supreme Pontiff to read all kinds of books without exception, as I am a known controversialist theologian, and nevertheless, I did not bring more than two or three prohibited books, precisely because I was challenging them; and the Inquisitor Tirado, with the challenge in hand told me that it does me much honor. How does one challenge the evil books without reading them? How does one combat the enemies of religion without knowing their weapons? These are evident injustices.

Therefore, I ask Your Highness, order the prelates of Santo Domingo to return my library and my doctoral insignias to me. Moreover, it was already ordered by the Council of the Indies, because of the dispute that I won, that they return my goods to me; my library had nothing to do with those priests. Since my youth I had them, and I had bought them with money from my family. To my family and not to the friars, I owe that which I spent for the doctoral degree. The Archbishop's sentence should not have fallen upon my goods; and thus, the priests ought to return them to me, or if they have disposed of them, they should pay me their total cost.

Second, I ask that you order my baggage stolen in Soto la Marina be returned to me, whatever can be found; and I am informed that in the Secretary of the High Court, today resident in Saltillo, exists a beautiful map of North America designed by [Aaron] Arrowsmith, divided into two parts that cost me very dearly.

Third, I ask that you order the Archbishopric's Vicar General return to me all my books, papers, documents, and manuscripts, principally those that I have mentioned written in the Inquisition, according and as appears on the lists that has passed to him, and if he has something to expound on these books etc. tell me and I will listen. If the Vicar General has lost anything, or the Inquisitors, they can gather it, and they must return it to me, or they must pay me for it. I know that some of my papers were passed to the Government or their petty officers; I have heard that many of mine ended up in the control of the quartermaster. It will serve Your Highness to order that they return to me all my things in whatever control they may be found, and I plead to you, pardon me for having interrupted your serious businesses with such a long exposition.

Governor José Eleuterio González Writes —

From the beginning of this speech, one sees what Dr. Mier's opinion was on the form of government that he believed suits us. He could not hide his feelings, and when he presented himself to the Emperor, neither did he wish to give him the title of Majesty nor did he hide from him his desire that Mexico should become a Republic. In Congress he always sustained the same ideas and he worked all he could so that the Nation could be free and republican. He contributed more than anyone to spread the opinion for republicanism, which brought about Iturbide's animosity to whom, finally, he was his most fervent enemy, as he had promised him. Dr. Mier highly condemned Itrubide's acts of despotism and tendencies of absolute power, he ridiculed his consecration and coronation, saying with much humor and greater malice, that the consecration of the kings was the application of the medicine called *The Four Thieves' Vinegar*. He also mocked the clothes, insignias, and ceremonies of the Guadalupe Order, comparing them to a company of ridiculous theatrical extras, called *Huehuenches*, with which the Indians were accustomed to solemnizing their festivals, for which for many years the Knights of Guadalupe were known by the burlesque nickname *Los Huehuenches*.

The 28th of August [1822] a conspiracy of the Republicans against the Emperor was discovered, and the latter believing that some Deputies took part in it, gave a verbal order to Don Luis Quintanar to apprehend them, among them Doctor Mier, and to take them prisoners to the Santo Domingo Convent, whose Provincial Carrasco had Iturbide's great confidence. On this same night, Quintanar carried out the order. From his prison, Father Mier continued satirizing Iturbide and preaching republicanism in whatever manner he could. In December of that year, the revolution erupted in Veracruz led by Santana proclaiming the Republic, which is why the care of the prisoners was redoubled. Doctor Mier fearing some misbehavior by the Imperialists sought to flee and he achieved it, leaving from among the guards without being recognized, dressed with the habit of Father Marchena; but, to his misfortune, he went to hide in the home of some nuns, who for conscientious scruples and counseled by a Filipino Father, denounced him, and he was again apprehended and taken by twelve grenadiers to the Court's jail, where they put him in a cell called *Oblivion*. At the end of some time, they took him from there and took him to the Inquisition's ancient building. Here it appears that High Providence, sympathetic to the miserable luck of the persecuted Doctor, decided that this would be the last time that he would lose his liberty, and that now he would be permitted to enjoy in peace the last years of his unfortunate life. It was announced February 11, 1823 that a body of troops of Mexico City's garrison by Santana's design and taking Doctor Mier from prison they put him at liberty, and now he never returned to be a prisoner. He left the City and joined with a party of patriots who fought against the tyrant. In his first letter to Monterrey's Provincial Council with much emphasis he says: "When I entered

Toluca, because my troop shouted *Republic*, the garrison resorted to their weapons." When Iturbide, stunned with the frenzy that he had caused and giving a proof of his weakness, he again convened the same Congress that he had dissolved, reinstating it, as he did the 20th of March, Doctor Mier hurried and came to occupy his Deputy's seat. Before this Congress, Iturbide abdicated the crown. Señor Mier defended, with all the vehemence of his character, that in no way should the tyrant be banished, but condemned to death; to cut the evil root, to assure peace and to take away any other ambitious person the hope of realizing his intentions. The contrary opinion prevailed, and Iturbide was banished; shortly thereafter this same Congress issued a decree declaring him outside of the law.

Chapter 9, Notes

1. The speech, first published by Manuel Payno in: *Vida, aventuras, escritos, viajes del Dr. Servando Teresa de Mier*, Mexico D.F., Imprenta Abadiano 1856.

2. Doctor Mier was born in Monterrey, Nuevo Reyno de Leon. Monterrey is the capitol of Mexico's State of Nuevo Leon.

3. February 23, 1822, Mier falls as a prisoner of General José García Dávila, Royal Commandant of San Juan Ulúa Castle, Veracruz, Mexico. While a prisoner in the Castle, he writes *Exposición de la persecución que he padecido desde el 14 de junio de 1817 hasta el presente de 1822*. March 5 and 15, Mexico's First Constituent Congress discusses and votes to demand that General Dávila release Fray Mier.

4. *"If Pergama* (the fortress of Troy) *could be defended by a right hand, indeed it would have been defended by this."* —Virgil, *Aeneid II*. Fray Mier's Latin, with no Spanish translation while waving his broken right hand before Mexico's Constituent Congress, clearly shows he is a scholar not a politician.

5. *Should the whole frame of Nature round him break, in ruin and confusion hurled.* Horace, Odes, 3. 3. 7-8), This is an ancient metaphor of

the falling sky.

6. King James Bible; Colossians 1:23, Matthew 26:12, Acts: 1:8 are the sources of the translation. These verses in the Reina-Valera Biblia most closely match Fray Mier's Spanish. Fray Mier probably translated from a Latin Bible to Spanish. There are other New Testament verses with verisimilar language. What is most noteworthy is Fray Mier cites Bible scripture and testifies to Mexico's Constituent Congress that the Gospel of Jesus Christ was preached by Apostles to every part of the earth, even unto America.

7. King James Bible; Proverbs 17:6; *The glory of children are their fathers.*

8. *Straightway throughout... the cities fly rumors; – the report of evil things than which Nothing is swifter; it flourishes by its very activity and gains new strength by its movements...* —Virgil, Aeneid, IV, 173.

9. *Mitote* is an ancient round dance of the Aztecs, also a Toltec dream ceremony. *Teponaxtle* is a Mesoamerican drum.

10. King James Bible; Psalms 2:2; *The rulers take counsel together.*

11. *"In pasione"* is Palm Sunday, the Sunday before Easter, the beginning of Holy Week.

12. Prebend is a stipend paid to clergy or canon by a cathedral or collegiate church. A prebendary is a Roman Catholic clergy or canon receiving a prebend.

13. The Second letter is translated and published in *Christianity in the Americas Before Columbus*, Gary Bowen, in Chapter 4, "Eleventh Note of the Second Letter from an American, On the Representation to the Courts from the Consulate of Mexico, by Fray Servando Teresa de Mier."

14. Fray Mier references two volumes of works by Bishop Bartolomé de las Casas (1484-1566), while titling it *4th Volume, The History of the Revolution of Anáhuac or New Spain.* Fray Mier much admired Bishop de las Casas. Both were Dominican Friars. Bishop Casas was born in Spain, 279 years before Fray Mier was born in New Spain. Bishop Las Casas, one of the earliest emigrants to the Americas, became the first Bishop of Chiapas, New Spain. Las Casas like Mier traveled back and forth between Spain and the Americas. Bishop Casas's chronicles on the first decades of the colonization of the West Indies, Venezuela, Guatemala, and Mexico focused on the atrocities the Spanish committed against the native peoples. His pro-Indian policies and activist religious

stance earned Bishop Las Casas the title "Protectorate of the Indies." Bishop Las Casas criticized the Spanish colonial encomienda system as slavery, and the forced conversion of the Indians to Christianity as a denial of their free will. Bishop Casas, like Fray Mier, had his critics. The most quoted is the Franciscan Fray Toribio Motolinia who excoriated Las Casas in his "History of the Indians of New Spain" written 1540. Fray Mier's publication of Bishop Casas's writings evidences that Fray Mier was a disciple of Bishop Casas's ethics, humane policies, political freedom, legal rights, religious free will, and belief of Christianity in Ancient America.

15. Fray Mier probably references Pope Benedict XIV's, July 9, 1753 Bull, *Sollicita ac provida*, which set standards for investigating, condemning, and censoring books.

Chapter 10

"Prophecy of Doctor Mier on the Mexican Federation" Delivered to Mexico's Second Constituent Congress, December 13, 1823

In Doctor Mier's letters, directed to the Deputation and to Doctor Cantú, one sees how much he worked in Congress to establish the republican regime. The Deputies met in his house and discussed the basics, they wrote the plans in his house, in his house they spread the sentiments and studied them and resolved the doubts. He initialed, supported, and obtained, in order to better prepare the Nation to receive a representative and popular government, that established Provincial Deputations in the provinces that did not have them, that in all things the military headquarters would be separated from the political leadership, that in place of the Deputations they then put in place Provincial Congresses, before dealing with the Constitution; and that in all parts they organized the governments with the greatest amount of authority. This Congress declared in session, contrary to Doctor Mier's opinion, and expedited the official announcement for a new Constituent Congress. Dr. Mier worked hard in the elections to assure that the wisest men and best patriots came through elected. He, himself, was re-elected by Nuevo Leon, and his works in this Second Congress were no less assiduous or less useful than in the First. All the Deputies were Republicans, all wanted the federation; and nevertheless, they formed two parties within the Congress: the few led by Doctor Mier wanted a federation somewhat centralized, in which the general government would stay with more power than the provinces, so that the people would not pass suddenly from a government of absolute monarchy to the most liberal possible, which is to make a sharp turn from the darkness to the light: the others, led by Doctor Ramos Arizpe, wanted to have a federation even more lax than that of the United States of America. The 13th of December 1823, the 5th Article of the Constituent Act was discussed—Doctor Mier pronounced the following speech that was printed and reprinted with the title of: *Prophecy of Doctor Mier on the Mexican Federation.*

Señor: (Before beginning I say that I am going to challenge the 5th Article, that of a federated republic in the sense of the 6th, that proposes a joining of sovereign and independent States. And thus, it is indispensable that I touch upon this; what I warn so that I am not called to order. When it deals with discussing without passion the most important matters of the homeland, to subject one trivially to rituals would be to let the means become the end.) No one, I believe will doubt my patriotism. My writings in favor of America's independence and liberty are known; my long sufferings are public, and I bear the scars on my body. Others will be able to claim services to the homeland equal to mine, but none greater, at least of its kind. And with all this, I have asked for nothing, and they have given me nothing. And after 60 years, what do I have to hope for but the tomb? Assisting me, therefore a right, so that when I speak of what ought to decide the fate of my homeland, one may believe me unselfish and impartial. I can error in my opinions this is man's heritage; but you will have done me a great injustice to mistrust the purity and rectitude of my intentions.

And will you be able to doubt my republicanism? During the Imperial regime, almost never did a paper come to light in which I was not reproached for the crime of republicanism and of being the republicans' spokesperson. It would not be much of a move forward if I told you that six thousand copies of my *Memoria política-instructive* ("*Instructive Political Memoir*") [1] were scattered in the nation, written from

Philadelphia to Anáhuac's independent leaders, in it, they spread the idea of the republic that until the other day was confused with heresy and impiety. And it was hardly legal to utter the word "republic," when I stepped forward to establish the federate into one of the foundations of the constitution project ordered circulated by the previous Congress.

Permit me to here note, that even though some provinces have boasted of having obliged us to take this step and to publish the convocation letter, they are deceived. The tyrant barely brought down, Congress was reinstalled, when I convened at my house a large meeting of Deputies, and I proposed to them the declaring of a republican form of government, as various Deputies had already put forth asking for it in formal arguments. And left around the government, so that it could be addressed, the flower of the liberals, a provincial Senate, the rest withdraw convening a new Congress. All received my proposition with enthusiasm and wanted to do it the next day in Congress. There are various deputies in their hearts of those who concurred and can serve me as witnesses. But the circumstances were then so critical for the Government that some of its members trembled to see themselves deprived of a moment of the lights, the support, and prestige of the national representation. It was for this reason that we resolved to work immediately on a project of constitutional foundations, which gives testimony to the nation that if until then we had resisted to provide a constitution, even though Iturbide demanded it of us, it was to not consolidate his throne, but later that we might come to liberate ourselves and to liberate the nation from the tyrant. We could have dedicated ourselves to fulfil the task of creating it. A commission of my friends named by me that later ratified the Congress, worked in my house for eighteen days on a project of foundations that did not come to be discussed because the provinces began to shout that we lacked the faculties for creating the nation. Say what you wish, in that project there is much wisdom and common sense; hopefully the nation will not someday throw it away.

It has censured us from proposing a federal government real in name and central. I have heard the same criticism made of the new commission's constitutional project. But why, is there not more than one way to become federated? There is a federation in Germany, there is one in Switzerland, there was one in Holland, there is one in the United States of America. In each part there has been, or it is different, and it could even have been one of other various manners. Whatever may be most suitable to us *hoc opus, hic labor est ("This is the task, this is the labor").* [2] I am going to spin my speech around this subject. The old commission opined, and still does I believe, that the federation and the principles ought to be very compact, by so being more analogous to our manners and customs, and more appropriate for the war that threatens us, until the passage of these circumstances in which we need much union, and progressing in the race of liberty, we can without risk let go of the baby-walkers of our political infancy until arriving at the height of social perfection that has so much captured our attention in the United States.

The prosperity of this neighbor republic has been, and it is, the trigger of our Americas so that the immense distance that comes up between them and us has not been weighted enough. They were already, one from another, separate and independent States and they federated themselves to unite against the oppression of England. To federate ourselves being united, is to divide ourselves and to bring upon us the evils that they sought to remedy with this federation. They had lived under a constitution that by only deleting the king's name is that of a republic: we bowed 300 years under the yoke of an absolute monarchy; we were barely able to take a step without a stumble in the unknown study of liberty. We are like children who have barely had their bandages removed, or like slaves we end up kicking off chronic chains. That one was a new people, industrious homogeneous, laborious, learned, full of social virtues, as educated by a free nation; we are an old people, heterogeneous, without industry, enemies of work and wanting to live from investments like the Spanish, as ignorant in the general mass like our parents, and infested by the vices connected to three centuries of slavery. That one is a tough, tenaciously brainy people; we are a nation of capricious persons, if I may be allowed this expression, as alive as quicksilver and as fickle as it. Those States form at the seashore a coastal strip and each one has the ports necessary to their commerce; among us only in a few provinces are there a few ports or anchorages, and nature itself, so to speak, has centralized us.

What tires me is indicating to Your Sovereignty the enormous difference of the situation and circumstances that has been and there is between us and them, to deduce from there that their same federation cannot suit us, even if the experiment has already been demonstrated to us in Venezuela, and in Colombia. Bedazzled as are our provinces with the prosperous federation of the United States, they imitated it to the letter, and they lost. Streams of blood have flowed ten years toward byway of recovering and standing up, leaving laying in the sand almost all your wise men and all your white population. Buenos Aires followed your example; and while it was involved in the whirlwind of its interior tumult, the federation's fruit, the King of Brazil with impunity seized the major and best part of the Republic. Will all these events be lost on us? Can we not learn out of the head of our brothers from the South, until the lightning thunderclap falls upon ours, when already our evils have no remedy, or could it be very costly to us? The cautious ones have centralized: will we throw ourselves without fear to the sea of our misfortune, and will we imitate them in their error in place of imitating them in their repentance? To want from the first attempt at liberty to even rise to the peak of social perfection, is the craziness of a child who intends to make himself a perfect man in one day. We will exhaust ourselves in the effort; we will succumb under a load unequal to our strength. I do not know how to adulate, nor do I fear to offend, because the fault is not ours, but of the Spanish; but it is certain that in most of the provinces there are few apt men to send, to the General Congress; and they want to have them for the Provincial Congresses, executive and judicial positions, city councils, etc. etc. The Provinces are not able to pay their Central Congress Deputies; and they want to assume the whole train and the enormous weight of the employees of sovereignty!

And what do we have to do, will he answer back to us, if they want it like this, so they ask for it? Tell them what Jesus Christ said to the ambitious sons of Zebedee: *Ye know not what ye ask: Nescitis quid petais.* [3] The peoples call us their fathers, let us treat them as children who ask what is not suitable to them: *Nescitis quid petais.* "One needs courage," says a wise politician, "to oppose an entire people, but at times it is necessary to go against their will to better serve them." "Reach out to their representatives to enlighten them and direct them about their interests or be responsible for their weakness." The people need to be led, not to obey. Deputies are not their errand boys, who have come here at such cost and from such long distances to present the ticket of our masters. For such a low office there were more than enough footmen in the provinces or halls of Mexico. If the people have chosen men of letters and integrity to send them to deliberate in a General Congress on their dearest interests, it is so that gathering the intelligence in the meeting of so many wise men we decide what best suits them—not so that we servilely follow the provincials' short-range goals restricted by their territories. We come to the General Congress to put ourselves as upon a watchtower, from where seeing far off the whole nation, we can provide with better discernment its universal well-being. We are their arbitrators and representatives not their errand boys. Sovereignty resides essentially in the nation, and not putting your Deputies to be elected in mass, the election is distributed through the provinces; but once verified, they are no longer the elected deputies precisely of such or such province, but of all the nation. This is the axiom recognized by many publicists who have dealt with the representative system. Otherwise, the Deputy from Guadalajara could not legislate in Mexico City, or the one from Mexico City to determine the affairs of Veracruz. Yes, since we are all and each one of the Deputies from the whole nation, how can a fraction limit the powers of a General Deputy? It is an absurdity, for not saying a usurpation of the sovereignty of the nation.

I have been astonished to hear some gentlemen from Oaxaca and Jalisco say they are not free to vote as their conviction and conscience suggests, that having limited their powers, they are not envoys or representatives of the sovereignty of their provinces. In truth, we have received them here as Deputies, because the election is who gave them the power, and gave it to them for all the nation; the role one abusively calls power, is no more than a constancy of their legitimate election the same way as the ordination is what gives the priests the faculty of confessing. What one calls a license is no more than a testimony of their aptitude to exercise the faculty they have by their character. Here from God. It is a known rule of law, that every absurd or contradictory or illegal condition that is imposed by whatever power, or contract, etc., annuls it and irritates, or ought to be considered as not set. It is thus that I have proven that the restriction set by a province on the powers of a Deputy of the entire nation is absurd. So, it is contradictory, because the Constituent Congress implies with foundations already constituted whatever they may be, as a federated republic is already determined in these limited powers. So, it is illegal, because in convocation's decree, all restriction is prohibited. Then or the powers that they bring to it are void, and those that have come with them ought to then come forth from Congress, or ought to be considered as not set, and those Deputies remain in full liberty to vote with the others without any impediment. I do not reach the solid response one ought to give to this argument.

But returning to our issue: is it true that the nation wants a federated republic and on the terms that the 6th Article tries to present to us? I would not want to offend anyone; but it appears to me that some intellectuals in the capitals, foreseeing that because of the same, the orders and the duties of the provinces will fall on them, they are the ones that want this federation and have made the people say that they want it. Some noble Deputies have engaged in proving the provinces want a federated republic; but no one has proven nor will ever prove that they want a species like an Anglo-American federation, and more than Anglo-American. How have the people desired that which they do not know? *Nihil volitum quin præcognitum* ("*Nothing is desired that is not first known*."). [4] Call one-hundred men, I do not say from the countryside, nor from the towns where there are those who barely know how to read, nor who even exist in the Anglo-American world, the same in Mexico, from these galleries make them bring down one-hundred men, ask them what breed of animal is a federated republic, and I give my neck if they do not respond with thirty thousand foolish remarks. And this is the pretended general goodwill with which you want us to take communion like children! This numerical general goodwill is a sophism, a mere sophism, a sophism that one can say was condemned by God when he says in the scriptures: "*Thou shalt not follow a multitude to do evil; neither shalt thou speak in a cause to decline after many to wrest judgement*." "*Ne sequaris turbam ad faciendum malum, nec in judicio plurimorum acquiescas sententiæ, ut á vero devies*." [5]

This general goodwill is what Iturbide puts forth in his favor, it could be found in all the common means establishing it; shouts, festivals, acclamations, oaths, congratulations to all the Nation's corporations who compete to pay him homage and frankincense, calling him Liberator, Hero, Guardian Angel, Pillar of the Religion, the Only Man Worthy to Occupy the Throne of Anáhuac. My faith does not doubt this to be the general will, one of the most passionate defenders of the federation that is claimed, when Iturbide's coronation was asked for here.

And was this the general will? Señor, it was not the legal

will only that it must be investigated. Such is what the legitimate representatives of the people emit, their arbitrators, their delegates, deliberating in full and upright liberty: as that is the will and belief of the faithful, what the Bishops and Priests, your representatives in a free and general Council or Congress of the Church, pronounce from which has been taken the representative system unknown by the ancients. The people have always been victims of the seduction of the turbulent demagogues; and so, their numerical will is a very dark beacon, a very uncertain compass. What the people truly want is their well-being, in this there is no equivocation: but it would be very large and pernicious if it were desired, to establish this well-being, to follow as a norm the will of gross and ignorant men; which is the general mass of the people, incapable of entering the political, economic, and public rights discussions. With reason, since, the previous Congress, after a long and prudent discussion, ordered that the Deputies be given the powers to constitute the Nation *according to what they understood to be the general will.*

This numerical general will of the peoples, this degradation of their representatives to errand boys and physical organs, this natural state of the nation and many other similar trifles with which the provincial's political poor are pounding our heads, are nothing more than rancid, decayed, and detested principles with which the Jacobins lost France, and they have lost Europe and as many parts of our America that have embraced their principles. Principles, if one wishes, and metaphysically truthful; but inapplicable in practice, because they consider man in abstract, and such a man does not exist in society. I also was a Jacobin, and it is evident in my two *Letters from an American to the Spanish in London,* because in Spain we did not know more than what we had learned in the revolutionary books of France. I saw it 28 years in a perpetual convulsion, seen submerged in the same, so many people who adopted their principles; but to me it looked like the same evidence— I worked to find other reasons to which so many disunions, so much inquietude, and so many evils could be attributed. In the end I went to England, which remained tranquil in the middle of the European convulsion, as a delighted ship in the middle of a general tempest. I tried to find the cause of this phenomenon, I studied in that old school of practical politics, I read their[Edmund Burke] Burkes [sic], and their [William Paley] Paleis [sic], their [Jeremy] Bentham and many other authors, I listened to their wise men, and I became convinced that the damage came from the Jacobin principles. [6] This is the Pandora's Box where the evils of the universe are locked up. And horrified, I backed down recanting like my celebrated friend the Spaniard Blanco White has already done in his 6th Volume. [7]

If it was only the matter of agitating the people in rebellion against their rulers, there is not a means more suitable than said principles, because they flatter the natural pride and vanity of man, drinking a toast to him with a scepter that foreign hands have snatched from him. From what one reads in the first chapters of Rousseau's social pact, [8] one is irritated against all government like against a usurpation of their rights; it jumps, tramples, and breaks all the barriers, all the laws, all the social institutions established to restrain their passions, like many other unworthy impediments of their sovereignty. But as each one of the ambitious multitude want their piece, and in the society it is indivisible, they are the ones who divide and tear apart, they rob, they take away, they kill, until tired and depressed about them, they raise a crowned despot, or a clever demagogue, and he restrains them with a scepter, not metaphysical, but of true iron, the last stop of the ambition of the people and of their intestinal divisions.

There have been, there are, and I know some demagogues of good faith, who seduced themselves by the brilliance of the principles and the beauty of the Jacobin theories, they imagine that given the first impulse to the people, they will be the proprietors of restraining it, or the people will restrain themselves in a reasonable streak. But experience has demonstrated that the principles once in place, the passions bring out the consequences; and the same drivers of the people who refuse to accompany them in the excess of their extravagances, loaded with shameful names, such as deserter and apostates of liberalism and of the worthy cause, the first are those who perish drowned among the tumultuous waves of a people pushed beyond the limit. How many great wise and excellent men died on the guillotine raised by the French people, after having been their leaders and their idols?

What then, must we conclude from all this? You will tell me. Do you want us to constitute ourselves into a central republic? No. I have always been for the federation, but a reasonable and moderate federation, a federation convenient to our little learning and to the circumstances of an imminent war that ought to find us very united. I have always opined for a medium between the lax confederation of the United States, whose defects many writers have made evident that there likewise it has many antagonists, since the people are divided between federalists and democrats: a medium, I say, between the lax federation of the United States and the dangerous concentration of Colombia and Peru: a medium in which leaving to the provinces the very precise faculties to provide the necessities of their interior, and promote their prosperity, does not destroy the unity, now more than ever indispensable, for us to be made respectable and fearsome to the Holy Alliance, nor weakening the action of the government, that now more than ever ought to be energetic, in order for all the forces and resources of the Nation to do its work simultaneously and promptly. *Medio Tutissimus ibis* ("*You will go most safely by the middle course,*"). [9] This is my vote and my political testament.

The Lords of the Commission will say, because someone has already told me, that this medium that I opine is the same that their lordships have tried to find, but despite their talent, lights, and healthy intention, no doubt of that, it appears to me that they have not yet found it. They have condescended with the anarchical principles of the Jacobins, the pretended numerical general will, or the chimera of the provinces, and the ambition of their demagogues. They have converted the federation of our provinces into a league of potency. Give to each one this partial sovereignty, and by the same absurdity that is proposed in the 6th Article, and they will truly seize it. The scepter grasped in the hands they will know from right-hand to right-hand to mock the obstacles with which it intends in other Articles to turn it illusory. Sanction the principle so that they will understand the consequences, and the first Querétaro already expressly deduced, is not to obey Your Majesty and the government but that you take account of them. Zacatecas installing its Constituent Congress already is prohibited to call itself provincial. Jalisco published some instructions in order that their deputies could avoid the edict, and against that which in this case was ordered, three provinces limited the powers to their own, and we are almost sure that Yucatán will not be so obedient. The excesses are notorious which the provinces have transgressed since they imagined themselves sovereigns. What will it be when the General Congress authorizes them? Ah, we would not even find ourselves in this if an army had not appeared!

Do not be frightened, they tell me, it is a question of name. The sovereignty of the States remains so reduced by other articles that it comes to being in name only. Without going into the profundity of the question, what is suitable for Article 6, and of showing the sovereignty residing essentially in the nation, it cannot be agreed to by each one of the provinces that is already determined they compose. I agree that every country that does not do enough itself to repel all exterior aggression, is a very silly and comical sovereignty. But the people adhere to the names, and the idea that ours have the name of sovereignty is that of a supreme and absolute power, because no other thing has been known. With this it is enough in order that the demagogues muddle it up, they are irritated by whatever decree of the general government that does not accommodate them, and they are induced to insubordination, disobedience, schism, and anarchy. If this is not the object, why then so many boasts and threats, if we do not concede to them this sovereignty in name only, in such a way that Jalisco does not even get it, has refused to lend us help for the common defense from the risk that encircles us? Here there is a mystery: *Latet anguis cavete* ("A snake lurks beware.").

It is well expressed in the same Article 6, it will be said to me, that this sovereignty of the provinces is only respective to their interior. In this sense a father of a family can also be called sovereign in his home. And what will we say if some of them come to us boasting because we did not issue a decree that sanctions this sovereignty in name only respective to their family? *Latet anguis, cavete, iterum dico, cavete* ("A snake lurks beware, again I say, beware."). This of the interior has significance as vague as immense, there will be more than enough voluntary interpretations, that altering the boundaries of the Provincial Congresses, according to their interests, restricts each step and confounds the central government. This province already believes in its interior responsibility to reestablish maritime customs and to name their employees; those will take charge of the mineral wealth or of the tobacco monopoly, and even of the funds from California's missions. One raises regiments to oppose those of the supreme executive power, another two reduce in their plans all the grand affairs of this and of the General Congress to deal with foreign powers and their ambassadors. Thank you very much. We should not leave ourselves to hallucinate, Señor: Remember Your Sovereignty that the names are everything for the people, and that France with the name of sovereign ruined everything, plundered it, killed it, and destroyed it.

No, no. I am for the plan of foundations of the old Congress. There it is given to the people the federation that they request, if they request it, but organized in a manner less damaging, in a manner more adequate, as I previously said, to the circumstances of our limited learning, and of the war that hangs over our heads, and the most perfect union is required for our defense. There also Provincial Congresses are established even though not so sovereign; but with enough attributes to promote their interior prosperity, to avoid the arbitrary actions of the government in the provision of jobs and to restrain abuses of those employees. In those Congresses, the provinces will go on learning the tactics of the Assemblies and the step of progress on the path of liberty, until progressing in it, ceasing the present danger and recognizing our independence, the nation revises its constitution, and guided by the experience it was expanding the powers of the Provincial Congresses, up to reaching to the height of social perfection without a stumble. To pass suddenly from one extreme to the other, without practicing well the medium, is an absurdity, a delirium; it is to decide, in a word, that we break our heads. I protest before the heavens and earth that we lose if the article of partial sovereignties is not abolished. *Actum est de republic.* ("*It is all over with the Republic.*"). Señor, by God, now that we want to imitate the United States in the federation, we should imitate them in the good sense with which they abolished the article of States sovereignty in their second constitution.

Señor, the tyrants do not instill fear in me. Such a tyrant can be the people as well as a monarch; and much more violent, rash, and sanguinary, as it was in France in its revolution and its experience in each tumult ; and if I did not fear to put myself in front of Iturbide in spite of the cruel dungeons in which he jailed me and of his threatening me with death, also I will know to resist an unteachable people that intends to dictate as oracles their capricious ambitions to the fathers of the homeland, and refuse to be within the line demarcated for the general good and utility.

Nec civium ardor prava jubentium
Nec vultur instantis tyrani
Mente quatit solida. [sic]
("Is not shaken from his firm resolve by the frenzy

of his fellow citizens clamoring for what is wrong,
or by the tyrant's threatening countenance.") [10]

There will be civil war; I will be a conscientious objector, if we do not concede to the provinces what they want that looks familiar. And that isn't there already this war?

Seditione, dolis, scelere, atque libidine, et ira,
Iliacos intra muros peccatur, et extra.
("Sedition, deceit, crime, together with lust and anger, made a
tale of sin within and outside the wall.") [11]

There will be civil war, and will it be delayed in happening if we sanction this federation, or even better the league and alliance of independent sovereigns? If as the proverb says, two cats in a sack are incompatible, will there be much peace between such a petty sovereign, whose interests for the contiguity necessarily must cross over and run into each other? Are a sovereign people perhaps less ambitious than a sovereign individual? The Roman people may say it, whose ambition did not stop until the world was conquered. To this add the total inequality of our supposed principalities. One province has one and a half million, another sixty thousand inhabitants: some a half million, others little more than three thousand such as Texas; one already knows that the large fish always has always swallowed the small one. If we intend to equalize their territories, where ought we to commence in the case of this federation—we already have a civil war because no large province will allow that their territory be cut back. Witness the canons of Guadalajara against Zapotlan, and their complaints about Colima, even though according to their principles, these parties have as much right to separate themselves from their pervious capital as Jalisco must constitute itself independent from its ancient metropolis. Small provinces, even though not in ambition, also refuse to unite themselves to other large ones. The representation of Tlaxcala has here read against their union to Puebla. It is clear in the instructions of various Deputies, that other small provinces also do not want to unite themselves to other equals for forming a State; be it for the ambition of the overseers of each one or be it for ancient local rivalries. Of whatever manner all will flame up in gossips, envies, and divisions; and we will have need of an army that walks from Pilate to Herod to pacify the provinces' differences, until the same army devours us according to custom, and their general will become our Emperor, or to a river turned upside down a king will fish us from the holy alliance. *Et erit novissimus error peiro priore* ("*So, the last error shall be worse than the first.*"). [12]

It is important that this alliance, holy by antiphrasis, finds us constituted: if not, we are lost. Better and much sooner we will be, say I, if one finds us constituted in the manner that is intended. What matters is that it finds us united, and by the same stronger *virtus unita fortieor* ("*Virtue is stronger when united.*"); but this federation is going to divide us and plunge us into an archipelago of discords. The mode that we are trying to establish, was it not that of Venezuela, Cartagena, and Cundinamarca? Well then it was precisely when, despite having as their head a general as great as Miranda, by the hindrance of the federation (even though other secondary causes had intervened) a *quidam* ("*kind of*"), Monteverde, with a handful of soldiers, and a military parade, destroyed the Venezuela republic, and a little later Morillo, who had only been a marine sergeant did the same with the republics of Cartagena and Santa Fé.[31] In the same manner that it is intended we constitute ourselves, the provinces of Buenos Aires tried it without gathering other fruit in many years of incessant civil wars, and while they battled for their particles of sovereignty, the King of Portugal extended the claw without contradiction over Montevideo and the immense territory to the left of the Rio Plata. They observe judicious vigor that neither could the United States support against a central power that attacked them on their continent, because every federation is weak by its nature, and for this they could not advance one step on the bordering part of Canada dominated by England. Far, therefore from guaranteeing us the proposed federation against the holy alliance, it will serve to better secure the dam. *Divide ut imperes* (*"Divide and rule"*).

When Doctor Becerra concluded his wise and judicious vote, he was heard to say, that we were not even in the season of constituting ourselves, and this most grave business ought to be left for when the nation was more enlightened, and our independence recognized; I saw several smile in compassion, as if he had uttered an absurdity. And nevertheless, he said nothing strange. The United States did not effectively constitute itself until the war with Great Britain concluded, and their independence was recognized by Great Britain, France, and Spain. And in the meantime, with what did they govern themselves? With the maxims inherited from their fathers, and even the constitution that they later produced is no more than a collection of them. Where is the constitution of England written? Nowhere. Four or five fundamental articles, such as the law of *habeas corpus* make up their constitution. That sensible nation does not like general principles or abstract maxims, because they are impertinent for the government of the people, and only serve to heat the heads and rush it to erroneous conclusions. It is appropriate for the French people's comical genius to fabricate constitutions arranged as comedy scenes that in no way have served them. In thirty years of revolution, they formed so many other constitutions and all were no more than the almanac of that year. The same happened with the several that Venezuela and Colombia considered. And why? Because they were still not in a state of constituting themselves, but of learning and fighting against the exterior enemy as we are. And meanwhile with what do we govern ourselves? So far with the same thing, with the Spanish constitution, the laws left in our codes not repealed, the decrees of the Spanish Courts until the year 1820 and those of the Congress that has gone and will go on modifying all this in conformity to the present system and to our circumstances. The only thing that we lack is a decree from Your Majesty to the supreme executive power that they must respect all this. If dissolution of the State is threatening, it is because we have with the lack of this decree, paralyzed the Government.

No, it is not the lack of a constitution and laws, what is going on with so much agitation is the insistence of snatching from us the decree of partial sovereignties, so that later the provinces do what their demagogues fancy. The enemies of the order want the principle that we consecrated to develop consequences, which they hide in their hearts, to confuse the people with the name and to lead them to dissension, to chaos, to anarchy, to anger, to the detestation of the republican system, to the monarchy, to the Bourbons, or to Iturbide. There is something to this in the *mitote* [uproar] to which they have provoked the innocent people of some provinces. I tremble when I see that in those where the fire burns most briskly are the most fervent and declared Iturbidistas at the head of the government and of the businesses. I do not want to explain myself anymore, a word to the wise is sufficient.

Protect us, Señor, from condescending to each shout that may resonate in the mistaken provinces, because we will ruin them like a spoiled child whose whims have no end. Protect us from those who believe that their threats intimidate us, because each day the insolence will grow, and the charlatans will multiply. Protect yourselves, said Gaius Claudius to the Roman Senate, from acceding to that which the people ask while they remain armed on Mount Aventine, because each day a new symbol will form to ruin the Senate's authority and to destroy the Republic. To the letter, the prophesy was fulfilled.

Firmness, Fathers of the Homeland! Deliberate in a prudent calmness, according to the counsel of Augustus, *festina lente* ("*Make haste slowly*"); enact fearlessly the constitution that in God and in your conscience you believe to be most suitable to the universal good of the nation and leave to the care of the government to make it be obeyed. He does not cease from protesting that he has the powers and enough means to force the compliance of all that Your Majesty decrees, be what will be, if authorized, use them. Washington also raised the sword to make the province of Maryland obey the second constitution, *si vis pacem, para bellus* (*"If you wish for peace, prepare for war"*). [14] There is not a better ingredient for obedience: *si vis pacem, para bellus.* And we will not have much to do because our people are by their nature not very disobedient, nor do they resist that which has been provided, except for some military and ambitious demagogues, that being unable to appear in the metropolis, have gone to tricking the provinces, to agitate them and to take away their voice, to make themselves respectable and mix in their personal interests, *si vis pacem, para bellus.*

Four are the dissident Provinces, and if they want to separate, then separate, not much damage and little argument. Parents, also, abandon obstinate children, until disillusioned they return playing the role of the prodigal son. I have no doubt that in the end what happens to these provinces is the same as to those of Venezuela and Santa Fé. There also they put up quite a ruckus for constituting themselves into Sovereign States, and after incalculable disgraces, sending to Cúcuta's General Congress their deputies to give them a new constitution that frees them of so many evils, they gave them very wide powers, except, they say, for making many little governments. So chastened, they have stayed with their partial sovereignties. What is certain is that the sanguinary Morales, [15] this inhuman Caribbean, this fierce beast, is embarking with his troops in Havana, and it is probable that he could be against Mexico since even Puerto Cabello reduced to extreme ends asks for help that commanding officer surrendered in Maracaibo; and he must be sworn in to not return to fight in Costa Firme. What is certain is that the Duke of Angoulême has pronounced that France with a conquered Spain will launch an expedition against America, and it is already known that Mexico is the coveted child. We will see then if Jalisco, which has refused us their help, even though it has taken advantage of the resources of Mexico's government, is able, once it is lost, to save its particle of metaphysical sovereignty.

I conclude, Señor, begging Your Majesty, become fully aware of the circumstances in which we find ourselves. We need union, and the federation tends to disunity: we need force, and every federation is weak by its nature; we need to give the major energy to the government, the federation multiplies the obstacles to coordinate early and simultaneously the nation's resources. In every republic when a close and grave danger that has menaced a dictator has been created, so that the powers are reunited into his hand, the action may be one, quicker, firmer, livelier, and decisive. We are with the colossus of the holy alliance on top, we shall do precisely the contrary, dividing ourselves into such small sovereignties! *Quæ tanta insania, cives* ("*Oh, unfortunate citizens who has brought such a great madness upon you?*")? [16]

Sir if such sovereignties are adopted, if the project of the constitutive act is passed in its totality, from now on I wash my hands, saying like the President of Judea when a tumultuous people asked for the death of Our Savior, without knowing what he was doing: *Inocens ego sum á sanguine justi huyus: Vos videritis* ("*I am innocent of the blood of this just person: see ye to it.*"). [17] I will protest that I have had no part in the evils that are going to rain upon the people of Anáhuac. They have seduced them so that they ask for what they do not know nor understand, and I foresee the division, the jealous rivalry, the disorder, the ruin and the disorder of our land even to its foundations. *Necierunt neque intellexerunt, in tenebris ambulant, movebuntur omina fundament terræ* ("*They know not, neither will they understand; they walk on in darkness; all the foundations of the earth are out of course.*"). [18] My God save my homeland! *Pater, ignosce illis, quia nesciunt quid faciunt* ("*Father, forgive them; for they know not what they do.*"). [19]

Chapter 10, Notes

1. *Memoria política-instructiva enviado desde Filadelfia en agosto de 1821 á los gefes independientes del Anáhua llamado por los españoles Nueva-España,* Mier, Noriega y Guerra, José Servando Teresa de, (1763-1827), published by J. F. Hurtel, Philadelphia, PA, August 1821, and R. Ayuntamiento de Monterrey, N. L., (Monterrey City Council, Nuevo Leon, MX), republished in Spanish 1977.

2. *This is the task, this is the labor;* Virgil, Aeneid, VI, 126.

3. King James Bible, Matthew 20:22; Fray Mier quotes the verse in Spanish and Latin; witnessing that his sermons were in Spanish, but he read and studied the Latin Bible.

4. *Nothing is desired that is not first known.* The quote has been attributed to the Greek Aristotle, the Roman Marcus Aurelius, and numerous Catholic authors including Thomas Aquinas, of the Dominican Order as was Fray Mier.

5. Fray Mier quotes King James and Latin Vulgate Bible, Exodus 23:2 in Spanish and Latin.

6. Burkes, likely Edmund Burke (1729-1797), was a political theorist, author, and philosopher who served for many years in Great Britain's House of Commons and was hostile to the French Revolution. Paleis, likely William Paley (1743-1805), was a religious philosopher, author, and a lightning rod in his life and even today in the conflict between science and religion, a formidable opponent of slavery. Bentham, likely Jeremy Bentham (1748-1832), was a social reformer, author, and philosopher, and a leading theorist of Anglo-American philosophy on law and a political radical of welfarism. Fray Mier's reference to Burkes, Paleis, and Bentham merits an explanation for the following reasons. First, his reference to Burke, Paley, and Bentham witness that whether the topic of his writings or discourses was religion, history, or the politics of Spain, France, England, United States, or Mexico; Fray Mier did his research, he was very erudite, and his sources are credible. Second, this may be the first published English translation of *Prophecy of Doctor Mier on the Mexican Federation.* It appears when reading the Spanish copy of his *Prophecy* that the text is a transcription of the oral presentation, because the style of spelling, grammar, language patterns, and apologetic comments to the presiding authority are quite different from Dr. Mier's written texts. Third, his *Prophecy* delivered

before Congress December 13, 1823, is found on the Internet archived as an important document of Mexico's Revolution of Independence. All Spanish copies use the same spelling for the referenced persons: Burkes, Paleis, and Bentham. His *Prophecy* is a respected political document in Mexico with no editing or research. "Paleis" is the Dutch word for "Palace." William Paley connected with Joseph Blanco White. The Burkes and Paleis misspellings with no editing corrections or research notes to original copies of the *Prophecy* speech is an emblematic fingerprint of how Fray Mier is honored in Mexico while his account of Mexican history is hidden behind curtains for fear of unveiling the thesis of his Guadalupe Sermon, the beginning of his fight for independence; which was — *there is no doubt of the ancient preaching of the Gospel in America.*

7. Joseph Blanco White (1775-1841); born in Seville, Spain of an Irish father and Spanish mother, sailed from Cadiz, Spain to England in 1810. He was a theologian, poet, advocate of Latin American independence from Spain and studied for the Catholic priesthood.

8. Jean-Jacques Rousseau, Republic of Geneva, (1712-1778), Fray Mier probably references: *Du contrat social ou Principes du droit politique.*

9. *You will go most safely by the middle course;* Ovid, (43 BC-17 AD), Metamorphoses, II, 137.

10. *Is not shaken from his firm resolve by the frenzy of his fellow citizens clamoring for what is wrong, or by the tyrant's threatening countenance;* Horace, BC 65-BC 8, Odes III, iii, 1.

11. *Sedition, deceit, crime, together with lust and anger, made a tale of sin within and outside the wall;* Horace, BC 65-BC 8, Epistle II, Book 1, 15-16.

12. King James Bible, Matthew 27:64: *so, the last error shall be worse than the first.*

13. Francisco de Miranda (1750-1812), a Venezuela revolutionary, was a forerunner to Simón Bolívar. Juan Diego de Monteverde (1773-1832), leader of the Spanish forces in the Venezuela war of independence was defeated by Simón Bolívar. Pablo Morillo (1775-1837) was the Spanish expedition commander and general captain of the provinces of Venezuela, who signed a truce with Simón Bolívar. The history Fray Mier references took place while he was an exile in Europe. Reviewing Fray Mier's biography, we learn that that in 1801 Fray Mier met Simón Rodríguez in Paris where they founded a Spanish language academy. Rodríguez was a teacher to Simón Bolívar. Fray Mier's eyewitness

account of the South America revolutions was very probably learned from his Paris academy partner, Simón Rodríguez.

14. *If you wish for peace, prepare for war;* Publius Flauvius Vegetius Renatus (4th - 5th Century A.D.), quoted from "De Re Militari," Book 3, ("Concerning Military Matters").

15. Francisco Tomás Morales (1781 or 1783-1845) a Spanish military officer born in the Canary Islands. Fray Mier references revolutionary battle in Columbia, Venezuela, Central America, Mexico, France, and Spain.

16. *Oh, unfortunate citizens who has brought such a great madness upon you?* Virgil (70 BC-19BC), Aeneid III, 43.

17. King James Bible, Matthew 27:24; *I am innocent of the blood of this just person: see ye to it.*

18. Vulgate Latin Bible, Psalms 81:5, King James English Bible: Psalms 82:5; *They know not, neither will they understand; they walk on in darkness; all the foundations of the earth are out of course.*

19. King James Bible, Luke 23:34; *Father, forgive them; for they know not what they do.*

Chapter 11

Honors and Memorials to Fray Servando Teresa de Mier by Governor José Eleuterio González

Despite all of this, the 5th and 6th Articles of the Constitutive Act were approved, and the partial sovereignties remained decreed. Doctor Mier, far from being offended because his opinion was not followed, always worked with the utmost determination because the federation could plant and consolidate such as had been decreed. Later Doctor Ramos Arizpe proposed, that of the four internal Eastern Provinces which are Coahuila, Texas, Nuevo Leon, and Tamaulipas, they could form a single State. Here Doctor Mier opposed it with all his strength, and in the end achieved that it was not so, and that Nuevo Leon will form one State by itself.

Both the government as well as all his companion deputies dispensed much appreciation and many considerations on Señor Mier: before dissolving, the Constituent Congress issued the following decree, found in the "Collection of Orders and Decrees,"
1829 edition, Volume 3, page 162:

Decree of the 23rd of December of 1824. —Pension to Señor Don Servando Teresa de Mier. — The Sovereign General Constituent Congress, taking into consideration that by the law on the 19th of July of 1823 the Government was authorized so that it rewards to those individuals who in the first insurrection offered their services to the cause of Independence; and besides being notorious the very important loans because of Señor Don Servando Teresa de Mier, no less than his sensitivity in not having demanded any recompensation; and satisfied with the opinion of the Government, who consulted upon this point a Commission at its very heart; it has been well decreed that to the expressed Señor Don Servando Teresa de Mier is granted a pension of three thousand pesos annually.

In addition to this pension that was always religiously paid to him, the President of the Republic, Don Guadalupe Victoria, assigned him a very decent abode in the National Palace, where he went to live and there passed the remaining years of his life. Three years of a peaceful and tranquil life loved and respected, in contact with the best society of Mexico and in relations with the most notable men of the nation, were the last of his life. It is to say, he had three years of rest for thirty of outrageous persecutions, jails, labors, and sufferings. He was very highly respected by President Victoria and his ministers, as well as by Vice President Don Nicolas Bravo who consulted with him on their gravest concerns. From all the States, or as he says in his letters, from the entire kingdom, inquiries were directed to him, and he came in this time to be the most popular man in Mexico.

He had the very great satisfaction of seeing his homeland independent, free, and republican, which had been the golden dream of his whole life. At the same time, he also had the satisfaction and consolation of having worked as much as he could in helping to constitute it, as well as he had helped to liberate it. To see his homeland free and to have been able to work on his gift was the prize Providence now gave him who with so much constancy suffered a life of unspeakable persecutions and misfortunes. He was honored and attended to not only in Mexico, but also abroad: he was a member of the National Institute of France, that was then the most honorable literary forum to which one could aspire; we have already seen that in Galveston they treated him as a Bishop; the Municipality of Monterrey, as appears in its acts, when it was writing to him gave him the title of Most Illustrious Señor. In one of his letters directed to Doctor Cantú, when he speaks of the installation of the Second Constituent Congress, he says that he attended dressed episcopally; and in his letters to Monterrey's Provincial Deputation it is signed: "Servando Archbishop of Baltimore." I think that he could have been nominated and presented to be Baltimore's Archbishop of the Church, where he had many good friends: but nowhere is there evidence that he was recommended in Rome, for which he stayed only with the title of Archbishop-elect and nothing more.

In the last days of the month of November 1827, feeling that an infirmity that he suffered was much worst, he knew that his end was approaching. He rode in a carriage and went in person to invite his numerous friends, in order that the following day they could attend his sacraments, those that he desired to receive with the most possible solemnity. Indeed, the following day, in the middle of a most brilliant assembly and after having made a solemn declaration of faith and a very tender speech, he received the sacred last rites with all the devotion and fervor of a good Catholic. He died the 3rd day of December of the same year, with the serenity of a philosopher and the resignation of a Christian, fulfilling in him literally the saying of Cicero: *The truely wise man dies with a very calm courage.* He lived sixty-four years and one and a half months.

Very great honors are attributed to the mortal remains of the distinguished Doctor Mier: his interment was very, very crowded. Señor Payno speaking of this says:

General Don Nicolas Bravo, who was Vice President of the Republic, presided at the wake and there was not a respectful person of the City who would not order his carriage and attend the funeral. The people crowded around in such a way on the streets where the funeral procession passed, that persons keep the memory, assuring that not even in the Corpus processions has there been seen such a crowd. The Doctor's body was entombed in the chapel of the Santo Domingo Sepulchers, beside his brothers who persecuted him and rested as did he amongst the dust of nothingness and oblivion.

Commonly the vicissitudes of men end in the tomb; but this did not happen to the celebrated Doctor Mier. As if the unfortunate luck that pursued him in his life could not have been satisfied with his death, still it prepared him for a strange turn of events even after death and burial. Fifteen years he was at peace in his grave, and in the year 1842, to bury another body, there, they removed that of the good Father Mier perfectly mummified and dried: they put him in the convent ossuary to the East side in the first place between other religious mummies that were put in that place for the same reasons. Nineteen years the Doctor's body remained in his new place of rest. In the year 1861, after the suppressed religious communities and the appropriated convents, there spread in Mexico the rumor that in the Santo Domingo Convent there were many dry bodies, about which everyone had diverse commentaries: according to some they were of persons for their great incorruptible sanctity, according to others they were of unhappy persons who had been victims of the Inquisition's cruelties, and there was no lack of those who said that the Friars had confined those persons to exert upon them private revenge. Doctor Orellana of the military medical corps, who examined those bodies with the proper attention and took all the available information, proved that thirteen mummies were extracted from the graves at various times and put there. He also proved that all were of well-known religious Dominicans, he had them lithographed, and published a little notebook with short biographical notices of each one of the Fathers of whom those bodies were, Doctor Mier being one of them.

The same Doctor Orellana says that four of these mummies were taken to Buenos Aires and another gifted to Mexico City's school of medicine, without specifying which they were. Señor Payno indicates that one of those taken to Buenos Aires was that of Doctor Mier; and Señor Rivera

Cambas says: "It is believed that a traveler bought it to take it to Buenos Aires, even though there is no lack of some who assure that the Dominican Friars had changed the body for that of a layman named Sumaita." There remains, therefore, the question of whether the body of Señor Mier stayed in Mexico or if it went to Buenos Aires. If it is true that a traveler from that country bought it, it is probable that he found reason to take that of Doctor Mier, because there he is, as a writer, better known than among us for reason of having sent there almost every edition of his "Anáhuac's Revolution," whose reading in that republic spread much and contributed singularly to the development of liberal and republican ideas in that country.

The Congress of Nuevo Leon wanting to honor the virtues and to perpetuate the memory of such an illustrious man of Nuevo Leon ordered by its Decree of July 27, 1849, that the new town, founded where before was the San Antonio de Medina hacienda, shall be called: "Villa de Mier y Noriega," which name it has, the same as the Municipality of which it is the head; and that forms the extreme South of this State.

APPENDICES

Appendix A

Distinguished Mexican Introductions and Prologue[1]

The following introductory notes are translations from José Eleuterio González's "Biography of the Distinguished Mexican Don Servando Teresa de Mier Noriega y Guerra," Commemorative Edition. These notes and the credentials of the authors manifest the profound respect, in which Mexico's academic community holds Dr. Mier. The publication and personal embracing of Fray Mier and his message by the Governors and the Mexican State of Nuevo Leon as authors, financial contributors, public supporters, and introducing endorsees in 1876 and again in 1977 validates the credibility of Fray Mier as a recorder of Mexican history, largely unknown outside of a small circle of Mexican scholars, or what Dr. Carlos R. Cantu Cantu calls "Mexican idiosyncrasy."

By Way of Explanation

Dr. Carlos R. Cantu Cantu, Member of the Nuevo Leon Historical, Geographical, and Statistical Society, wrote this Introduction to the 1977 Commemorative Edition of Governor José Eleuterio González's Biography of Fray Mier.

It is my very great honor and reason for profound satisfaction to have contributed with the use of my books to make this facsimile edition of the Biography of the eminent leader of the National Independence, our illustrious Fray Servando de Santa Teresa de Mier Noriega y Guerra, whose knowledge of Mexican idiosyncrasy gains more validity each day.

Father Mier is perhaps the most important man at the dawning of Mexico's Independence and unquestionably the most representative of the raucous and libertarian character of the settlers of this frontier.

To remember him, one hundred fifty years of his spectacular transition, by the wise Distinguished Nuevo Leones, Dr. José Eleuterio González, Gonzalitos,[2] his biographer, of Jalisciense origin, without doubt the most notable of the adopted sons of this Nuevo Leon, splendid and generous corner of Mexican soil, that holds with special love the many men of different nations of the world who have chosen to build here, under its bright sky, the home of their life.

To evoke their lives and their works, and for causal coincidence, the honorable Attorney Don Genaro Garza Garcia,[3] Governor of the State, to whom this volume is dedicated, who saw that this facsimile copy was done; they recall better times and men, Eternal Luminaries; a name for men who lived exemplary lives, without flaws; strong characters with souls of steel and a kind heart, free, serene, honest to the last letter, who were and are the pride and character of these regions.

Anyway, the remembrance is opportune, meritorious, and perfect. Honor to whom, in the name of the Government of the State; have shouldered the funding of such a laborious and meritorious task. The honor that reaches me for having intervened in the laudable proposition is minimal, but it is more than what I need to be happy and I accept it with great gratitude.

Introduction

Governor Pedro G. Zorrillo Martinez of the State of Nuevo Leon (1973-1979), wrote and signed this Introduction to the 1977 Commemorative Edition of Governor José Eleuterio González's Biography of Fray Mier.

To think about Fray Servando Teresa de Mier—his life, his work, his death—is to meditate on the nationality, the patriotism, and the selfless dedication to an ideal, the constant fight for what with intimate conviction becomes a glimpse of truth.

Father Mier, a man profound in his historical-political thought and slight in contempt for his pain. Endowed with a spirit sufficient to interpret the past and bring it into the future, he did not skimp effort or struggle to get attention to be heard. Not for egotism. But with the pathos of a prophet, aware of the difficulty of his language.

A conflictive friar, a problematic man, and compromised with his reality, Mier responds with unifying spirit to the dispersed and disconnected world in which he lived. He prefers the rough and hard road of liberty, to the comfortable position that his doctorate gave him.

One hundred fifty years after his death, Fray Servando keeps reminding us of our commitment and struggle for unity. Division gives chaos. We need to be only one; by compensating the needs of others, giving up the power of another fortifies the weakness we bear. It is this interweaving of actions which holds the world in its place, that which permits it to exist, to be, without strategies or desolations.

The prose of Fray Servando is always charming, sparkling, without regard to ideologies. This facsimile of his Memoirs goes with the support of the Government of the State of Nuevo Leon making for unity. There is not a better homage to Father Mier than to maintain alive what he wanted to maintain all his life.

The Distinguished Mexican Prologue

Governor José Eleuterio Gonzalez, Governor of the State of Nuevo Leon (1870, 1875-73,1874) and a Medical Doctor wrote: *Biografia del benemérito mexicano D. Servando Teresa deMier Noriega y Guerra* the source of *Fray Servando Teresa de Mier: Writings on Ancient Christianity and Spain's Evangelism of Mexico.*

Great men are a mark of honor and a beautiful adornment of the nations that produce them: their biographies come to be the most pleasant, useful and instructive part of history. Linked in an insoluble manner to the events of their time, simultaneously and of importance they offer us illustrious examples to follow and perilous errors to avoid. In all times, there have been biographers who have given us to know the most eminent men of the people, thus doing a very great service to humanity.

Among the men of merit that Nuevo Leon has produced, none is comparable to Dr. Don Servando Teresa de Mier Noriega y Guerra, whose services to the independence of the Nation and to the Republic, and whose knowledge and very unfortunate life, have given him not a little fame. It was not easy that such a notable man should be left to find who will be responsible for transmitting to posterity his name and his services, his feats, and the various adventures of his life: thus it is that in 1861 Dr. Orellana wrote a short biography of Dr. Mier, on the occasion of the mummies found in the Santo Domingo ossuary of Mexico City. I in 1863 Dr. Don José Angel Benavides published in the *Revista de Nuevo Leon* a few Notes for the Dr. Mier biography, Don Manuel Payno wrote a life of the same Doctor the 1865 "New Year." And Don Manuel Rivera Cambas read in the Hidalgo Lyceum the night of February 9, 1874 a biography of Dr. Don Servando Teresa de Mier. Neither the circumstances in which these writers found themselves, nor the scarce case documents that they had to view, enabled them to give their works the extension and exactitude that are to be desired. For this I now count on that which they wrote. I live in Monterrey where I have been able to gather some data from the very many relatives of Dr. Mier, who still live, and from the archives of the city, that I can get from the *Apologia* or *Memoirs* of his life, that the Doctor himself wrote and that I owe to the favor of Señor Licentiate Don Emilio Pardo. I own twenty-one autograph letters from Dr. Mier to Dr. Cantú and to Monterrey's Provincial Delegation in the time that Mr. Mier was a Deputy in the first two Congresses of the Nation, resulting in a biography of such a celebrated personage, the most complete and the most exact to the truth that will be possible. I believe there are sufficient materials for such an arduous undertaking.

The work will prove to be very voluminous, because in order to publicize such an extraordinary man with the appropriate clarity, it is necessary to insert his unabridged speeches, his *Apologia*, and his letters, pieces that I believe cannot fit in less than a hundred printed sheets; but only in this way can one come to know perfectly the inexplicable candor, the immense erudition, the festive genius, the style so easy as elegant, the untarnished patriotism, and the other uncommon talents that characterize such an interesting subject. Moreover, his *Apologia* and many of his letters remain unedited, at the risk that they are lost forever, it will be good that case documents that so much honor Monterrey as well as the Mexican Nation are brought to light in the same place that saw born their author.

Dr. Mier's history is of interest not only to Mexico, but also to all the Americas. With the same ardor that he defended the independence and rights of his native land, he defended the independence and the rights of Venezuela, and of all the American nations, so that anyone who without knowing who he was, who read his "First Letter to the Spanish" will believe him a Venezuelan. Finally, the works of Dr. Mier, by his gracious style, by the prodigious extension of his historical news and by the profundity of his theological knowledge, interest every kind of person, since they will find in them very various and very solid instruction, without the annoyance of the gaunt forms of didactic works.

Appendix A, Notes

1. Appendix A, *The Distinguished Mexican*, Introductions, Prologue, The Mier Family, and Dr. Mier, are translated from *Biografia del benemérito mexicano D. Servando Teresa de Mier Noriega y Guerra*, José Eleuterio González, published 1876, Monterrey, Mexico with a Commemorative Edition, Facsimile of the Original, published by the State of Nuevo Leon, Mexico, and the Autonomous University of Nuevo Leon, Sesquicentennial of the Death of Father Mier, 1827-1977, pp. 3-9.

2. Jose Eleuterio González served three times as Governor of the State of Nuevo Leon: 1870, 1872-1873. and 1874.

3. Genaro Garza Garcia served five times as Governor of the State of Nuevo Leon: 1871-1872, 1876-1877, 1877-1879, 1881-1883, and 1885

ACKNOWLEDGMENTS

This book would not have been written without the encouragement of Dr. Paul Y. Hoskisson, appointed 2008 as Director of the Laura F. Willes Center for Book of Mormon Research, and the Foundation for Ancient Research and Mormon Studies (FARMS). I shared my research with Paul and his wife Joaquina at a 2009 luncheon meeting in Provo, UT with my wife Herlinda Briones Bowen. After the luncheon, Paul told me he knew of no one else who was studying the research sources I had shared with him. He said, "You need to get this written."

In 1967, visiting Herlinda's family in Los Mochis, Sinaloa, MX, she insisted I buy a book she had studied as a student, *Servando Teresa de Mier Escritos y Memorias* ("*Servando Teresa de Mier Writings and Memoirs*"). This was my introduction to 50 plus years studying Dr. Mier and his research sources on ancient Christianity in the Americas. Much of the book is translated from Spanish. Herlinda earned a Bachelor of Art in Spanish and a Teaching Licensure at the University of Utah. She is my Spanish Editor in Chief.

While writing, I came to know Deirdre Paulsen and Colleen Whitley retired Brigham Young University Professors of English, Writing, and Folklore. I was done writing when Deirdre Paulsen, Colleen Whitley and Paul Hoskisson recommended that I divide my writing into two books; an academic work, *Fray Servando Teresa de Mier, Writings on Ancient Christianity and Spain's Evangelizm of Mexico*, a translation of Fray Mier's defense of his December 12, 1794 Guadalupe Sermon, and *Christianity in America Before Columbus, Unfamiliar Origins and Insights* that gives historical , geographic, and cultural authenticity to *The Book of Mormon*. Deirdre Paulsen and Colleen Whitley did the final editing, polishing my translation and writing to publishing standards.

Deirdre Paulsen, Colleen Whitley, and Paul Gardner coached me as I stumbled down the road to find a publisher. I finally contracting with Elite Online Publishing. I appreciate the work of Jenn Foster, Chief Executive Officer, and Melanie Johnson, Elite Online Publishing, for launching and publishing my books.

To all of you, *muchísimas gracias* (translation: "thank you very very much") for being my Author Mentor Team.

BIBLIOGRAPHY

de Acosta, Joseph, Prologue and selections by Edmundo O'Gorman. *(Historia natural y moral de las Indias) Vida Religiosa y civil de los Indios.* Biblioteca del Estudiante Universitario No. 83. Mexico, D. F.: Universidad Nacional Autónomoa de México, 1963, published in Spain, 1590.

de Alva Cortés Ixtlilxóchitl, Fernando. *Historia de la nación chichimeca.* Linkgua ediciones S.L., Barcelona, 2008. Original written circa 1614.

de Alva Ixtlilxóchitl, Fernando. *Obras históricas de don Fernando de Alva Ixtlilxóchitl.* Volume 1 and 2. Reprint from the collection of the University of Michigan Library. Original written circa 1608-1611.

Bataillon, Marcel, trans. by J. Coderich and J. A. Martínez Schrem. *Estudios sobre Bartolomé de las Casas*, Serie Universitario, Historia/Ciencia/Sociedad 127. Barcelona: Ediciones Península, First Edition: 1976. The original French edition, *Études sur Batolomé de las Casas*, published by Centre de Recherches de l'Institut d'Études Hispaniques, Paris, 1965.

Bennett, Robert F. *Leap of Faith, Confronting the Origins of the Book of Mormon.* Deseret Book, Salt Lake City, Utah. Copyright and published 2009.

The Bible. King James translation. Distributed by The Deseret Book Company, Salt Lake City, Utah, U.S.A.

The Book of Mormon. The Church of Jesus Christ of Latter-day Saints, Salt Lake City, UT, U.S.A. First edtion published in 1830.

Bowen, Gary. *Christianity in the Americas Before Columbus: Unfamiliar Origins and Insights* and *Fray Servando Teresa de Mier: Writings on Ancient Christianity and Spain's Evangelism in Mexico.* Salt Lake City, UT (Publication not yet determined.)

de las Casas, Bartolomé, Prologue Olga Camps. *Brevísima relación de la destrucción de las Indias*. Mexico, D. F.: Editorial Fontamara, S. A., 1984. First edition 1552, Sevilla.

de las Casas, Fray Bartolomé., trans. from Latin Atenógenes Santamaría 1942, Forward by Agustín Millares Carlo and Introduction by Lewis Hanke. *Del único modo de atraer a todos los pueblos a la verdadera religión*. Mexico, D. F.: Fondo de Cultura Económica, 1942, 1975.

de las Casas, Fray Barolomé, ed. Prologue, Appendices, and Notes by Edmundo O'Gorman, with collaboration of Jorge Alberto Manrique. *Los indios de México y Nueva España, Antología*. Mexico, D. F. Editorial Porrua, S. A., Sixth Edition 1987.

de Cervantes Saavedra, Miguel., trans. Edith Grossman and Introduction by Harold Bloom. *Don Quixote*. New York: HarperCollins Publishers, Inc., 2003.

de Cervantes Saavedra, Miguel., *El Ingenioso Hidalgo Don Quijote de la Mancha*, Editorial Ramón Sopena, S. A., Barcelona, Spain, 1962.

The Church of Jesus Christ of Latter-day Saints. *The Book of Mormon, Another Testament of Jesus Christ*. Salt Lake City, Utah, U.S.A. 1992, First published 1830.

Clavijero, Francisco Javier. R. P. Mariano Cuevas, Prologue and Editor. *Historia Antigua de México*. Mexico D. F.: Editorial Porrua, S. A., Fourth Edition 1968. Published from the original Spanish text 1945, 1968. First published title: *Storia Antica del Messico*. Cesna, Italy, 1780, Original Spanish text translated to Italian by the author; *The History of Mexico*. Translated from Italian, published London 1787; Richmond, Virginia 1806, London 1807, and Philadelphia, 1817. Translated from Italian to Spanish; *Historia Antigua de México*. London 1826; Mexico, D. F. 1844, 1853, 1861-62, Jalapa 1868, Mexico, D. F. 1833, 1917, 1944.

Cortés, Hernán, Edition annotated by Dr. Julio Le Riverend. *Cartas de relación de Hernán Cortés*. Mexico, D. F.: Editorial Concepto, S. A., 1983.

Diamond, Jared. *Guns, Germs, and Steel, The Fates of Human Societies.* New York & London: W. W. Norton & Company, 1997.

Frost, Robert. *The Poetry of Robert Frost.* Edited by Edward Connery Lathem. New York, Chicago, San Francisco: Holt, Rinehart and Winston, 1969.

González, José Eleuterio. Juan Peña, ed. *Biografia del benemérito mexicano D. Servando Teresa de Mier Noriega y Guerra.* Monterey, Mexico: José Saenz, published, 1876. Commemorative Edition, Facsimile of the Original, Government of the State of Nuevo Leon, Autonomous University of Nuevo Leon, Sesquicentennial of the Death of Father Mier, 1827-1977, 1977.

Herring, Hubert. *A History of Latin America from the Beginnings to the Present.* New York: Alfred a. Knopf, 1961.

de Humboldt, Alejandro., trans. from French and study by Jaime Labastida, *Aportaciones a la antropología mexicana.* Mexico, D. F.: Editorial Katún, S. A., 1974.

de Landa, Fray Diego. *Relación de las Cosas de Yucatán.* Merida, Yucatán, Mexico: Ediciones Dante, S. A.,1983. Previous editions 1864, 1881, 1900, 1928-29, 1937, 1938, 1938, 1941. An abridgement of Landa's writing, believed to have been first published about 1660.

Lane, Helen., trans., and Susana Rotker., ed. and Introduction. *Fray Servando, The Memoirs of Fray Servando Teresa de Mier.* New York and Oxford: Library of Latin America, Oxford University Press, Inc., 1998.

Maxwell, John Francis. *Slavery and the Catholic Church.* Chichester & London: Barry Rose Publishers in association with the Anti-Slavery Society for the Protection of Human Right, 1975.

Motolinia, Fray Toribio de Benavente or Motolinia. Edmundo O'Gorman. Critical Study, Appendix, Notes & Index. *Historia de los indios de la Nueva España.* Mexico D. F.: Editorial Porrua, S. A., Fourth Edition 1984, Previous editions 1858, 1969.

Nibley, Hugh. *Lehi, in the Desert, The World of the Jaradites, There were Jaredites.* Salt Lake City, Utah: Deseret Book Company; and Provo, Utah: Foundation for Ancient Research and Mormon Studies, 1988.

O'Gorman, Edmundo. *Servando Teresa de Mier, escritos y memorias, Biblioteca del Estudiante Universitario 56.* Prologue and Selection by Edmundo O'Gorman, Ediciones de la Universidad Nacional Autonoma, Mexico, D.F., 1945.

Paz, Octavio. *El laberinto de la soledad.* Mexico, D. F.: Fondo de Cultura Economica, First Edition 1950, 1983.

Paz, Octavio. *Sor Juana Inés de la Cruz o Las trampas de la fe.* Barcelona: Editorial Seix Barral, S. A.1982.

de los Rios, José Amador. *Historia social, politica y religiosa de los judios de España y Portugal.* Madrid, Spain. Aguilar, S.A., 1960 Edition, republished 1973. Original text first published 1848.

Secretaría de Educación Pública de México. *Mi libro de Historia de México.* Mexico D. F.: Comisión de los Libros de Texto Gratuitos, 1992.

Vickery, Paul S. *Bartolomé de las Casas Great Prophet of the Americas.* NewYork/Mahwah, N. J.: Paulist Press, 2006.

About the Author

Gary Bowen earned degrees in Economics and an MBA from the University of Utah. His career began in egg marketing, when hired by Jon M. Huntsman Sr.. His experiences included agricultural wholesale marketing and financial consulting. He was a Utah State Division Director and a Securities Examiner.

Gary's studies began in 1962-64 as a Church of Jesus Christ of Latter-day Saints Missionary to West Mexico, where he learned Spanish and Mexican culture. In 1964, he married Herlinda Briones-Vega, who introduced him to Mexico's hidden history. Reading Spanish history books, having coincidental meetings over decades with a member of Mexico's Congress and Mexican Jesuit Priests, Gary came to know a history of Mexico that other than Herlinda and Mexican Catholic Priests is largely unknown. Gary likens his historical research to the idealistic dreams of Don Quixote of La Mancha for a better world.

Before his 2011 retirement, Gary met Dr. Paul Y. Hoskisson, Director of the Laura F. Willes Center for Book of Mormon Research and The Foundation for Ancient Research and Mormon Studies (FARMS) at Brigham Young University. They discussed Gary's studies on Mexican history and its evidence of the authenticity of *The Book of Mormon*. At the end of the meeting, Dr. Hoskisson said: "Gary, you have to get this written. No one else in the Church studies what you study." *Christianity in The Americas Before Columbus* and *Fray Servando Teresa De Mier: Writings on Ancient Christianity and Spain's*

Evangelism of Mexico were written upon Dr. Hoskisson's wise counsel.

Gary and Herlinda are parents of four children, ten grandchildren, and one g-grandchild. In 2017, Gary was elected to the Emigration Canyon Metro Township Council, which keeps him very involved in community activities in Salt Lake County, Utah.

Follow Gary

Twitter.com/GaryBowenAuthor

fb.me/GaryBowenAuthor

Linkedin.com/in/garybowenauthor

www.ingramcontent.com/pod-product-compliance
Lightning Source LLC
Chambersburg PA
CBHW021824090426
42811CB00032B/2009/J